It's Never Too Late to Begin Again

ALSO BY JULIA CAMERON

A TarcherPerigee book

an imprint of Penguin Random House

New York

It's Never Too Late to Begin Again

*Discovering Creativity and Meaning
at Midlife and Beyond*

JULIA CAMERON

with EMMA LIVELY

An imprint of Penguin Random House LLC
375 Hudson Street
New York, New York 10014

Most TarcherPerigee books are available at special quantity discounts for bulk purchase for sales promotions,
premiums, fund-raising, and educational needs. Special books or book excerpts also can be created to fit specific needs.
For details, write: SpecialMarkets@penguinrandomhouse.com.

Library of Congress Cataloging-in-Publication Data
Names: Cameron, Julia, author. | Lively, Emma, author.
Title: It's never too late to begin again : discovering creativity and
meaning at midlife and beyond / Julia Cameron, Emma Lively.
Other titles: It is never too late to begin again
Description: New York : TarcherPerigee, 2016. | Includes bibliographical
references and index.
Identifiers: LCCN 2015050216 | ISBN 9780399174216 (paperback)
Subjects: LCSH: Creative ability. | Aging. | BISAC: SELF-HELP / Creativity. |
SELF-HELP / Aging. | FAMILY & RELATIONSHIPS / Aging.
Classification: LCC BF408 .C17555 2016 | DDC 155.67/19—dc23

Printed in the United States of America
11   13   15   17   19   20   18   16   14   12

Book design by Gretchen Achilles

Some names and identifying characteristics have been changed
to protect the privacy of the individuals involved.

This book is dedicated to Jeremy Tarcher,
whose lifelong creativity inspired us all.

Contents

Introduction

Twenty-five years ago I wrote a book on creativity called *The Artist's Way*. It spelled out, in a step-by-step fashion, just what a person could do to recover—and exercise—their creativity. I often called that book "The Bridge" because it allowed people to move from the shore of their constrictions and fears to the promised land of deeply fulfilling creativity. *The Artist's Way* was used by people of all ages, but I found my just-retired students the most poignant. I sensed in them a particular problem set that came with maturity. Over the years, many of them asked me for help dealing with issues specific to transitioning out of the work force. The book you hold in your hands is the distillate of a quarter century's teaching. It is my attempt to answer, "What next?" for students who are embarking on their "second act." In this book you will find the common problems facing the newly retired: too much time, lack of structure, a sense that our physical surroundings suddenly seem outdated, excitement about the future coupled with a palpable fear of the unknown. As a friend of mine worried recently, "All I do is work. When I stop working, will I do . . . nothing?"

The answer is no. You will not do "nothing." You will do many things. You will be surprised and delighted by the well of colorful inspiration that lies within you—a well that you alone can tap. You will discover that you are not alone in your desires, and that there are creativity tools that can help you navigate the specific issues of retirement. Those who worked the Artist's Way will find some of the tools familiar.

Other tools are new, or their use is innovative. This book attempts to address many taboo subjects for the newly retired: boredom, giddiness, a sense of being untethered, irritability, excitement, and depression, to name just a few. It seeks to give its practitioners a simple set of tools that, used in combination, will trigger a creative rebirth. It attempts to prove that everyone is creative—and that it is never too late to explore your creativity.

When my father entered retirement after a busy and successful thirty-five years as an account executive in advertising, he turned to nature. He acquired a black Scottie dog named Blue that he took for long, daily walks. He also acquired a pair of birding binoculars and found that the hourly tally of winged friends brought him wonder and joy. He spotted finches, juncos, chickadees, wrens, and more exotic visitors, like egrets. He lived half the year on a sailboat in Florida and half the year just outside of Chicago. He enjoyed the differing bird populations and was enchanted by their antics. When it got too dangerous for him to live alone on his boat, he moved to the north permanently, settling into a small cottage on a lagoon. There he spotted cardinals, tanagers, blue jays, owls, and the occasional hawk. When I would visit him, he would share his love of birding. His enthusiasm was contagious, and I found myself buying Audubon prints of the birds my father was spotting. Mounted and carefully framed, the prints brought me much joy. My father's newfound hobby soon became my own, if only in snatches.

"It just takes time and attention," my dad would say. Retired, he found he had both. The birds kept my father company. He was thrilled when a great blue heron established a nest within his view. Visiting my father, I would always hope for a glimpse. The herons were lovely and elegant. My father waited for them patiently. His patience was a gift of his retirement. During his high-powered and stress-filled career, he had no dog and no birds. But nature had called to him, and it was a call he was only able to respond to fully once he retired.

At age fifty-four, I moved to Manhattan. At age sixty-four, entering my own seniority, I moved to Santa Fe. I knew two people who lived in Santa Fe: Natalie Goldberg, the writing teacher, and Elberta Honstein, who raised champion Morgan horses. It could be argued that I had my two most important bases covered. I loved writing and I loved horses. In my ten years in Manhattan, I had written freely, but I didn't ride. It was an Artist's Way exercise that moved me to Santa Fe. I had made a list of twenty-five things that I loved, and high on that list were sage, chamisa, juniper, magpies, red-winged blackbirds, and big skies. In short, a list of the Southwest. Nowhere on the list did New York put in an appearance. No, my loves were all Western flora and fauna: deer, coyotes, bobcats, eagles, hawks. I didn't think about my age when I made my list, although I now realize that the move from New York to Santa Fe might be my last major move.

Allotting myself three days to find a place to live, I flew from New York to Santa Fe and began hunting. I made a list of everything I thought I wanted: an apartment, not a house; walking distance to restaurants and coffee shops; mountain views. The first place the Realtor showed me had every single trait on my list, and I hated it. We moved on, viewing listing after listing. Many of the rentals featured pale carpeting, and I knew from my years in Taos that such carpeting was an invitation for disaster.

Finally, late on my first day of hunting, my Realtor drove us to a final house.

"I don't know why I'm showing you this," she began, winding her way through a maze of dirt roads to a small adobe house with a yard strewn with toys. "A woman with four children lives here," she apologized. I peered into the house. Toys and clothing were strewn every which way. Couches were shoved chockablock.

"I'll take it," I told my startled Realtor. The house was nestled among juniper trees. It had no mountain views. It was miles from restaurants and cafés. Yet, it shouted "home" to me. Its steep driveway would be treacherous in winter, and I sensed that I would have to become accustomed to being snowbound. But it also featured a windowed, octagonal room surrounded by trees. I knew my father would have loved this "bird room." I made it my writing room, and I have appreciated my daily dose of aviary enlightenment every day that I have lived here.

I have lived in this adobe house halfway up the mountain for almost three years now, collecting books and friends. Santa Fe has proven to be hospitable. It is a town full of readers, where my work is appreciated. Often, I am recognized from my dust jacket photo. "Thank you for your books," people say. I put my life in Santa Fe together in a painstaking way. My friendships are grounded in common interests. I myself believe creativity is a spiritual path, and my friends number many Buddhists and Wiccans among them. Every three months, I go back to Manhattan, where I teach workshops. The city feels welcoming but overwhelming. I identify myself to my students as "Julia from Santa Fe." I love living there, I tell them, and it's true.

My mail comes to a rickety mailbox at the foot of my drive. I have to force myself to open the mailbox and retrieve it. So much of what I receive is unwelcome. In March of my first year in Santa Fe, I turned sixty-five. But it was in January that my mail became infested with propaganda related to aging. Daily, I would receive notices about Medicare and special insurance targeting me as a senior. The mail felt intrusive, as if I were being watched. Just how, precisely, did the many petitioners know that I was turning sixty-five?

I found myself dreading my birthday. I might have felt young at heart, yet I was officially categorized as a senior. The mail went so far as to solicit my payment on a gravesite. Clearly I was not only aging, I was nearing the end of my life. Did I want my family saddled with burial costs? No, I did not.

The mail became a mirror that reflected me back in a harsh and unforgiving light. My laugh lines became wrinkles. My throat displayed creases. I thought of Nora Ephron's memoir *I Feel Bad About My Neck*. When first I read it at sixty, I thought it was melodramatic. But that was before I felt bad about my own neck, before I turned sixty-five and became a certified elder.

The term "senior" officially applies to those sixty-five and older. But not everyone who is called a senior feels like a senior. And not everyone who retires is sixty-five. Some retire at fifty, some at eighty. Age is a relative thing. Most working artists never retire. As director John Cassavetes put it, "No matter how old you get, if you can keep the desire to be creative, you're keeping the man-child alive." Cassavetes himself was a fine example of what might be called "youthful aging." He both acted and directed, making and attending films that reflected his own convictions. Working with an ensemble of actors that included his wife, Gena Rowlands, he told tales of intimacy and connection. As he aged, Cassavetes cast himself in his films, portraying troubled and conflicted men. His passion was palpable. Even if he played the oldest character in the movie, he was always young at heart. Taking a cue from Cassavetes, we can retain a passionate interest in life. We can throw ourselves wholeheartedly into projects. At sixty-five, we can still be vibrant beginners.

I'm told the median age in Santa Fe is sixty. It's true that when I go grocery shopping I note many elders pushing carts. People retire to Santa Fe. I have almost become used to the question, "Are you still writing?" The truth is, I cannot imagine not writing. I go from project to project, always frightened by the gap in between. I catch myself distrusting my own process. No matter that I have forty-plus books to my credit, I am afraid that each book will be my last, that I will finally be stymied by age.

Recently, I went to talk to Barbara McCandlish, a gifted therapist.

"I'm sad," I told her. "I'm afraid I'll never write again."

"I think you're afraid of aging," said Barbara. "I think if you write about that, you'll find yourself writing freely again."

The answer is always creativity.

Theater playwright Richard Nelson throws himself into new projects. His age is not an issue. One of his more recent works, the theatrical cycle *The Apple Family Plays*, sets an example of just what is possible with commitment.

Excellent writer John Bowers published his first novel, *End of Story*, at age sixty. At age sixty-four, he is hard at work on a second novel, longer and more ambitious than his first—and he's quick to remark that Laura Ingalls Wilder published *Little House in the Big Woods* when she was sixty-four. John opened his recent book signing in Santa Fe by remarking that the bright stage lights revealed his many wrinkles. An attractive man, he carries his age lightly—despite his jokes. To my eye, his active creativity is keeping his spirit far younger than his calendar age.

My friend Laura, in her midsixties, takes strenuous classes in the dance form Zumba at her local Chicago gym. "I manage to keep up," she says modestly. In truth, she does more than keep up. Her posture is proud and her energy is electric. "It's just three times a week," she tells me. But it is clearly enough to make an impact on both her physique and her optimism. Laura has always loved to dance—ever since her childhood ballet classes—and in finding an exercise routine that delights her playful and creative nature, she's positively glowing—and exercising more consistently now than she ever has before.

Silver-haired but fit, Wade recently retired from a long career in academia. Well-known for his charismatic lectures in the philosophy department at his university, he still surprised himself in retirement when he felt a strong pull to take an acting class. As a young man, he had enjoyed being an active member of his local community theater. Now, he pursues acting with passion, recently undertaking the Jack Nicholson role from *As Good As It Gets* in the very same community theater he once haunted in his youth. "My return to the stage," he chuckles. His excitement is palpable, and the younger members of the troupe are eager to hear his stories of days past.

In their retirement, both Laura and Wade saw themselves returning to passions from their youth. There is no mistake here. There are clues in all of our lives that point to what will bring us joy in our own "second act."

My friend Barry, who loved to take photographs as a child on his Brownie camera, rediscovered this passion almost immediately after retiring from a long career in communication technology. He began taking photos, enjoying learning about the magic of digital cameras, and soon playing around in Photoshop to alter the images he took. He now posts his photos daily on Facebook, and they are mysterious and beautiful, sometimes capturing a more literal image, and sometimes showing a manipulated version of the original shot to convey his own unique impression, his own artist's eye. Often he will adjust an image until it is reminiscent of a classic painting.

"When I was about five," he tells me, "I would sit in my dad's lap as we looked through Rockwell Kent's *World-Famous Paintings*. He would read me the captions. We did this for several weeks, and I looked at a lot of art. It stuck with me." When his friends remark that he has always known his calling, he is humble. "I just didn't know that I knew it," he says. "That's probably true for a lot of people."

As Picasso remarked, "Every child is born an artist. The trick is remaining one as an adult." Passion, commitment, and most of all, the courage to be a beginner, are the qualities that it takes—and qualities that are well within our grasp.

Recently I had dinner with an artist friend. Now sixty-seven, he still works daily as a writer, radio personality, and teacher. The conversation wandered to my current writing and my musing on the subject of retirement.

"Artists don't retire," he said simply.

It's true. Tom Meehan, at eighty-three, had two musicals on Broadway in one season. Today, at eighty-six, he has a new show in the works. Roman Totenberg, an esteemed violinist and teacher, taught—and performed—until his final days, well into his nineties. Frank Lloyd Wright passed on at ninety-one with an unfinished building standing in Oak Park, Illinois. B. B. King toured until six months before his death, at age eighty-nine. Oscar Hammerstein II lived until he was only sixty-five, but just long enough to see *The Sound of Music* open on Broadway. His final song, "Edelweiss," was added to the show during rehearsal.

What do we all have to learn from this? Self-expression is something that does not—and should not—ever stop. Each of us is creative. Each of us has something unique to bring to the world. We have both time and experience on our side. Retirement is a time to tackle projects and unlock dreams, a time to revisit the past and explore the unknown. It is a time to design our future.

BASIC PRINCIPLES FOR CREATIVITY RECOVERY

1. Creativity is the natural order of life. Life is energy—pure, creative energy.
2. There is an underlying, indwelling creative force infusing all of life—including ourselves.
3. When we open ourselves to our creativity, we open ourselves to the creator's creativity within us and our lives.
4. We are, ourselves, creations. And we, in turn, are meant to continue creativity by being creative ourselves.
5. Creativity is God's gift to us. Using our creativity is our gift back to God.
6. The refusal to be creative is self-will and is counter to our true nature.
7. When we open ourselves to exploring our creativity, we open ourselves to God: good, orderly direction.
8. As we open our creative channel to the creator, many gentle but powerful changes are to be expected.
9. It is safe to open ourselves up to greater and greater creativity.
10. Our creative dreams and yearnings come from a divine source. As we move toward our dreams, we move toward our divinity.

How to Use This Book

It's Never Too Late to Begin Again is a twelve-week course for anyone who wishes to expand his or her creativity. It is not meant only for "declared" artists. It is aimed at those transitioning into the second act of life—leaving one life behind, and heading into one yet to be created. For some, this may mean retiring from the formal work world, for others this may mean facing an empty nest once the children have grown up and left home, for still others this may simply mean rejuvenating the creative spirit when suddenly branded "senior citizen."

Each week, you will read the week's chapter and complete the tasks within. You will work with four basic tools: the daily tool of Morning Pages, the once-weekly Artist Date, and twice-weekly solo Walks. The Memoir will unfurl over the entire twelve weeks, as you revisit your unique story one manageable section at a time.

Twelve weeks—three months—may seem like a long time, but think of it as a few-hours-weekly investment in the next phase of your life.

Basic Tools

MORNING PAGES Three daily pages of longhand, stream-of-consciousness writing done first thing in the morning, "for your eyes only"

MEMOIR A weekly, guided process of triggering memories and revisiting your life in several-year increments

ARTIST DATES A once-weekly, solo expedition to explore something fun

WALKING A twenty-minute solo walk, twice weekly, without a dog, friend, or cell phone

xix

Morning Pages

The bedrock tool of a creative recovery is something I call Morning Pages: three pages of longhand morning writing about absolutely anything. They are to be written first thing in the morning and shown to no one. There is no wrong way to do Morning Pages. I like to think of them as windshield wipers, swiping away anything that stands between you and a clear view of your day.

The pages may seem petty and trivial—"I forgot to buy birdseed. I'm not impressed with the new dishwashing liquid. I need to renew my AAA membership. I'm out of printer paper. I need to call my brother back."—but they forge the trail for further adventures in creativity.

The pages notify both us and the universe precisely where we're at. I often think of them as a form of active meditation. Another way to think of them is as a tiny whisk broom that dislodges dust from every corner of our life. Many times, people resist Morning Pages, claiming lack of time, only to find them increasingly doable as empty time looms on the horizon.

Make no mistake: Morning Pages are ideal for retirees.

"Julia, I have no time" gives way to "Julia, I have plenty time—and I know how I want to use it." I explain that the pages are like a spiritual radio kit. As we write out our resentments, fears, joys, delights, dreams and wishes, we are notifying the universe who we really are. As we write freely, we find ourselves freer in our lives, seeing choice points in our day that we may not have noticed before. We begin to hear the universe responding back to us. We have hunches and intuitions that tell us what our next steps should be. We are led carefully and well. Often, Morning Pages are a tough-love friend. If we are avoiding action on an important issue, the pages will nag us until we comply with their suggestions.

"Julia, I did Morning Pages and cornered myself into sobriety," I have often been told.

"Julia, I did Morning Pages and found myself willing to take a rigorous look at my eating and exercise habits. I've lost fifty pounds."

It is very difficult to complain about a situation morning after morning, page after page, without being moved to constructive action.

Morning Pages lead us to a conscious contact with our creator. They forge a bridge over which we can walk into new lives—lives better suited to our dreams and aspirations.

"Julia, I'm afraid of pages," I sometimes hear. Pages are gentle, I reassure the timid.

"I don't see how they can work," the doubters sometimes say.

"Just try them," I urge. There is no wrong way to do Morning Pages. The pages are an experiential tool. Practicing them makes us believers.

Just as travelers on a jet may not appreciate the speed at which they are moving unless there is turbulence, so too, those writing Morning Pages may be unaware of the velocity at which they travel. It is impossible to write Morning Pages without effecting change, and yet, some protest that while they are doing Morning Pages, the pages themselves are merely boring.

"Keep writing," I advise these defiant ones. "If you keep writing, you will have a breakthrough."

"But Julia, really. Nothing's happening," I will sometimes hear from a student who, to my eye, is changing at the speed of light. Often, our creative recovery remains invisible because it is changing us in directions we do not expect. I have seen writers begin to paint, lawyers begin to write, teachers begin to sing. Everyone unblocks in the direction they are meant to. I often say that when you use these tools, you shake the apple tree—and the universe delivers oranges.

Not all unblocking happens in the arts. Carol found herself volunteering at an adult literacy program. It gave her great joy and filled her empty hours. Anthony joined a chess league. Monty joined a bridge club. A new appreciation of our hobbies is a frequent fruit of Morning Pages. So the next time you catch yourself thinking "nothing" is happening, think again.

Writing Morning Pages is an act of attention. The reward for attention is always healing. Many embark on Morning Pages without realizing their therapeutic value. All of us carry wounds; some severe, some less so. Some may have suffered harsh blows as a child. Others carry wounds acquired in adulthood. By writing, we quite literally "right" the wrongs we have encountered.

Morning Pages hold hope for the future. They do this by focusing on the present: each day's march holds many choice points. As we see our choices, our moods lighten—and so do our lives.

For the first-time practitioner of Morning Pages, the impact of many previously avoided emotions may be overwhelming. We are accustomed to being vague. But this no longer serves us. We are accustomed to saying, "I feel okay about that," when actually we may feel something quite different. The pages dare us to be specific. Instead of saying, "I feel okay," we may find ourselves saying, "I feel angry, annoyed, threatened"—any of a number of things—none of them "okay." As we learn to name—and claim—our feelings, those feelings become less overwhelming. As we admit our negative emotions, we begin to stop thinking of them as bad. "I'm threatened," we may find ourselves writing, or "I'm jealous," or "I'm mad." Feeling our previously ignored emotions gives us a leg up in dealing with them. We are no longer ambushed. As we use our Morning Pages to explore and express our difficult feelings, we are teaching ourselves the valuable art of authenticity. First on the page, and then in life, we draw new boundaries. We no longer people-please with white lies. We show up for ourselves on the page, and soon see that we are standing up for ourselves in the world.

Writing Morning Pages, we are pointed toward our own "true north." We clarify our own values. We become more honest, first with ourselves, and then with others. Once fearful that our honesty might push others away, we find that the opposite is actually true: relationships heal and grow as we heal and grow.

Morning Pages are written by hand. Why? Every time I teach, a student will point out that they are much faster on the computer. Wouldn't it be more efficient if . . . ?

No, I don't think so.

For Morning Pages, writing by hand is essential. When we write by hand, we go slowly enough to record our thoughts with accuracy. On a computer, we whiz along, dashing our thoughts to the page. Writing by hand, it is as if we are driving our car at thirty-five miles per hour. "Ah," we say, "here comes my exit. And look—there's a convenience store."

Typing on a computer, it is as if we are driving at seventy-five miles per hour. "Oh dear—was that my exit?" we wonder. "Was that a convenience store or a gas station?" Our perceptions are fleeting. We're not quite sure what we see or feel. We miss important signposts and details. Writing by hand, we know precisely what we encounter. Writing by hand yields a handmade life. Many of us feel we can write faster by computer, but fast is not what we are after. We write by hand to connect ourselves precisely with what it is we are thinking and feeling. Writing by computer, we speed along, telling ourselves that we feel "okay" about the events of our life. But what does "okay" really mean?

That is what is answered when we write by hand.

I feel sad, and my handwriting tells me why. I miss my dog Tiger Lily, who died two months ago. I miss my daughter, who is in New York visiting with her father. There is specificity in what I miss: my dog's habit of dozing on the Oriental rug; my daughter's sweet voice as she catches me up on the events of her life. No, I do not really feel "okay." "Okay" was a smokescreen, a haze that stood between myself and my reality. Pen to paper, my honesty is palpable. Though word for word it may be slower than typing, I am directly in touch with my own questions—and answers—much faster.

The Morning Pages tutor us in patience as we work through difficult relationships. They tutor us through our resistance as we embark on new goals and projects.

TASK
Morning Pages

Every morning, as close to waking as possible, write three pages about absolutely anything. These single-sided pages are handwritten, and for your eyes only. I suggest using 8.5-by-11-inch paper—smaller, and you will crimp your thoughts. Please do write by hand—it is not the same when we write on a device, even though we may feel we can go "faster." I am often asked whether these must be done before coffee. As a coffee lover myself, I would never get between someone and their morning pick-me-up. I would say, though, do not spend forty-five minutes brewing the perfect cup. Get to the page as quickly as possible. The faster you begin writing, the greater the effect of the pages will be.

Do not show these pages to loved ones or well-meaning friends. These pages are private, completely free, and strictly stream-of-consciousness. They perform a type of spiritual chiropractic; they clear us for the day ahead. They are not meant to be "writing" or even journaling, where we are more likely to explore a single topic in a structured fashion. Morning Pages clear the psychic debris standing between us and the day ahead. Done consistently, they will alter the trajectory of our lives.

Artist Dates

The second major tool of a creative recovery is something I call an Artist Date. It is a once-a-week, solo expedition on which you explore something that interests or entrances you. Expect to meet resistance when you propose to yourself doing something fun. Morning Pages are work, and we undertake the work willingly. We seem to understand the notion of "working" on our creativity.

Artist Dates, by contrast, are assigned play. And even though we give lip service to the phrase "the play of ideas," we don't always truly understand how fun can help us. Those who undertake Artist Dates report insights, hunches, and breakthroughs. They report a heightened sense of well-being. Some go so far as to say that Artist Dates give them a conscious contact with a power greater than themselves. So it is worth our while to resist our resistance.

Plan an Artist Date ahead of time—that's the "date" part of Artist Date. Then watch how your inner killjoy swings into action. Suddenly, there are a million things that should be done instead. Our significant other begs to join us. But no. Artist Dates are to be undertaken by ourselves, alone. When we stick to our guns, we are rewarded by a heightened sense of autonomy.

An Artist Date need not be expensive or exotic. It can be something as simple as stopping into a pet store. A favorite Artist Date of mine is a visit to a children's bookstore. After all, our artist may be seen as an inner child. I find that a children's bookstore offers "just enough" information to scratch the surface of a topic I find interesting, and the playful nature of the store encourages me to play—exploring many different topics, dipping my toe in here or there.

The point of the Artist Date is that it is something that feels fresh and exciting to *you*.

Charles took himself on an Artist Date to a plant store. There he viewed many exquisite orchids but settled on a pink-and-blue bromeliad the clerk assured him would last for months.

Muriel took herself on a musical Artist Date. She went to hear her church choir as they performed Handel's *Messiah*. "It was glorious," she relayed. "I had no idea they were so talented."

Gloria visited an art supply store that featured a 250-pound snake in a plexiglass enclosure. "I was scared of the snake," Gloria reported. "But it made my shopping spree an adventure."

Antoinette took a lively Artist Date: a kickboxing class at her gym. "I got winded quickly and couldn't keep up," she reports, "but I resolved to keep going, knowing my stamina would increase. After all, the teacher was overweight, and she could set a strenuous pace. I enjoyed that our instructor wasn't perfect. It gave me courage."

Artist Dates require courage. But their reward is renewed vigor and inspiration.

One of the first fruits of Artist Dates is increased stamina. As we undertake play, we find that we do not tire so easily. The world is an adventure and we are adventurous souls. It is important, in planning our adventures, that we think in terms of mystery rather than mastery. You don't know how to ice-skate? It's never too late to learn! The youthful part of ourselves has often long been starved. We need now to think in terms of beauty rather than duty. We are seeking to reawaken our sense of wonder. Often a zoo, aviary, or aquarium is an ideal place to start. There we encounter living creatures that may regard us with as much curiosity as we do them. In planning our adventures, we may want to invent an imaginary youngster who we must seek to entertain. But don't bring along a real youngster—the point of the Artist Date is for us to recapture the wonder and excitement that we had when we were young, uninhibited by the responsibility of taking care of a flesh-and-blood child.

As you progress through your Memoir, you may wish to take an Artist Date that evokes a memory of the time you are revisiting. These "remembering" Artist Dates can be very powerful indeed. One student of mine remembered visiting her grandmother's house as a young child each summer, and the tall bin of "Granny Cookies" that resided high on the shelf. Years later, working with her Memoir, she took a specific Artist Date to re-create the experience.

"I went to several antique stores with the hope of finding a tin that reminded me of the one Granny had. Amazingly, I did find something that evoked that memory. I realized I didn't know exactly what Granny's tin had looked like, but a tall blue-and-white cookie jar sparked something childlike in me. I got the recipe from my aunt and made 'Granny Cookies' myself, painstakingly lining the cookie jar with waxed paper to protect the pink-frosted sugar cookies from sticking together. The experience was very moving for me. The smells and tastes of the project took me back to a very simple and happy time."

Another student of mine took an Artist Date to a more painful memory—with surprising results. "I lost my brother to alcoholism," Chris tells me. "For a long time I was his caretaker. It was a scary time of very mixed emotions—at times I was afraid that I was losing both him and myself. He lived with me in Greenwich Village and there was no telling what each day would bring. It was a chaotic, unstable few years." Chris took himself to the Chinese restaurant he used to order from when he had lived with his brother in Greenwich Village. "I hadn't been to that restaurant since—It had been years," he remembers. "I ordered the dumplings I used to always order. There they were—just the same as always. The taste and smell just brought me back. I walked through the old neighborhood, past the apartment where we lived. I was overwhelmed with memories—my dog as a puppy, my brother at lots of different ages, on his good days and his bad days. The times we shared those Chinese dumplings and the times I ate them alone, fighting back tears as he sat nearly comatose, drunk on the couch. I went into an office supply store I used to frequent during that time. Sometimes, when I felt at a loss, I'd go in and just stand there, looking at the colorful pens, trying to distract myself with something I liked. I stood there in that office supply shop, years later, staring at the pens. I felt really sad thinking of my brother, thinking of my own darkest hours. And then something incredible happened. I realized I could be there for my former self. That guy who had stood there, idly testing pens years before—he was me. It was like I could look back at him and say, 'Hey, it's going to be okay. You're going to make it through.' It was some kind of closure for me. I bought myself a pen that day. It actually makes me really happy each time I use it."

Courting ourselves, wooing ourselves, exploring new or historic sites—an Artist Date typically takes only about an hour. As much effort as it might seem to take to get up and go out and do it, the hour is likely to be very memorable.

TASK
Artist Date

Make a list of ten possible adventures. Once a week, take yourself on one. It may be something from this list or something that occurs to you during the week. The Artist Date is for *you alone* to explore what might delight *you alone.* Plan to spend about an hour once a week—more if you like—and schedule your Artist Date as you would a meeting with someone important. Resist canceling the plans or inviting others along. This is your date with your inner artist. You may sense great resistance to doing this task, but the rewards will undoubtedly surprise and inspire you.

Walking

One of the most valuable creativity tools is also the simplest. I am talking about walking. When I wrote *The Artist's Way,* I put exercise in Week 12. I knew it was important, but I hadn't yet realized how important. Now, twenty-five years later, I assign two weekly walks whenever I teach. I have learned that walking quells anxiety and allows creativity to bubble to the surface.

"But, Julia, I don't have time to walk," students sometimes protest. They do so because they don't realize the importance of the activity. Very often, those students who protest the hardest become walking's biggest fans. As one explained to me, "It's as though I have communicated with the universe and the universe uses walking as the chance to communicate back."

Walking is an exercise in receptivity. As we walk, we fill the creative well. We notice new images and make new connections. From the cat seated in the window box to the dog tugging at the owner's leash, we register our connection with all creatures. From the shriek of glee from the child at play to the merry *chirrup chirrup* of a visiting songbird, we knit together many notes in the melody of life. Walking makes a quilt out of the silken patches of our experience. So yes, it is important that we walk.

"*Solvitur ambulando*," Saint Augustine remarked. In plain English, "It is solved by walking." The "it" can be almost anything. For many of us, walking solves the problems of daily living. Not only does it bring structure—it brings answers, too. We may walk out with a problem, but the odds are excellent that we will walk back in with a solution.

Mona resisted walking. She considered it a waste of her valuable time. When I insisted that she must try it, she became grumpy, even hostile. "Julia, *you* may have time to walk, but *I* don't," she protested.

"Mona," I told her, "we're only talking about twenty minutes. Surely you can find that amount of time."

Angrily, Mona took the first of her twenty-minute walks. She walked seven blocks down the street and seven blocks back—ten minutes each way. As she walked, a squirrel scampered across her path and a red-winged blackbird lilted on the branch of an apple tree. The blackbird was rare in the city, Mona noted to herself. Spotting it gave her a sense of satisfaction. Reluctantly, Mona admitted to herself that perhaps there was something to this walking business. On her second walk of the week, Mona happened upon an elderly pair of lovers who walked, hands entwined. Spotting them, Mona felt a sense of faith and optimism. "Maybe aging is not so bad," she caught herself thinking. More rapidly than she would have thought possible, she took to walking. Although the assignment was to walk twice weekly, she found herself walking daily and finding a sense of adventure on every walk.

Diplomat Dag Hammarskjöld believed in long, daily walks. On them, he would ponder complex questions of statesmanship. Novelist John Nichols writes every day and walks every day, as well. Esteemed writing teacher Brenda Ueland swore by long, daily walks—"I will tell you what I have learned myself. For me, a long five- or six-mile walk helps. And one must go alone and every day." Walking aerobicizes not only our minds but also our bodies. We walk for free, without an expensive gym or trainer. Walking brings us gently to mental and physical fitness.

Lisa found herself entering retirement overwhelmed and overweight. She began a regime of daily walking, which she undertook to, as she put it, "clear my mind," and because it was "only for twenty minutes." Within two months, she had shed ten pounds. "Walking is addictive," she told me.

Frances, a composer, found herself stuck halfway through an operetta. At my suggestion, she tried walking and happily reported after two weeks, "I'm full of melodies again."

Gerald, a New Yorker, often walks to his destination, taking in the architecture of Manhattan's many varied neighborhoods along the way. An optimist by nature, he credits his walks for his many good moods.

A habit of daily walks becomes a habit of daily health. Twenty minutes is long enough, although many people find themselves walking longer.

Katie, a high-powered literary agent, believes in walking. She goes on what she calls "urban hikes" through the city, often logging ten or more miles in a day. "Walking brings me peace and clarity," she says. "The fresh air is exhilarating, and I find insights and intuitions often come to me as I walk."

TASK
Walk

Twice a week, take yourself on a twenty-minute solo walk. Allow yourself to walk without a dog, spouse, friend, or cell phone. This is time for you to move—and move into clarity. Walking alone creates the open space in your mind for insights to land. I often like to listen for "ahas" on my walks. Listening, I always find them.

Memoir

One especially heartbreaking sentence I have heard over and over from my newly retired students is, "Oh, my life wasn't that interesting."

The truth is that every life is fascinating. And when we are willing to look at, and thus honor, the life we have led, we inevitably bring ourselves to a place of both power and self-appreciation.

If it sounds like magic, it is.

The Memoir is a weekly exercise that builds upon itself. You will divide your life into sections; as a rule of thumb, divide your age by twelve, and this is the number of years you will cover each week. By answering a "jot list" of questions each week, you will trigger vivid memories, discover lost dreams, and find unexpected healing and clarity. Don't worry—you aren't required to write a magnum opus of your life, unless of course you want to. Everyone's Memoir will be different—you may choose simply to answer the questions and list the memories they evoke in standard prose form; alternately, you may sometimes find your answers coming out as poems, drawings, or songs. Along the way, you will find dreams you wish to return to, ideas you are ready to discard, wounds you are ready to heal, and most of all, an appreciation for the life you have led. There will be topics you wish to dig into more deeply. I have had students quilt periods of their lives, write songs about lost loves, send letters of gratitude to people whose influence they now appreciate, write short stories based on people they have known or essays on experiences they have had.

As you become open to revisiting your life, your life will become open to revisiting you. I have had students worry that they "don't remember anything"—but this has never turned out to be true. Each week, at the end of the first essay, there will be questions for you to answer. This guided process to gently revisit your life to date—with a good dose of fun and adventure—brings powerful insight. By revisiting—and reigniting—the many deep, complex, creative parts of yourself and your story, you will arrive at a place of clarity and purpose—a jumping-off place for the rest of your life.

It is with great excitement that I present to you these tools. Using them, your life will be transformed. I hope you will find yourself in the stories in these pages. It is my belief that what I call the second act of life can be the most exciting and fulfilling time of all.

Reigniting a Sense of Wonder

This week you will delve into early childhood memories as your creative adventure gently begins. You will reconnect with the wonder of a familiar—but perhaps long-ignored—sense of possibility. You will start to examine and discard old ideas that may be stopping you from exploring new horizons: the inner blocks of skepticism and self-censorship; the outer societal assumptions that creativity is a rare gift granted only to few; the idea that it's "too late" to begin something new. You will begin to look at yourself—and your story—with more compassion. With wonder, you will begin to recognize yourself as a unique being with much to contribute to the world.

Returning to the Wonder of Childhood

Youth is happy because it has the ability to see beauty.... Anyone who keeps the ability to see beauty never grows old.

—FRANZ KAFKA

The part of us that creates is childlike. It is filled with awe, alert to new experiences, and mesmerized by the sensory wonders of our environment: the otherworldly blanket of fresh white snow, the enticing smell of chocolate chip cookies baking in the oven, the crispness of a new pencil, the delightful allure of a colorful paperweight. For me, Victorian houses awaken a strong memory: the fascinating corners within my childhood home in Libertyville, Illinois. The house was built by a woodworker whose artistry appeared in secret compartments, elaborate carvings, and hidden panels. It was thrilling to tap a special spot on the wall and watch it spring open to reveal the stereo behind it. Roaming through the house was its own adventure—there was an artful effect around every corner just waiting to be discovered.

Young children discover one thing at a time. The tiniest detail sparks wonder. Because a young child doesn't have the same awareness of time as an adult does, there isn't a sense of "hurrying" to learn something. Each new discovery builds upon the last as an exciting body of knowledge, and experience is formed. Adults have often forgotten this natural perspective, and they put pressure on themselves to learn quickly or impatiently expect themselves to come to a solution immediately.

Just-retired adults are often leaving a structured life where they were an expert—and entering a non-structured life where they may feel, to some degree, at loose ends. The shock of retirement can be startling. Suddenly, endless bolts of empty time loom on the horizon. The possibilities are infinite—and this can be a very overwhelming proposition. Just-retired people almost unanimously describe the early days—even months—of retirement as an acute adjustment.

Richard, on his first day of retirement after a long stint as a re-creation director, woke up feeling aimless after many years of daily agendas. When his wife asked him what he might do that day, he replied, "I think I'll take a bike ride." And when she asked where he might go, he realized he didn't have an answer. "I don't have anywhere to go," he admitted.

Victor ended a career as an engineer, and in the early days of his retirement he repeatedly wandered into his home office, looking through his books from work. His daughter called to check in, asking how he was enjoying his retirement. "I'm not sure what I'm supposed to do," he told her.

Wonder is the beginning of wisdom.

—SOCRATES

It is important to be very gentle with yourself, especially in the early days of a transition. In fact, there is no such thing as being too gentle with yourself at this time.

Many retirees haven't realistically anticipated the trauma that may be caused by excessive free time. Suddenly left to their own devices, they may find themselves moody and depressed, which in turn leads them to judge themselves negatively. "I should be doing much better," they tell themselves, struggling to find self-compassion. How much better it would be if, instead of harsh judgments of their failings, they could say to themselves gently, "Of course I'm in shock. I'm in the midst of a huge adjustment."

It is human nature to crave a sense of purpose, and without one, it is natural that panic might set in as you begin to feel adrift. This is where Morning Pages, Artist Dates, and Walks become a lifeboat. These three basic tools create a structure for your day and for your week. Within this structure, new ideas and opportunities will arise. At the same time, as you answer simple questions to build your Memoir, you will begin to discover new interests, desires, and direction. You may find yourself reawakening long-lost dreams and passions. A rich and thrilling journey awaits.

Sally retired after thirty years as an accountant. At first, she floundered. "I wanted to do something creative," she says, "but I considered myself completely noncreative. I worked with numbers. Everything was black-and-white."

As Sally began working with Morning Pages, she experienced unexpected bursts of creative energy. "My Morning Pages had all kinds of ideas for me," she reports. "I changed all the colors in my house and I threw away almost all my work clothes. I felt like wearing things that were colorful. I wanted to plant a garden."

She began her Memoir with reluctance, only to make an unexpected discovery. "I was intimidated by the word 'Memoir,' but I thought, why not answer the questions? It seemed easy enough. There were lots of memories that came up for me—my grandfather was a mural painter, and I loved to go to his sites with him. I remembered the thrill I felt when I did that—like I was entering a secret world. I had really forgotten about how magical that experience was." Continuing to excavate, Sally remembered a time she got in trouble for painting on the kitchen wall as a young child. "I had my paints and I thought what I was doing was beautiful. I sure was having fun. But Mother came in halfway through, and she saw red. I had messed up her wall and it was expensive for her to fix. We didn't have a lot of money. I remember feeling so guilty about it, just devastated."

In her own defense, Sally argued that Grandpa painted on walls, too. But her mother replied, "Well, he's a real painter. That's something else."

Sally had forgotten about this exchange, but in looking back, she could see that her mother's words had stuck with her. "I didn't do very well in art class all the way through school," she says now. "It was like a self-fulfilling prophecy. There was such a thing as a 'real' painter and all I knew was that it wasn't me. I think without even realizing it, I decided then and there that I'd better do something as far from that as I could."

It took a great deal of courage for Sally to take an Artist Date to an art supply store. "I was so nervous to walk inside. I walked past the

The most sophisticated people I know—inside they are all children.

—JIM HENSON

door four times before I went in," she admits. "I know it sounds crazy. But I think I just didn't believe I was allowed to go in there."

When she did, she was overcome with memory. "The colors, the brushes, the canvases just brought me back to that place with my grandfather," she says. "Even some of the types of paints still have the same packaging." Sally chose a few simple supplies, took them home, and allowed herself to paint. "I was laughing with delight," she reports. "I had no idea what I was doing, but I really wanted to do this. It was pure, imperfect, exhilarating fun."

Sally returned to that art supply store a few months later to find a beginning mural painting class in session in the back. She asked the clerk if it was still possible to sign up for the class late, and was told that she was welcome to join. A few months later, Sally proudly showed off a small mural she had begun on her screened-in porch: simple tree branches with birds. Also on her porch? A photograph of her grandfather at work.

"Turns out it's still thrilling for me to paint on the wall," Sally admits with a laugh. "I'm convinced that if I can find a lost passion, anyone can. It's just a bit of work to get back to that pure place. But it's worth it. And I feel like I'm visiting with my grandpa again, too."

So, where to start? At the very beginning, of course! It is helpful to remember ourselves as children, naturally open to exploration. Our early memories are specific, and we often find there are clues there to our true passions, if we are willing to search for them.

TASK
Memoir, Week One

Divide your age by twelve. This is the number of years you will cover each week in your Memoir exploration. For example, if you are sixty years old, you will revisit birth through age five this week. Start by filling in the following "jot list," allowing yourself to move quickly through the questions. They are designed to trigger your conscious and subconscious mind. You may discover memories in this list that are exciting, painful, resolved, unresolved—there are no wrong answers. This is *your* story, as only you can tell it. Memories that come loaded with emotion are excellent material for Artist Date ideas, fuel for an extra-long walk, or motivation to reach out to a long-lost friend. If you are moved to dig deeper into a certain memory, now or later, do. Over the course of the week, revisit your answers and, if you feel so moved, expand upon one or more of the memories they evoke. You may want to describe what happened in narrative form, or perhaps let the memory inspire another form, perhaps a poem, a painting, or a song. But be gentle with yourself. There is no right or wrong way to create your Memoir.

AGES: _____

1. Where did you live?
2. Who took care of you?
3. Did you have any pets?
4. What is your earliest memory?
5. What was your favorite book? What was your favorite toy?
6. Describe a smell you remember from this stage of your life.
7. What was your favorite food?
8. Describe a sound from this period of your life (a voice, a song, a train whistle, a dog's bark, etc. . . .)
9. Describe a location where you remember spending time.
10. What other memories occur to you from this period? Did you discover anything in your Memoir that you'd like to explore in an Artist Date? (For example, if you remembered the smell of fresh-baked bread, a visit to a bakery could be a wonderful Artist Date.)

Never Too Late

The joke runs like this:

> Question: Do you know how old I will be by the time I learn
>   to play the piano?
> Answer: The same age you'll be if you don't.

A year from now you will wish you had started today.

—KAREN LAMB

I posted on Facebook recently that it was never too late to be a beginner. A flood of "likes" came back to me. One woman wanted me to know that her dad had begun piano lessons at age seventy-six—and his lessons were going well. I began my own piano lessons when I turned sixty. At age sixty-five, I still considered myself a beginner, although my teacher said I had made great strides. Every week, I went to my lesson armed with a small notebook. In it, my teacher recorded the assignments of the week:

"Practice the C major scale. Practice the G major scale. Practice, period . . ."

I still take piano lessons. Every Thursday I show up at my lesson, bringing a record of the week's practice to my teacher. I love my piano lessons. I am undoubtedly still a beginner, but I have made progress. And any progress is satisfying. As a child, I was considered one of the "nonmusical" children in a large family, where three of my six siblings went on to become professional musicians. The piano was often "taken," with one of my brothers or sisters playing more advanced pieces than I was capable of. I happily immersed myself in words and books, but a bit of me longed to be a part of the melodies that danced through the house. I have always loved a home filled with music. Today, even at my early stage of learning, it is thrilling to be the one adding music to my home.

Often, when we say it is "too late" for us to begin something, what we are really saying is that we aren't willing to be a beginner. But when we are willing to dip our toe in, even just a little, we are rewarded with a sense of youthful wonder.

Gillian enjoyed a long and successful career as an actor. But as she approached her seventies, she found acting opportunities were fewer and farther between. Telling herself she was just filling time, she began writing poetry. "I'm just a beginner," she told people who asked about her newly discovered passion. "I'd like to know more," she told me. I suggested she consider a writing program. "I'm a little bit old to be pursuing higher education," she replied. I told her that in the creative arts, age did not matter. After all, Robert Frost won his first Pulitzer Prize at age fifty—and his fourth at age sixty-nine.

Gillian screwed her courage to the sticking point and applied to an online poetry program. To her surprise and delight, the program accepted her. She told me, "I'll be seventy-five by the time I finish—and I'm really intimidated by the idea of using the Internet." I told her, "You'll be seventy-five anyway—and there are lots of people who can help you become computer literate." She accepted her place in the program and asked her teenage granddaughter to tutor her twice weekly on the computer for a modest fee. Her granddaughter was happy to help, and happy to make a little bit of extra cash. By the time Gillian began the intensive poetry workshops, she was proficient in the online skills she needed to know. She loved learning more about poetry and loved trying her hand at the different forms. To her surprise and delight, her teachers liked and appreciated her work.

And, when she inevitably did turn seventy-five, she had a master's degree in poetry, a fiery enthusiasm, and a real sense of ease with the computer that had once intimidated her.

Gillian was nervous about beginning a new art form—but maybe even more nervous about using the computer and the mysterious Internet. But as she took small steps to learn, she realized that they were simply new tools—and ones that were, in fact, a lot more user-friendly than she had presumed.

Often, the hurdle that blocks us from beginning something is

Never give in, never give in, never, never, never, never.

—WINSTON CHURCHILL

smaller than we realize. It takes only a tiny step in the direction of our dream to start the process. "It's too late" is a powerful block for many, but in fact, it is rarely an actual block to exploring the desired activity.

"I'm sixty-five and I've never exercised," says Patti. "I could say it's too late for me to be an Olympic gymnast, and decide I've done all I can. Or I could start taking walks, join a gym, hire a trainer, and enjoy watching the Olympics on television for inspiration. Just saying 'I could never do that' when I watch teenage girls flip over the bars on the TV is a bit defeatist. And is my goal really to be an elite athlete? No, my goal is to be just a bit more fit than I am. I can be satisfied by small steps—in fact, very satisfied."

We are always the same age inside.

—GERTRUDE STEIN

In exploring new realms, we often find that our life experience serves us very well. We have learned patience. We are able to see the long game. We are able to identify expertise and seek out those who can help us find efficient routes to our goals. And, no matter our age, the thrill of beginning something new is universal.

Ron is seventy years old. He still works full-time as a tenured academic, although retirement is on the horizon for him. Last year, he turned his focus to a book idea he had had for forty years. Writing daily, he fleshed out his idea. He then sent a proposal to a writer friend, who in turn sent it on to his agent.

"This book is great," the agent responded. "I'd like to represent it myself."

And so, Ron, a beginning writer, found himself in possession of a first-rate agent and a whole new set of challenges. He knew how to navigate in the academic world, where he was well respected as a professor. But how to navigate the publishing world was another story.

Fortunately, his years in academia had taught him the value of research. He reached out to seasoned professionals. To his delight, he was met with encouragement. He had a large project in front of him, but it was one he looked forward to. "I love the learning environment," he says. "And now I will become the student of this process which is so new for me."

He was not "too old" to be a beginner. And by allowing himself to begin this project just before he expected to retire, he set up his next phase nicely, anticipating that the change from the highly regimented academic calendar to the vast freedom of retirement would be smoother if he had a large project to help structure his time.

It's never too late to be a beginner.

TASK
Never Too Late

Take pen in hand. In a notebook, number from 1 to 5 and finish in the following:

1. If it weren't too late, I'd . . .
2. If it weren't too late, I'd . . .
3. If it weren't too late, I'd . . .
4. If it weren't too late, I'd . . .
5. If it weren't too late, I'd . . .

The Inner Censor

During our work lives, we customarily received criticism from our bosses and sometimes our colleagues. Many of us endured yearly or quarterly reviews, and we took in their frequent negativity as part of our job. Retired, we find ourselves continuing to receive negative feedback, but instead of coming from our employer, it is the product of our own inner Censor—that internal voice that tells us we are not doing well and that we could do better. Our Censor attacks us from out of the blue and its voice has a damning certainty. We could have, and should have, done better, states the Censor, and we often then repeat this criticism to ourselves. In dealing with the Censor, it helps to know that its negative voice is not the voice of reason. Rather, it is a caricature villain who will always be on the attack until we stand up to it and say, "Oh—that's just my Censor."

For many of us, this negative inner voice is a formidable foe. We have often spent many years buying into the Censor's negativity, believing what it says and using that negative belief to talk ourselves out of projects and delights. The scenario goes something like this:

The worst enemy to creativity is self-doubt.

—SYLVIA PLATH

I'd love to design clothes.

Censor: You're too old to learn fashion design.

I'd really love to design clothes.

Censor: You're not fashionable.

I think I'd like to try.

Censor: What a terrible waste of money.

I can afford it.

Censor: You're really a fool.

Afraid of feeling foolish, we often back down from our dreams. We take the voice of the Censor as the voice of reason. In reality, it is the Censor's voice that is foolish, talking us out of joys and future rewards.

The Censor is typically sarcastic. It pokes fun at our ideas and encourages us to give up. The Censor speaks in a "schoolyard bully" tone and often uses simplistic reasoning. Upon closer examination, we discover that our Censor is unreasonably negative—in fact, our Censor may criticize our best ideas. To the Censor, any original idea seems dangerous. Let's say our creativity is a verdant meadow. The Censor believes itself to be in charge of the animals that enter the meadow. It likes known, familiar beasts—an idea that's like a cow. But perhaps a novel idea strives to enter the clearing—say, a zebra. The Censor will begin its attack, poking fun at the very sight of a new idea. And so it rants and belittles: "Stripes? Who ever heard of stripes? Stripes look foolish."

It does no good to say soothingly, "It's a zebra. Zebras have stripes." The Censor doesn't want to hear it. "Send in a cow," the Censor commands. And, unless we back down, the Censor will continue its shrill attack on zebras. It's important to realize that the Censor saves its most vehement attacks for our most original ideas.

I am a seasoned writer with more than forty books to my credit. Yet, my Censor is alive and well—and plausibly believable. Every time I propose a new book idea, my Censor swings into action. "It's a bad idea," it tells me. That, and, "You'll never pull it off." I have named my Censor Nigel, and Nigel is almost impossible to outflank. I recently wrote a book that had Nigel up in arms. Every page I produced seemed to provoke ever more vicious criticism. As a younger writer, I might have allowed myself to become so discouraged that I would have abandoned the project. Older and wiser, I found myself angered by Nigel's attack. The anger gave me fuel to keep on writing.

I have learned to say, "Oh, hello, Nigel! What don't you like this time?"

My students have found they enjoy naming and describing their Censor. When they do so, their Censor is miniaturized, often turning into a cartoon character that they can easily dismiss.

We cannot eliminate our Censor, but we can learn to evade it.

When Annie retired from a career as a biologist, she knew she wanted to write a memoir. She dreamed of writing and sharing her life story with her children and grandchildren. Annie had written some prose in her life, mostly letters and short essays. But she truly desired to write a longer, polished piece as she revisited her life.

Her Censor told her that her idea was crazy—and that her life was boring. But, one page—one word—at a time, Annie persevered. Ignoring her Censor, she joked, "Thank you for sharing," whenever she heard its nasty voice in her head. Early in the process, Annie joined a women's writing circle. With the support of the group, she tackled her memoir gently and methodically, writing weekly installments.

"This is stupid," her Censor piped up. "Who would want to read this?" But Annie persisted. The members of her writing circle were enthusiastic about her tale. Week after week, recounting year after

If you hear a voice within you say you cannot paint, then by all means paint and that voice will be silenced.

—VINCENT VAN GOGH

year, Annie wrote her adventures, small and large. Eventually, she was able to neutralize her Censor's negativity more often than not. She worked hard to perform creative alchemy, converting each negative remark to a positive.

"No one will want to read this," the Censor opined.

"Somebody will love to read this," Annie shot back.

"Your life is dull," the Censor pressed.

"My life is filled with many small adventures," Annie responded.

A remark at a time, Annie trained herself to outsmart her Censor. The rest of us can learn to do the same. It takes a great deal of compassion for ourselves to stand up to our Censor. Knowing that the Censor exists—for us and for everyone—is a good place to start. Just because the Censor says something does not make it true. And the more actions we take on our own behalf that defy its doom-and-gloom predictions, the stronger we become. Actions build upon themselves. Each creative step we take gives us energy and guides us toward the next one. When we are in motion, our lives are in motion, no matter what the Censor might say. So start your project, yet be alert for the Censor's attack. Do not be discouraged. The Censor is a jerk.

Our doubts are traitors,
And make us lose the
good we oft might win,
By fearing to attempt.

—WILLIAM
  SHAKESPEARE

TASK
Shrink Your Censor

Take a few minutes to name and describe your Censor. Is it male, female, neither? How old is it? What does it look like? How does it speak? What are some of its favorite disparaging remarks and insulting moves? You may wish to quickly sketch your Censor, as well. My students have drawn beasts, witches, a fourth-grade teacher . . . Allow your Censor to take whatever form emerges. Humor is welcome here! Drawing, naming, and describing the nasty creature will automatically minimize its power in your life.

Battling Skepticism

Skepticism can appear in many guises. It can come from within us, in the form of doubts or concerns about our own abilities or about whether the tools will actually work. It can also come from outside of us, in the form of either societal beliefs that only a select few are creative, or the voices of those near and dear to us who chime in with cautionary tales as we embark on our creative journey. No matter the source, skepticism is both common and destructive. It is important to identify and dismantle these misgivings, and move forward despite our own negative beliefs or the negative beliefs of those around us.

Doubt kills more dreams than failure ever will.

—SUZY KASSEM

I still suffer from skepticism—from the fear that I will not be reliably guided. In teaching others, I find that skepticism is a block for them, as well. And so I have learned to ask, "How can I help people overcome their skepticism?" The answer always comes to me: "Tell them to do Morning Pages. Tell them to ask for guidance. Tell them to note and record the results." I have been writing Morning Pages for more than twenty-five years and have found them to be a reliable source of spiritual wisdom.

For many of us, the idea that we have a direct line to the creator seems to be too good to be true. We have been taught that we need a third party—a minister, rabbi, or priest—someone trained in spiritual matters—in order to contact the higher power. It is my experience that every one of us can directly contact the creator. All it takes is the willingness to try.

In my Morning Pages, I simply ask, "Please guide me," and then I listen and write down what I "hear." The voice of guidance is calm, gentle, and simple. I am told not to panic, that I am well and carefully led, that I am on track, and that there is no error in my path. I may be given a further directive: "Try _____." When I do try _____, I am rewarded for my faith with tangible results. When I demonstrate my trust in my inner wisdom through action, my inner skepticism diminishes.

Many people look forward to retirement, anticipating one long vacation. In their imagination, retirement is the time when they will finally pursue what might be called "forbidden joys."

"When I'm retired, I'll let myself breed puppies," Agnes told herself. But when she did retire, she found countless reasons not to pursue her dream.

"When I retire, I'll pursue acting," Howard daydreamed. But when he retired from his long career as a school principal, he found himself unexpectedly unwilling to be a beginner. He was used to a certain amount of respect and dignity.

"I'll look like a fool," he caught himself thinking. And so the dream of acting remained a dream.

James dreamed that when he retired, he would live aboard a sailboat, traveling port to port. A widower, he did manage to sell the family house and purchase the sailboat. But instead of sailing port to port, he kept his boat safely docked, instead pursuing adventure between the covers of mystery books.

Doing Morning Pages, we face down our inner skeptic, but we still must face down the skepticism of those around us. Skepticism is born of fear: well-meaning others focus on our fears and not on the joys our fulfilled dreams may bring.

For many retirees, what stands between them and experiencing their forbidden joys is the fear of looking foolhardy. Many of them have friends who are skeptical about their adventures. These friends have their second thoughts for them. "Raising puppies? That's so messy, and such a lot of work. And what if you don't sell the puppies? Then what?" "Acting? Consider the competition you'll face." "Living aboard a sailboat? It sounds dangerous." What most of us really need is a believing mirror—someone who will champion our adventures. "Raising puppies? That sounds like fun." "Acting? I've always thought you had a flair for drama." "Living aboard a sailboat? Ship ahoy!"

[T]he most terrible obstacles are such as nobody can see except oneself.

—GEORGE ELIOT

15

It is important to seek out those who will encourage our baby steps in the early days of retirement. Like the youngster discovering his world for the first time, we are free to play and daydream, to stretch in new directions and dabble lightly in areas that might be of interest. Practicing Morning Pages, we build the muscle that reminds us "there is no wrong way to do this." Taking Artist Dates, spending "just an hour" doing something fun, we poke our nose into a topic or area that expands us. In tandem, we grow. The trick to outwitting skepticism is to keep gently pushing ahead.

Success is most often achieved by those who don't know that failure is inevitable.

— COCO CHANEL

Harry had looked forward to being retired after many years of practicing law. In his imagination, retirement was pleasant, filled with projects and adventures. But when retirement came, it was not at all what Harry had envisioned. His days loomed long and empty. He had trouble getting started on any of his many intended projects. And as for adventures, he found himself fearful, filled with second thoughts and the second—and third—thoughts of his friends. "I didn't realize how skeptical I really was," he says. "I had trained myself to take things apart, always trying to anticipate the worst possible scenarios. As a litigator, I had lost cases that I should have won. Over the course of my career, I had learned to distrust 'justice'—and this inner skepticism became my intellectual stance. I surrounded myself with people who felt the same. I think in the name of being 'smart'—or at least sensible—we really just reinforced each others' negativity."

Dispirited, he finally sought the counsel of a wise friend who was what he would call "successfully retired"—active, pursuing projects that interested him, both large and small, and content with his life.

"Retirement takes getting used to," his friend told him. "I'd give yourself two years. And it's okay to fall out of touch with people who are making this harder on you with their doubts. Give them—and yourself—a break. This isn't a time for nitpicking. It's a time to be a little goofy. See what comes to you."

Harry found the conversation, although radical, a source of great relief. It was true. What good was it doing him to consult with people who he knew would try to warn him of the flaws in his ideas, only deepening his own sense of limitation? He needed to spend time with people who would encourage him to expand—and he needed to spend time encouraging himself. "This may take a little time," he realized, "and that's all right. New lives don't just form overnight."

Harry began to explore his new life with Morning Pages. Any day he accomplished them, he felt a sense of productivity. He slowly found that the pages were an excellent tool both for processing the shock of retirement and for dreaming of the possibilities ahead. "The pages give me a sense of hope," Harry admitted. "I'm intimidated by doing Artist Dates, and I am afraid if I look at my life story I'll find a lot of regret and missed opportunity. But what do I really have to lose? This, too, can be done in small steps." A day at a time, he began to build the foundations of his future, eventually adding Artist Dates, Walks, and a Memoir to his agenda, and was rewarded with a sneaking sense of growing optimism. When he did reconnect with his friends, he knew they would sense a shift in him. "I may wait, though," he confessed. "I think I'll keep this to myself for a while."

TASK
Active Kindness

Skepticism is rooted in fear, and fear is healed by compassion. Being gentle with ourselves helps us move through our vulnerability and toward our dreams. A little active kindness toward ourselves can take us a very long way, indeed.

List three kind actions you could take on our own behalf. For example:

1. I could buy candles and wonderful bubble bath and take a long, luxurious bath.

2. I could take an afternoon and finally clear out the bookshelf that has been bothering me with the same clutter for the past ten years.

3. I could allow myself to go and see the comedy at the local theater that got poor reviews and might be "a waste of time"—but that I have secretly wanted to see ever since I laughed my way through the trailer.

This week, choose one of these actions and accomplish it.

WEEKLY CHECK-IN

1. How many days did you do your Morning Pages? How was the experience of doing them?

2. Did you take yourself on an Artist Date? What was it? Did you discover anything in your Memoir that you'd like to explore in an Artist Date?

3. Did you take your Walks? What did you notice along the way?

4. An "aha" is an insight or realization that may occur seemingly out of nowhere as you work with these tools. What "ahas" did you discover this week?

5. Did you experience any synchronicity this week? (Synchronicity may appear as "accidentally" being in the right place at the right time, hearing from a long-lost friend you'd just been thinking about, discovering information on a topic you'd been interested in, etc.) What was it? Did it give you a sense of connection?

6. What did you find in your Memoir that you would like to explore more fully? This exploration could take many forms. This could be expressed in a quilt square, a painting, a goofy dance, a song, a simple poem. Remember not to judge your early efforts. Some people are compelled to write a polished essay about a specific time or memory. Others are moved to "move"—a

particularly emotional memory may inspire a long, solo bike ride or a walk through the woods. You may wish to revisit music from this period of your life, adding an album to your collection that was played in your home in your early years. If you aren't sure what additional action to take, don't worry about it. Just keep moving forward.

Reigniting a Sense of Freedom

This week, you may find that you simultaneously crave freedom and feel baffled by it. Diving into the next phase of your Memoir, you will encounter your younger self at a time when you desired—and received—increased independence. Gone is your feeling of inertia. You have a new influx of energy, energy to use for change. As you come into contact with a new sense of freedom in your present as well as your past, issues of time, space, and routine became more important to you. There is a parallel to be found between the expansion of later childhood and the expansion of retirement. Is there such a thing as too much independence? Too much—or too little—time? How do you want to live? Does your space feel cluttered, outdated, friendly, depressing? You may find that making small changes in your home environment will better serve your expanding persona. As your sense of freedom increases, your environment will reflect your new perspective. Productive freedom requires a balance: it is easier to thrive and flourish with a sense of structure in place.

Increased Independence

Entering retirement, we are in a place of sudden independence. No longer subject to the schedules or demands of our jobs, we are in the complex position of being our own boss. Whether we have looked forward to this with anticipation or in some way dreaded the lack of structure, our increased independence is a new reality that we are now free to shape.

Independence can be both something to celebrate and something we find we fear. We're on our own, which is exciting, but we also lack the backup support that our colleagues provided us for so many years. Morning Pages and Artist Dates can help strengthen our ability to support ourselves. The pages teach us how to be honest and compassionate toward ourselves. Artist Dates teach us how to venture forth into the world and take risks. Undertaken together, they are a powerful catalyst for change as we discover our true and varied colors.

The next phase of life that you revisit in your Memoir will focus on your early school-age self and contain memories of newly growing independence. Remembering the simplest steps of increased independence—your first day of school, your first night away from home—it is likely that you will be flooded with memories that are strangely close to the experience of rediscovering your own independence in retirement.

"I took guitar lessons as a kid," Jeff says, "and when I was about ten years old I really didn't want my mother to wait and watch during my lesson anymore. I wanted to do it by myself, and I didn't want her getting on my case about practicing. I begged and begged to go to my lessons alone, and eventually she conceded. But the problem was, I really didn't practice enough, and if she hadn't seen the lesson, she didn't know what I wasn't doing. It was a constant struggle between us. She'd always ask me if I was really serious about it, if it was worth her hard-earned money for me to go. I did like my lessons, but I just struggled to discipline myself to practice. Eventually I quit the lessons." Jeff, now retired, wonders about trying his hand again at the guitar. "It's a loaded memory for me," he says, "but actually revisiting that in my Memoir, I see that my resistance then and my resistance now are not so different. My mom wasn't doing anything wrong. I just wanted to exert my independence by saying, 'I'll do what I want with this.' I realize that now I'm doing exactly the same thing—just to myself. I'm holding back what I'd enjoy just to prove I can." Jeff found the excavation of this memory, while painful, very powerful. "It's like in some small way I broke the code on myself. I don't have to keep up my same patterns just because it might be my default. And who knows—I may look into buying a used guitar on my next Artist Date."

When I discover who I am, I'll be free.

—RALPH ELLISON

Artist Dates are very powerful avenues to an almost immediate sense of freedom. They can be misleadingly small adventures that deliver a profound return on the investment of an hour of your time. It just requires being willing to take that step out the door.

Even if you feel that you know your city or town so well that there is nothing left to discover, allow yourself to explore. The solo aspect of the Artist Date also casts the "old" into a new light. Perhaps you have visited a restaurant many times in groups, but you have never gone alone. The restaurant you think you are tired of may in fact be a source of interest and delight when visited solo. Free to order whatever you like, to order dessert first or not at all, to try the menu item you noticed but never mentioned, to sit in a new corner—the experience, taken alone, is a small but enlightening risk.

Kara found that the transition to being in charge of her own days—every day—was harder than she thought. "I don't think of myself as a codependent person, but suddenly spending so much more time alone, and not being part of a group effort like I always was at work, made me feel uneasy." It was ironic that her willingness to use the tool of the Artist Date—done very much alone—was what started to break down her sense of isolation.

"I was amazed at the level of excitement and adventure I felt trying the simplest things," Kara confessed. "I had gone to my local movie theater dozens of times, but I had never gone alone. Going alone, the entire experience felt heightened to me. I saw a movie only I wanted to see, bought candy I hadn't eaten in years, and was almost giddy doing it. It was amazing how unfamiliar that simple excursion felt when I actually went out and tried it alone. After I had done it, it was like I had a secret with myself. I started to learn that I could be a companion to myself—and that when I did that consistently, it was actually easier to reach out and connect to others."

The greatest thing in the world is to know how to belong to oneself.

—MICHEL DE MONTAIGNE

When Natalie retired, she had, for the first time in her life, the time and money to travel. For years, she had been enamored of all things French, but she never thought she would actually travel outside the country. She couldn't imagine anyone in her life who would like to make the trip with her, and she certainly couldn't imagine making the trip alone. Instead, she allowed herself to explore French culture in the tiniest ways—ways she could manage on French-themed Artist Dates in her own town. Her Artist Dates included a movie with French subtitles, then a cooking class on French cuisine, then a wine-tasting class on French vintages. She excitedly saw that opportunities to experience French culture existed everywhere she looked, from online language courses to imported soaps and perfumes at her local apothecary.

"Maybe it was just because I had France on the mind, but I began to see France everywhere. When I spotted a notice on a community bulletin board that read 'Bicycle through France!' I was sure it was meant for me." Natalie called the number listed and learned that her cycling skills were good enough, and her age—sixty-six—was not an obstacle. "Because I had taken a few small steps, this larger one, by the time I got to it, didn't feel like such a big deal," she says.

The price was modest for such a grand adventure, and she got off the phone determined to go. "That was four years ago," Natalie says. "I've gone back four times, for four weeks at a crack. This year I've rented an apartment in Paris and I'll be staying on another four weeks."

Natalie would never have imagined being as independent as she is, traveling alone to a foreign city that now feels like a friend to her. "I'm not only comfortable with it, I love it," she beams. She has met many like-minded friends on her adventures. "They see me as a free spirit, a bold adventurer," she says, and laughs. "That wouldn't have been my self-definition before—but I guess actions speak louder than words." And positive actions toward our dreams, large or small, add up to an expanded—and more accurate—sense of what we are capable of.

Small steps lead to larger ones. And the next step is always within your grasp. "My goodness, I could try _____," you may catch yourself thinking. You may paint a room, reupholster a chair, purchase a new table for your kitchen. You may find yourself "window-shopping" through a catalog and buying yourself new sheets and a lovely scarf. Such small but significant changes give you a sense of freedom. You sense, as Leo Tolstoy remarks, that your life is lived by tiny changes. Each tiny change empowers you as you act on your authentic interests. Each small change prepares the path for you to make larger changes in a life that you are free to build to your own unique design.

TASK
Memoir, Week Two

Pick up where you left off last week in terms of your age. As always, if you are moved to dig deeper into a certain memory, now or later, do.

AGES: _____

1. Where did you live? Describe your bedroom.
2. Who were the major players in your life? Did you have a particularly influential teacher?
3. Did you try your hand at any new art forms in this period?
4. What new freedoms did you experience during this time?

5. What were you bored by?

6. Describe a smell you remember from this stage of your life.

7. Describe a close friend from this time—real or imaginary.

8. Describe a favorite treat from this period.

9. Describe a location where you remember spending time.

10. What other memories occur to you from this period?

And in the end it's not the years in your life that count. It's the life in your years.

—ABRAHAM LINCOLN

Time

During our work life, before we retire, many of us find ourselves too busy to pursue our creativity. We dismiss ideas as not possible in the moment, something to be saved for retirement. Retired, we find ourselves swimming in time. It seems to stretch in all directions. And yet, planned-for projects often go uninitiated, much the same way academics find that they cannot write during their sabbaticals. Too much time proves to be just as daunting as too little.

It is all too easy to put undue pressure on ourselves and criticize how we use our time. We rush from this to that. We call ourselves "lazy" when we "waste time doing nothing." We don't have "enough" time or we have too much. We regret past uses of time—time spent worrying about things beyond our control, time "lost" doing something we didn't love, or endless obsession over "does he/she love me?" We are trained as a society to "use time wisely" and constantly reminded that time is money, time is short, time is . . . ultimately ours to shape and use.

Many of my students, in going through their Memoirs, discover that the time they thought was "wasted" was in fact well spent. Alternatively, I have watched people realize that the time they spent digging themselves into holes of depression or self-doubt was not just wasted, but in fact self-destructive. One student of mine in particular told me that he realized that he had often used his (considerable) creativity "just writing worst-case scenarios in my mind and living in the wreckage of my future." Articulating this realization turned out to be the first step toward avoiding this behavior. By consciously directing his time and creativity toward a purpose, he found that he felt much less anxious. "I beat myself up, and then beat myself up for wasting time doing it," he says. "Pretty crazy cycle, but the thing that broke it for me was changing what I was *doing*. I realized that even in small ways—like cleaning the kitchen—I could be useful. Slowly I came to see what I wanted to do, how I really wanted to spend my time, instead of berating myself for not knowing."

The only reason for time is so that everything doesn't happen at once.

—RAY CUMMINGS

It is okay not to know how we want to spend our time at first. We abruptly have more than enough time to pursue our creativity, but that doesn't necessarily make it easy. In fact, it is at this time—when we have time—that we must be most gentle with ourselves. There is no need to be perfect. It is important to simply take one step after the next and trust that we are led. One of the most powerful things we can do is seek to put structure into our days. Morning Pages are the first step toward building a creative life. Done daily, they create a gentle structure. Daily and cumulatively, they suggest direction, and soon we find ourselves not only doing Morning Pages, but also doing what those pages suggest.

Recent retirees often experience a combination of stressors related to time: the idea that time is short and also that their days are too empty. Neither of these need be true. It is important to stop pressuring ourselves not to waste a moment and to make every moment perfect. Many retirees harbor the thought that this time is a "last chapter" when, in fact, this period may be many, many chapters. Despite our fears, creativity is always with us. It doesn't mysteriously dry up when we hit sixty-five. Consider artists like Georgia O'Keeffe, working at the height of their powers into their nineties.

Claude retired from a busy practice as a certified public accountant. He went from having no free time to having great swaths of it. I suggested that he undertake Morning Pages as a means of gaining structure. He was reluctant but willing. "My pages are depressing," he told me. "I just see so many dreams I left behind."

"Keep writing," I encouraged him. "Keep writing."

A few weeks into his pages, one dream kept coming to the fore, and when he saw an ad for a film school promising that students would make their own films, he decided to enroll.

There are no secrets that time does not reveal.

—JEAN RACINE

His family and friends all thought he was crazy, beginning such a "left field" endeavor, but Claude felt a growing excitement. At sixty-five, he was forty years older than most of his classmates. But far from being a detriment, he found that his life experiences gave him certain advantages over his fellow students. He had many stories to tell, and he could tell them now from a place of humility and perspective. For his first short film, he tackled divorce, something he had long felt guilty about since his divorce in his thirties. His classmates applauded his bold and vulnerable topic choice. Many of them were not yet married, and many of them expressed gratitude for his forthright exploration of a subject that had not occurred to them as a possibility in their own lives. His twenty- and thirtysomething classmates were open to the lessons he had to teach. Claude found himself feeling surprisingly happy and fulfilled as he shared the pain of his own story. "I feel useful," he says, "and optimistic. I have stories to tell and the time to tell them. I think I'll make another movie."

When time becomes your own in retirement, the importance of structure is paramount—but your desired structure may not be immediately obvious to you. Morning Pages begin by helping you structure your day, but ultimately guide you to pursuits that structure your weeks and months. Morning Pages suggest small changes in how you use your time. For example, you may write, "I think I'd like to get up earlier. I always enjoy the early morning and I feel useless when I lounge around until noon. Maybe I'll set a gentle schedule for myself to do Morning Pages and walk daily, and be showered and ready for the day—even if I don't know what it will bring—by 9:00 a.m." Morning

Pages also suggest larger changes in how you invest your time: "Maybe I could volunteer at the local school. Maybe I'll read the book series I've been saving. Maybe I'll see if anyone would like to read it with me—a book club could be more fun than reading it alone. Maybe I could . . ."

Yes, maybe you could. And yes, you have "enough" time each day. It is all about spending it according to your own values and wishes. As you do, you will find your anxiety about time lessens. Time well spent contains its own reward. Looking back on each day and naming one productive thing accomplished, even if it's just phoning a friend who needed support, brings us energy and satisfaction. Morning Pages cue us into productive action. Working on our Memoir is one such action. The combination of Morning Pages and Memoir exploration lends positive structure to our days.

TASK
Time

Write quickly, without overthinking, and finish the following sentences.

1. If I had more time, I'd try . . .
2. If I had more time, I'd try . . .
3. If I had more time, I'd try . . .
4. If I had more time, I'd try . . .
5. If I had more time, I'd try . . .

1. If I had less time, I'd try . . .
2. If I had less time, I'd try . . .
3. If I had less time, I'd try . . .
4. If I had less time, I'd try . . .
5. If I had less time, I'd try . . .

Clearing a Path

With more time on our hands, we may find ourselves at home much more than we have ever been. Spending time in our homes, we notice the things we want to improve: the unfinished doorframe; the junk drawer in the kitchen that always seems to be jammed shut; the worn doormat that we've been meaning to replace. We also notice the beauty that we may have been blind to when distracted by busyness: the needlepoint pillow carefully stitched by Aunt Maude; the view of the lake we had come to take for granted; the wildlife playing in the trees whose antics we can now take the time to enjoy. Allowing ourselves to engage in and observe our surroundings, we are often both moved by appreciation and called to action.

The best way to find out what we really need is to get rid of what we don't.

—MARIE KONDO

There is creative potential awaiting us in our homes: decorating, furniture making, needlework, gardening . . . and now that we are home with time to experience and embrace our environment, it does us good to take care of our space.

In our work life, our work arena was often under scrutiny. As a result, many of us tended to keep our areas neat. After all, mess seemed disrespectful. Retired, we may now find ourselves the victim of clutter. With no one to scrutinize our behaviors, we find ourselves leaving our environments unchecked. Papers pile up on papers. Magazines create rubble. Is it any wonder that when we sit down to our desks, we find it difficult to think clearly? Clutter is the enemy of clarity. A few minutes spent decluttering our environment pays off in increased mental acuity. Most meditation practices favor twenty minutes of committed time. I have found twenty minutes of cleanup an effective form of meditation. As we toss out our papers and discard those that are extraneous, we begin to have clarity about our life's priorities. Straightening the piles of excess paperwork leads us to clarity about what really matters. A messy desk—or sock drawer—equals a messy mind, and of course, the opposite is equally true.

Decluttering and tidying powerhouse Marie Kondo speaks of keeping only those items that "spark joy" in our homes, and discarding the rest. While this perhaps sounds radical at first, the minimalist idea of not only taking stock of everything we own, but also keeping only those items that serve us, is very powerful indeed. Her belief that, by handling each item we own, we will know whether to keep it or to let it go, has provoked many, many practitioners of her methods to remove many, many bags of items from their homes—leaving only what "sparks joy" behind. It is a concrete, active way of honoring our possessions and respecting ourselves and our choices. For recent retirees, this process of "clearing the old to make room for the new" is especially powerful. When we clear our space, we clear room for new ideas. We make room for insight. We literally clear our minds.

One can furnish a room very luxuriously by taking out furniture rather than putting it in.

—FRANCIS JOURDAIN

The process of decluttering while revisiting our lives in the Memoir is doubly powerful. As we carefully consider each of our belongings, we trigger memories. As we revisit memories, many of our belongings take on more—or less—value. Esther worked through her Memoir while simultaneously preparing to move from her home of many years. "It was a trial by fire," she says now, "but I am grateful for the full-scale change. Just as I retired, I sold my house. I had planned to move, but I didn't expect the sale to happen so quickly. I had no time to think—I was forced to look at all of my belongings and decide which ones moved forward with me. It was overwhelming and also very freeing. Decluttering my belongings in concert with revisiting my story in my Memoir gave me great clarity about my life." As Esther moved thirty-five years' worth of "stuff" out of her house, she saw her life parade before her. "Stories my kids wrote when they were young, clothes I made for their first piano recitals, my college diploma, my kids' college diplomas—it was all there, with everything in between." Esther found that in revisiting her life in such a wholesale and dramatic way, she was quicker to come to conclusions. "When you look at everything you own—with the pressure to make a keep-or-throw decision—you realize how much you have and how much you don't really need. It's just being stored—not used or loved or looked at."

Getting rid of her things, Esther learned that the more she discarded, the easier it was. "I realized my mother always gave me beautiful cards," she says. "My impulse was to save them all. But then I thought, how much do I really want to store? Would I really go back and look at the cards? I was consciously downsizing to simplify my life. Instead of saving every card, I made a conscious vow to appreciate my mother's artful eye. And now, every time I give someone a card, I try to do it as thoughtfully as my mother would. I think, in a way, that honors her more than saving every card she ever gave me."

Many people retire only to feel overwhelmed by their own space, a space they may have been blind to while they were distracted by the busyness of their work life. Sam, a Broadway actor, began working with the Memoir tool when he turned seventy. "I was still auditioning," he says, "and still getting myself out there, doing voiceover work and some commercials. But I had less work and more time than I'd had before. Turning seventy gave me pause. I don't know what I expected to feel, but I actually felt pretty depressed. I looked at my contemporaries who had won Oscars. I had had a long, steady, solid career as an actor, but I couldn't stop playing the 'compare' game. What if I had stayed in LA in my thirties? What if I hadn't gotten my first Broadway show? What would have happened instead? Going back through my life with the Memoir, I very, very slowly started to honor my own career path. It wasn't someone else's. It was mine. I had done work I was proud of. I had met lots of people."

As Sam focused on seeing his life as it was, not as it might have been, he also focused clearly for the first time on his surroundings. He realized that he had become a real pack rat, saving the mementos of a lifetime. His home was cluttered with memorabilia—playbills and eight-by-ten glossies—beginning with his bit parts as a young actor and continuing, part by part, season by season, all the way to today. When I suggested to him that he might consider jettisoning some of

Have nothing in your houses that you do not know to be useful, or believe to be beautiful.

—WILLIAM MORRIS

his stash, he reacted with genuine horror. And yet, there was barely room for him in his crowded apartment.

Sam had to admit his home environment really wasn't serving him. "Working through my Memoir, I realized I'd always felt 'less than' this or that other actor. I actually think that I kept every memento to prove to myself I'd had a career: See? I danced with Mary Martin. I met Richard Rodgers. I got a mention here, a great review there. But the sheer volume was leaving no space for me to think, much less find perspective on what I'd done and what I'd still like to do. And most of what I had was packed in boxes, stacked to the ceiling. What good was it doing me, really?

"I went through it all," he continues. "What I couldn't have seen coming was the profound realization that it was the first time in my life I had honored my own career. I had always dismissed my accomplishments to some degree. I didn't even realize I was doing it."

Many of us routinely dismiss our own accomplishments, and this is why working with our own Memoir is so vital to moving forward as complete people, in touch with our own stories.

Sam got rid of almost all his mementos. "Ultimately there was only about a box of things that really spoke to me," he says. "It was very hard at first—an emotional roller coaster really—to look at these items, much less get rid of them. I felt like I was throwing my life away. But the opposite was true. I was honoring my own life by pulling out the fifty or sixty things that I truly loved and were irreplaceable. I recycled a bunch of stuff, and gave some playbills and photos to the library. And then I went and bought a giant, leather-bound scrapbook. I filled it with the highlights of my career." Gathering his thoughts and mementos into one organized place both consolidated and made more accessible the many stories he had to share. "For fifty years I didn't want to forget anything," Sam says, "so I held on to it all. But in letting go of it, I actually own it more."

His newfound freedom is clear to the outside eye. He has a visible lightness about him, and a palpable confidence.

"Instead of being cramped in boxes, out of touch, my cherished memories are on the shelf, being treated with respect," Sam explains. "I've shared the book with many friends and it's fun to see how much they enjoy it. One of my buddies even said I inspired him to do the same thing with all his old sports stuff that's been taking up half of his den. And my apartment is much more spacious now—I can think again. In fact, I'm thinking I may try writing my first play."

Letting go of that which you do not cherish—and bidding farewell to that which no longer serves you—leaves room for you to live in the day. Living in the day, you release the past, and open yourself to the potential of tomorrow.

TASK
Time and Space

Allow yourself a few minutes to sit in a place in your home where you may have been "too busy" to sit before. Look around from this spot and really see your home with a fresh perspective. What do you appreciate? What do you wish to change? If you see many things you wish to change or feel overwhelmed with emotion when doing this exercise, don't worry: your Morning Pages will help you prioritize and process these insights.

TASK
Twenty Minutes

All of us can stand to clear some clutter, and all of us can stand to do it for twenty minutes. Set the timer and, promising yourself that you will stop as soon as it buzzes, take twenty minutes to discard that which is no longer needed in your home. You may wish to go through the house with three bags: trash, recycling, giveaway. I like to make it a race against the clock: how much can I get rid of in twenty minutes? Tackling our clutter in bite-size segments, we make a dent in the seemingly impossible task. Making a dent, we are often inspired to make another.

Boredom

Boredom is a mask, one that we wear to tell ourselves, "Oh, what's the use?" In other words, boredom covers fear. We claim we are bored, but what we really are is frightened. We are afraid to take a risk, afraid to try something new. Many of us suffer from boredom, and I do mean suffer. When we feel bored, we feel stuck. Nothing seems to ignite our passions. We wonder if the feeling of boredom will ever pass. We feel desperate, as if we are grasping at straws. Not knowing what to do, we panic, and in panicking, we dig ourselves further into the dark place where we believe we have no ideas.

It is a terrifying thought to believe we have no ideas, and it is, in fact, never true. But when we are caught in boredom's grip, it can be very hard to pull ourselves out of it and gain some perspective. We need to jolt ourselves out of our inertia. Few ways accomplish this better than taking an Artist Date.

Caroline, age sixty-seven, lived in Santa Fe, a city rich in art and artists. But she could have been living anywhere because she didn't explore what her city had to offer. When I suggested that she undertake Artist Dates as a cure for the boredom she complained of, Caroline was resistant. She felt she couldn't think of even one thing that sounded fun to do. I told her not to worry—this didn't have to be done perfectly. If she could think of only one thing that *might* be fun, that would work just fine. Reluctantly, she suggested that she might visit a gallery. Santa Fe is known for Canyon Road, a winding street where galleries are tucked in every nook and cranny. Caroline had never been there in her four years of living in Santa Fe.

"It seems too simple, too obvious," she protested.

"It seems great," I retorted. "A perfect Artist Date."

She refused to be bored chiefly because she wasn't boring.

—ZELDA FITZGERALD

35

And so, Caroline planned her first gallery visit.

"I promised myself I would spend one hour looking at galleries," Caroline says. "That's what got me out the door. I guess I needed a time limit to be willing to begin. At first, I wasn't so sure about the artwork, or if it was sparking anything in me. But it had only been five minutes and I had said I'd give it an hour, so on I went."

The Beatles saved the world from boredom.

—GEORGE HARRISON

Imagine her delight when she found the work of several artists deeply interesting.

"By about the tenth gallery, I realized I was having fun," she says sheepishly. "My reluctance to explore was a denial of my own intellect. When I visited solo exhibits, I found myself inspired. I realized that these artists all worked alone, and yet somehow they were driven to create and create. Whole bodies of work existed because these artists kept working at it. I found it so impressive, and I realized I could take a lesson from them. There were plenty of places in my life where I could stand to push myself a little harder. I loved the idea that local artists were so gifted. I began to picture myself as part of a fascinating community, and that I could add something to it, too."

Caroline went home that day with her spirits lighter. She had long wanted to add a small flower garden to her front entryway and now realized it was well within her ability to accomplish—and an enticing idea to her creatively. "I couldn't wait to do it," she says. "Maybe it's a bit abstract, but the care all of the artists took in their work made me feel like it was important. I wanted to treat something as precious. I spent a really fun afternoon choosing, arranging, and then planting the flowers. And now I feel like I am adding a little color to Santa Fe, too."

It is important that we tend to our feelings of boredom and deal with them honestly. It may not be comfortable to feel bored, but it is possible to change how we feel when we are willing to admit our frustration and take action to address it.

We are all creative, and we all have an unlimited supply of creative energy. As we act on it—or "spend" it, so to speak—in positive ways, we expand and improve our surroundings. But if we contract instead of expand, we run the risk of wallowing in our own negativity.

When people are bored and not using their creative energy productively, they tend to cause trouble. I am thinking of a woman I know whose mother stopped working as soon as she started having children. Now, decades later, her children long flown from the nest, she is at a retirement age herself, but she never had a career to retire from. My friend—this woman's daughter—tells me that instead of working or even finding hobbies that she enjoyed, her mother has used her considerable intellect and creativity to meddle in her children's lives for nearly forty years.

"My mother is smart," says Cindy, "and I always thought it was a waste of her education—Ivy League education, by the way—that she never worked. As I watched her grow more and more miserable—and more and more difficult—I promised myself that I would always work. It was the only defense I could think of against the negativity I observed and received from her—and it has shaped my life. I honestly think my mother is bored. She is intelligent, but did not use her intelligence in ways that would have been satisfying for her. Instead, she micromanaged my life and my siblings' lives to a terrifying degree. We all know it is because she is 'just' bored, but it's still incredibly destructive."

Because our creativity has to go somewhere, it is important that we are making conscious decisions about how to spend it. Cindy's mother may have thought she was being admirably selfless, but spending an unhealthy amount of energy on others has ended up stifling both her and her children. Because she wasn't willing to think about what she herself might like to pursue, the dramas in her family's life became the focus of her days. It is not unlike a child who, bored, decides to stir up trouble for entertainment. The problem is that as adults, we are capable of seriously impeding the natural process of those we meddle with. In

Is not life a hundred times too short for us to bore ourselves?

—FRIEDRICH NIETZSCHE

37

the end, resentment and frustration often overshadow any initial good intentions.

When we are exercising our own creativity and expanding ourselves for the better, there is no time to muck around in other people's business. We are satisfied, and so we don't have an urge to make others unsatisfied. It may be uncomfortable to admit that we are bored and don't know what to do about it, but it is important to be honest with ourselves. Once we are willing to be honest, we are in a position to discover the answers we actually seek. Boredom is a sly foe: it begs us to ask large and scary questions like, "What am I doing with my life?" The cure for boredom is actually small. The correct question is, "What productive thing could I be doing right here, right now?" To that, we often already know the answer.

TASK
Boredom

Children instinctively react to boredom with imagination and creativity. Looking back, can you remember ways you confronted boredom as a child?

For example:

1. Putting on a puppet show
2. Building a sand castle
3. Creating a pots-and-pans band
4. Long conversations with imaginary friends
5. Playing dress-up

Select one memory and write on it, reentering your childhood world.

Routine

Recent retirees tend to speak of having mixed feelings about routine. On one hand, they enjoy being free from the externally imposed schedule of their work lives—they may choose to sleep later, to travel during the week, to eat meals when they fancy them instead of hewing to a strict timetable of meetings and business hours. On the other hand, the lack of routine can be a source of stress. If a person hasn't shaped his or her own days for decades, it can be a tricky adjustment to determine what exactly is the ideal routine for this new phase of life.

Retire from work,
but not from life.

—M. K. SONI

I ask you to be open-minded: although it may take some trial and error, it is possible to find a routine that can begin to feel like a spiritual practice, opening you to guidance, energy, and creativity. Creating routines for yourself that comfort you will quiet your mind, and it is this quiet mind that allows inspiration to spring forth.

My daily routine begins when I rise. I brew myself a cup of coffee, retrieve my notebook and pen, settle into my large leather writing chair, and write my three Morning Pages. Pages done, I turn to breakfast, and after breakfast I undertake the steps my pages have suggested. "Walk the dog, change the sheets, read my Ernest Holmes prayers, call my sister, write the foreword for Natalie's book . . ." It is a rare day when the pages fail to dictate the next right thing. "Call Domenica and listen," my pages may suggest. Most of the time the pages yield "good, orderly direction," for which I use the acronym GOD—God. Afternoon exercise keeps me mentally and physically fit as daily I hike the dirt roads surrounding my house, keeping an alert eye for coyotes and snakes. Late afternoon is an ideal time for working on my current writing project. Once a week, I schedule an Artist Date.

With such minimal structure in place, we find ourselves feeling serene and secure. We are led in directions that serve our spirit. We are once more given routine, but this time it is a routine of our own choosing that responds to our inner impulses, not an external taskmaster.

Routine brings us into contact with our own capacity for discipline. We learn inspiration from the regular practice of Morning Pages. As we daily invoke the higher power to communicate through our pen, we are nourished with new ideas.

The secret of your future is hidden in your daily routine.

—MIKE MURDOCK

The spiritual value of routine is nowhere more evident than in a monastery. Monks rise at a set time, pray a set morning prayer, then enter a day where bells chime at regular intervals, cuing them to move from activity to activity. Setting time for work, time for prayer, and time for relaxation yields a rewarding, fulfilling, and productive life. When we undertake Morning Pages, we undertake routine, but we also undertake a certain form of prayer. As we write, "Please guide me," we are given a flow of inspiration. We are indeed guided. As we write each morning about whatever is current for us—feelings of loss, confusion, excitement, wonder, regret—we are, in effect, praying on the page. And it is indeed as if a benevolent force beyond ourselves is listening, whether we choose to name this force or not. Morning Pages give us a path through the day, a place to set our own goals and deadlines. When I call my daughter, I find myself serving as a sounding board. Our exchange is mutually healing. Morning Pages also serve as a sounding board and a jumping-off place for the rest of our lives.

Tom took early retirement expecting to enjoy a multitude of adventures. His work life had been filled with successes, and he anticipated his retirement would be the same. Instead, he was shocked to find himself battling depression. He found the great swaths of time now available to him to be daunting. To his surprise, he missed work and the sense of purpose it gave to his life. Six months into his retirement, he found his depression so acute that he decided to seek therapy. His therapist struck straight to the core of his depression. "Tell me what a typical day is like," the therapist asked, and Tom found himself saying, "There is no typical day. I just muddle through."

"I think you need some structure," the therapist suggested. "You need to build a healthy routine into your day."

Tom heaved a sigh of relief. They were on the right track. He had missed his routine. It had given him a daily sense of accomplishment. Now, without routine, he realized he felt like a daily failure.

"You need to fill your day with meaningful structures. Do you think you can?"

"I feel like a bum sleeping in," Tom admitted.

"So set a time to rise and shine," the therapist suggested.

"I feel out of touch with the world," Tom complained. The therapist suggested he set a daily time for catching up on the news of the day. Tom found himself feeling slightly excited.

Routine, in an intelligent man, is a sign of ambition.

—W. H. AUDEN

"I could go to my local bakery for coffee every morning and bring the *New York Times* with me," he volunteered. "I always saw people having a leisurely coffee and thought that looked like the life. So why not try it?" As Tom started to establish his simple morning routine, he was quickly filled with more ideas. "I've also been skimping on exercise," he admitted. "I could join a gym and set some fitness goals. I could even head to the gym straight from the bakery—that would fill my morning! I could establish a beat."

Tom found even the gentlest structure rewarded him with a sense of purpose and optimism. As we set new routines for ourselves that are built around our true values, we are rewarded with clarity and ideas.

Carrie found that in exploring her Memoir, she was brought back to a time when she had a very clear routine. "When I was about ten," she says, "I took violin and piano lessons. I had to practice each week and complete my assignments. It was a struggle for me sometimes, but it was nonnegotiable in my household. My parents treated practice as equally important to schoolwork, and there was no bargaining out of it. After homework and practice were done, we were free to have some playtime, but not before." Carrie now sees the benefit of this discipline on her life. "I ended up with many years of music," she says, "and a sense of tenacity that carried through my entire career as a computer programmer. The idea of building skills piece by piece taught me

41

patience. I didn't put it together until now, but I am convinced that some of my greatest assets are a result of careful music training as a young person."

Carrie remembers this time fondly, not because it was easy, but because it was rewarding. "It also gives me an idea," she says. "Now that I am retired, I have time to learn new things. Why not learn the accordion? I've always wanted to, and I do know how to learn an instrument—I've done it before, with the violin and piano. And the practicing for me has always really been a spiritual practice. Slowly learning to move my hand from chord to chord is meditative. The building of skills, the process of learning, is a routine that feeds every-thing about my life. Practicing an instrument brings me perspective and makes me feel satisfied—like I've accomplished something. I go into my day calmer. I think I will open up the accordion case and make it a part of my day."

If we are unsure as to what routines might be satisfying for us, it behooves us to look back into our Memoir. There are, almost unfailingly, clues here. The point is not to find an instant perfect answer, but to try simple ideas that we feel might spark satisfaction for us. I have had students who decide to start their day with a six-mile walk, meditation, or taking an early hour of the day to tidy their home and thus put their thoughts in order. As we keep an open mind about trying a new rou-tine, we are rewarded with a sense of freedom within structure.

TASK
The Relief of Routine

Number from 1 to 5. Then finish the following:

1. I would be relieved if I made time to . . .
2. I would be relieved if I made time to . . .
3. I would be relieved if I made time to . . .

4. I would be relieved if I made time to . . .

5. I would be relieved if I made time to . . .

Now, look at your list. What clues are here? What are you wishing to include in your routine? Choose one activity; can it be part of your daily routine?

WEEKLY CHECK-IN

1. How many days did you do your Morning Pages? How was the experience of doing them?

2. Did you do an Artist Date? What was it? Did you discover anything in your Memoir that you'd like to explore in an Artist Date?

3. Did you take your Walks? What did you notice along the way?

4. What "ahas" did you discover this week?

5. Did you experience any synchronicity this week? What was it? Did it give you a sense of connection?

6. What did you find in your Memoir that you would like to explore more fully? How would you like to explore it? As always, if you have a loaded memory that you feel requires further attention but aren't yet sure what additional action to take, don't worry about it. Just keep moving forward.

Reigniting a Sense of Connection

This week, your Memoir is likely to reveal early relationships that you focused on with a new intensity. For some, it is a heightened relationship with a parent or favorite teacher, for others, close friendships or the beginnings of romances. You began to see yourself in relation to other people. Retirement also provides a time to reflect on past and present relationships. Who do you want to be close to? Who do you want to distance yourself from? Are there openings in your life for new relationships? This week, you will look at yourself in relation to others. Who is your community? Who would you like it to be? You will explore loneliness and isolation, common issues in retirement, as well as opportunities to connect with others through volunteering. You will experiment with asking for—and offering—support. As in your earlier years, you will be challenged with balancing relationships that exist outside your choosing (immediate family, former coworkers) and those you chose for yourself.

Choosing Our Companions

Friendship, I have said, is born at the moment when one man says to another, "What! You too? I thought that no one but myself..."

−C. S. LEWIS

In retirement, the intensity of our work relationships diminishes, and those that continue are for the most part by choice. On the one hand, this may be a relief on some levels—we may be eager to bid farewell to the inconsiderate coworker who brought small annoyances to the day, or the higher-ups we didn't agree with. On the other hand, we may have loved our work environment and may experience loss on a personal level: we now feel adrift from a community we held dear. In many cases, it is a combination of both.

Now that we have more free time, we also have choices to make. People in our lives may expect us to be fully available now—whether that is what we would choose to be or not. We may also have relationships we want to rekindle that we didn't have adequate time to nurture during our work life. It is time for us to consciously consider the community we want to surround ourselves with in retirement.

Jessica is sixty-six, and her Memoir during Week 3 focused on ages eleven to seventeen. "That was a very intense period for me in my intimate relationships," she says. "I had a complicated relationship with my father, who worked a lot. I wasn't much of a dater, but I did become very close to a tight-knit group of girlfriends as I entered my teenage years. I remember the intensity of those friendships. I was, of course, going through puberty and filled with hormones, but I was very, very angry at my father, who I felt was unavailable to me. I now see that I was pretty codependent with my school friends—we thought we were invincible and we were completely inseparable. The stress I felt from not getting enough attention from my dad was pretty similar to the stress I felt when I was somehow not a part of my group of friends— like I was missing out on something." Freshly retired, Jessica had gone through a similarly painful phase of feeling like she was "missing out." She panicked, joining too many groups that she wasn't actually interested in, and then proceeded to feel overwhelmed and unsatisfied by the meaningless busyness she had inflicted upon herself.

"Working on my Memoir, I realized this panic I felt was more historical than current," she says. "I've had a lifetime of building relationships that served me. But being 'cut loose,' I think I kicked up some old fear." Jessica found that by connecting the dots for herself, she was able to view herself with more compassion. "I dropped out of a few of the groups," she says. "It was pretty clear, once I stepped back and saw what I was doing, which ones would actually be fun for me. But when I was in my heightened emotional state, I was blind to all of it."

A dream you dream together is reality.

–JOHN LENNON

There is a saying that "if it's hysterical, it's historical," meaning that when emotions are overwhelming, they may not be fully relevant to the present situation. Revisiting our own stories and patterns in relation to other people is both prudent and empowering. It helps us know who to carry forward with us into this new chapter in our lives, where we are able to start fresh.

Especially as you begin to take on new creative endeavors in retirement, it is important to build a community that will support you. I call people who mirror back your most positive and expansive self "believing mirrors," and believing mirrors are important people to keep in— or add into—the mix. Creative endeavors are vulnerable, and it takes a great deal of courage to begin the delicate process of undertaking them. The people who will encourage our first small steps are the ones who are safe to share them with.

Our creative ideas deserve our protection. Bert discovered in his Memoir a disturbing pattern of handing his creative ideas—and the power associated with them—over to other people, especially those in need.

"I could see this as early as grade school," he says, "when I gave the credit for a science project over to my lab partner, who was struggling and getting upset. It seemed easier to just let him take the credit than deal with him crying in science class. But looking back, I don't know

47

why that was the best logic." Bert went on to become a successful businessman but continued this pattern of giving in to others—to some degree at his own expense—to avoid conflict or emotion. "Honestly, I'm embarrassed to see this pattern," he says. "But I'd rather see it than not see it. Over and over again I did this. Even last year, I made a judgment call about a business relationship that turned out to be wrong. She was a wealthy woman who said she wanted to be involved in a new project I was working on. Her skills were lacking, but she said she wanted to learn to be more than just an investor. Unfortunately, she turned out to be either unwilling—or unable—to learn. I guess it doesn't really matter which. I made a mistake getting involved with her at all, but we all make mistakes. The bigger mistake was the number of times I gave in to her when our ideas conflicted because she would get upset and it seemed easier to smooth it over for her than to deal with it. Dealing with it would have meant cutting the relationship loose, and that really would have been better. I called it 'giving her the benefit of the doubt'—but in this case, I had my doubts. I gave in to her emotion, and it was very expensive for me."

We are like islands in the sea, separate on the surface but connected in the deep.

—WILLIAM JAMES

In retirement, Bert is determined to learn from his mistakes. "I still landed on my feet," he says, "I mean, here I am. I am retired and I can afford to have some fun. But I really want to watch out for my tendency to take care of other people emotionally, especially at the expense of my own ideas and better judgment. I see now how I get in my own way when I do that." Bert's insight is an exciting one. He is in a position to start new projects and, with his new awareness, he is also in a position to protect himself as he pursues them. "I have an idea," he says, a twinkle in his eye. "I'm going to write a children's story about a kid who helps another kid in science class. Or—come to think of it—maybe a kid who *doesn't* help the other kid. Let's see if I can rewrite that story and improve on it."

Building community takes work, and fluidity is part of it. Trial and error is to be expected. Looking at our patterns, we will discover insights, and it will help in taking some of the guesswork out of our present choices. Examining our own lives, thoughts, and desires, we come into contact with how much community—and who in particular—we want to connect with as we go forward.

TASK
Memoir, Week Three

AGES:_____

1. Whom did you form new major relationships with in this period? Briefly describe the dynamic of the most important ones.
2. Where did you live?
3. What was your community in this period? Did you have one? Was it satisfying, complicated, dramatic, supportive?
4. Describe one sound from this period. Was there a song you listened to over and over? Try listening to it now. What does the experience bring up?
5. Describe one taste from this period.
6. Describe one smell from this period.
7. Describe a time you felt lonely during this period.
8. Describe a time you felt supported during this period.
9. What was a source of stress during this time?
10. What other memories feel significant to you from this time?

Loneliness and Isolation

Loneliness is a common aspect of the human condition, and it is something every person experiences, whether they are actually alone or not. Sometimes the most poignant loneliness is in the company of those with whom we struggle to connect. Other times, there is a "joyful loneliness" to be found in times of change. Artist Dates allow us to learn to be joyfully alone, yet they often end up helping us to make strong connections with others.

Mia retired from a career in photo editing to realize she was, in retirement, spending far less time alone than she had at work. At work, her job was fairly solitary, as she worked in a small office where most of the editors pursued independent projects. "I liked this way of working," Mia says. "I liked the quiet." When Mia retired, she joined her already-retired husband at home. Suddenly, she had no time to herself. "I actually felt abruptly lonely," she says, "losing my time alone." Her husband was now a 24/7 companion. "When I said I wanted to go out and take photos, he asked to come with me. I tried to explain that I wanted to do it alone, but he seemed hurt. I wanted to move from photo editing to photography, and it was a private endeavor for me. But my husband couldn't understand that, and we began to grow apart."

Mia said she had never felt lonelier than when she had no time alone. "I felt myself sinking into a murky place, getting into the habit of ignoring my own thoughts, feelings, and intuitions. Ultimately, I lost myself," she says. "It was devastating."

As Mia began to work with Morning Pages and Artist Dates, she found she had a place to dump her feelings as well as a framework for the alone time she craved. "When I explained to my husband that I was doing Morning Pages, and what they were, he seemed a bit intrigued. And when I shared with him that Artist Dates had to be undertaken alone, he seemed to understand that. I think the fact that these tools were part of a course, and defined by someone else, was helpful. I was just doing my homework. He didn't feel so abandoned by me."

Using the tools, Mia felt a sense of freedom and relief. But she also began to feel an unexpected sense of connection. "Taking Artist Dates, I actually felt more connected to my husband," she says. "I had something to bring home to him, an experience to tell him about. Sometimes I would go places he'd never want to go—like a quilting museum. Other times, I'd find treasures in our town that he'd love—like a tiny Thai

It was only a sunny smile, and little it cost in the giving, but like morning light it scattered the night and made the day worth living.

—F. SCOTT FITZGERALD

restaurant with coconut ice cream—and we would then visit these places together. Going on Artist Dates became normal—and from that, going off to take photographs alone also became normal in our dynamic. And now, paradoxically, my next photo series is going to be of us together."

I have had many students who resist Artist Dates because they tell me that they "already do everything alone." Perhaps they live alone and already spend a considerable amount of time by themselves. But often, a sense of loneliness or isolation arises not because we lack relationships or interactions with others, but because we lack a relationship with ourselves. Although it is hard to believe before experiencing it, Artist Dates break isolation even though they are undertaken alone. It's the relationship with ourselves that is cultivated in the Artist Date, and, establishing this habit, we are always in good company, even if we are physically alone. Part of this effect comes from the planning of each Artist Date. You choose an activity that entices you and is outside your usual beat. This is the "Artist" part of the Artist Date. You then plan it—this is the "Date" part—and enjoy the anticipation of it. Perhaps you buy a ticket to a concert or play or museum tour a few days in advance. Taking the Artist Date is a very different action from "just" spending time alone. You will experience a heightened sense of intimacy with yourself, and you will come home knowing yourself better than when you left. Artist Dates build on themselves—they become easier to take, and more exciting to anticipate. But what you are really building is a relationship with yourself—and this relationship is the core of all other relationships you will have. When you work to connect with yourself, your ability to connect with others is exponentially improved.

David retired and was dismayed to find he spent almost all of his time alone. At first he read books and caught up on things he'd been meaning to do, but soon he tired of his long empty days. He had dug up in his Memoir a very specific memory of a chocolate muffin he used to get at a bakery with his best friend when he was in medical school.

Loneliness ... is proof that your innate search for connection is intact.

—MARTHA BECK

He had lost touch with this friend years before but was reminded in his Memoir of the power of that friendship in his life. "It was the small things," he says. "My buddy was very, very attentive to detail. He'd keep his pencils lined up. His desk was always clean. He had tiny, precise handwriting. He was an artist in that way. And he became a great surgeon because of all of those qualities. People tell me I'm neat now, and I always think of him and his influence on me. I learned it all from him—and it really did affect my life. He inspired me."

Love is the bridge between you and everything.

—RUMI

David went back to the bakery he and his friend used to visit after class. "I went in there alone and was flooded with memory. I ordered the chocolate muffin and sat there. At first I felt really lonely. I didn't know what had become of my friend, really. I knew he'd had a good career, but we weren't in touch anymore. He was someone that I really regretted getting too busy to keep up with. I really missed him." As David sat, he watched as an old man behind the counter restocked the cabinet. He recognized that man—he was the owner, the very same person who ran the bakery when he had visited it thirty years before.

"I went and bought a notecard and I wrote my friend a note," David says. "It was pretty simple. Just that I'd gone back and gotten a chocolate muffin, and really regretted losing touch with him. I was shocked to hear back from him almost immediately. It had been more than three decades, but we reconnected and pretty much picked up where we had left off. He had just retired, too. What a gift it was to find someone whom I'd once had so much in common with, and learn that we still had worlds to talk about—past and present. We were still so connected. I know it sounds crazy, but even though I thought about the guy, I don't think I actually would have reached out to him without that chocolate muffin provoking me to."

Although stories like David's sound fantastical, synchronicity of this sort is the rule, not the exception, when using these tools. I believe that in our Morning Pages, we speak to a higher power, and on our

Artist Dates, a higher power replies. Following the guidance we receive, we make connections that we may have discounted as impossible—with ourselves, our environment, and other people.

Sister Mary Bernice, a Catholic nun, spent close to fifty years in the classroom. Under her careful tutelage, students prospered. When her mother superior told her the time had come for retirement, she inwardly panicked. Teaching gave her life meaning. If she wasn't a teacher, who was she, she wondered.

Long accustomed to urging her students to write, she decided that she, too, could benefit from putting pen to page. Casting back to her early days as a teacher, she remembered her troublesome students and the strategies she had devised to trick them into learning. As her teaching methods matured, her students began to flourish. She remembered the many prizes and honors they had gleaned. Looking back, she felt a sense of pride. Her students' honors felt, in part, to be her own.

Writing down her teaching strategies, she felt her loneliness start to dissipate. Once again, she felt a sense of purpose and a connection to the students she had held so dear. She could share the lessons she had learned with the younger nuns who were just embarking on their teaching careers. After more than fifty years of teaching, she finished writing what would become her version of a memoir: a book of teaching tools that she had discovered by trial, error, and experience. A young nun volunteered to type it into the computer. It became required reading for novice teachers.

Revisiting her life through words, she found her sense of isolation lessened. She reconnected in a concrete way with memories of students from the past, and forged a new and practical connection with those who followed in her footsteps.

Looking back through our lives, we have the chance to honor our unique choices and where they have led us. Befriending ourselves, we gain clarity on our values. Expressing ourselves in any way—writing a poem, singing a song, sketching our surroundings, sending a postcard—we connect with a greater power. In the moment of creation, we are never alone.

TASK
Loneliness

Take twenty minutes and allow yourself to write about a time in your life when you were most lonely. What were the circumstances? Were you surrounded by others or isolated? Working or not working? Now, take the time to write about a time when you felt connected to others. Who did you connect to? Over what? Can you reach out to that person now? Is there someone else who comes to mind who might fill a similar role? Twelve-step programs talk about "the phone that weighs a thousand pounds," meaning that it may be very hard to pick up that phone and reach out to another, but once we have, the burden is lightened immensely. Remember that the person you are calling may need to connect with you as much as you do with them.

Volunteerism

Possessed of more time and life experience, retirees are in an advantageous position in terms of volunteering their time and talents in their community. When considering volunteering, it is possible, although not necessary, to contribute skills formerly used professionally. A retired academic may help with grant writing for the local library, or a retired music teacher may produce and serve on the board of a local concert series. On the other hand, many have experienced connection with their neighbors by volunteering in areas they have no experience in: the computer programmer washing dishes in a soup kitchen, the physics PhD reading children's books with immigrants wishing to learn English. Volunteering is a spiritual—and therefore individual—

experience, and retirees have often found the connections they make through donating their time enrich all aspects of their lives.

We are, ourselves, creations of a higher power, and, serving others, we become conduits through which this higher power can enter the world. In this way, volunteering and expressing ourselves creatively are more alike than different. Opening ourselves to be a channel for good, we are rewarded with optimism and ideas. As we extend ourselves to others, we experience a flow of grace.

Daryn, an investment banker, retired and found great inspiration spending time volunteering at his local park. "I never considered myself creative," he says. "I worked at my job for forty years, and successfully, but when I retired I didn't have any ideas for myself." Daryn discovered in the early part of his Memoir a fond memory of working in the yard with his dad. "We would rake and clear and weed and when we were done, the yard was something to be proud of," he says. "I remembered the sense of satisfaction it brought me." Now, living in a city far from where he grew up, Daryn doesn't have a yard—but he has many nearby parks. "One day I just thought, why not see if they could use a hand," he says. "I'd like to get outside, and I'd like to help out." Daryn discovered a nearby park that was looking for willing volunteers. He now pitches in with the maintenance—raking, clearing—twice a week. "I'm getting to know some of the guys there," he says, "and they have some very interesting stories. I feel close to my long-passed dad doing this. And I feel rejuvenated. Doing this makes me think I could try other new things."

Volunteering can also involve using our long-honed skills. Decades of work experience have put us in a position to help people in need and teach others the tricks of the trade. Doing this, we feel both connected to our former work and useful to our community. For many, this is a very rewarding choice, especially for people who have retired earlier than they expected to or who found passion in the work they did as a career and want to maintain their skills. Keeping active and productive

Since you get more joy out of giving joy to others, you should put a good deal of thought into the happiness that you are able to give.

—ELEANOR ROOSEVELT

also provides a positive outlet for our creative energies that otherwise could be misdirected.

Leigh worked a full-time job as an interior decorator. Her clients were universally pleased by her artful touch. When she retired, she found herself focused on her own home. She redid it three times, and would have done it a fourth, but her husband protested.

"I liked it several times back," he said.

"I like it now," Leigh protested.

When Leigh told me this story, I found my sympathies lay with her husband. It would be upsetting, I thought, to have one's "nest" torn apart again and again. But I also had compassion for Leigh. She had creative energy that she needed to "spend." It was imperative that she find an outlet, lest her husband come home again to a foreign place.

"Why not volunteer your services?" I asked Leigh. She clearly needed the work more than she needed the money. With a little sleuthing, Leigh found a house for troubled teens badly in need of a facelift. Leigh's offer to help left the director of the house in tears of gratitude.

Leigh began a systematic redecorating of the house, starting with the common areas and reaching every corner of every bedroom. "I had never been in a place like this before," Leigh told me. "It was very humbling. There were teen girls who had eating disorders, who had attempted suicide—I was saddened and shocked to see the level of pain that such young people were trying to survive. And the place, while a lifesaver for them, literally, was so outdated. It was a safe place but not a beautiful place.

"I love creating beauty," Leigh told me. And that is just what she did. One room at a time, she shared her vision with the director, and one room at a time, she executed it. Her many local contacts were more than willing to help, donating paint, artwork, and even furniture to the cause. Leigh transformed the house from a decrepit building into a serene and healing oasis. "It became a labor of love," she said. "One of my proudest accomplishments. To see the difference it made in the lives of these girls was very exciting and moving for me. One of them,

We must use time creatively, in the knowledge that the time is always ripe to do right.

—DR. MARTIN LUTHER KING JR.

who struggled with anorexia, told me she started to see beauty in a new way watching me work, and that it made her think she could see beauty in herself someday, too—that beauty wasn't outside of our control, but something that could be built. I told her she was exactly right about that, and that many people saw beauty in a space—or a person—before the space, or person, in question was able to. I told her that, just as I saw potential in the house, I saw it in her. And then I went home and cried. I cried for her pain and I cried because I felt like my energy had gone in the right place. It was a deep, deep sense of gratitude that I hadn't experienced before in all my years of transforming spaces."

Morning Pages are likely to bring up areas of interest that we miss or would like to learn about. Sometimes the tiniest clue can lead to a fulfilling volunteer endeavor. John, for several decades a publisher, found that in retirement he missed his work. He wrote Morning Pages, developed his Memoir, and wrote a few short pieces of his own. But he still missed other people's words. He had spent his career diving deep into the authors he published. He loved "getting inside their minds," as he put it, and although his current writing was fun for him, he found it a bit solitary. He researched the outreach projects in his community and found himself drawn to an adult literacy program. There, he could freely share his love of words, but also reconnect to the magic within them—and to others while doing it. "I'm more enlivened than I have been in years," he says now, "seeing the excitement in the eyes of adults learning to read and write for the first time. Something I take for granted is a novelty to many, and I feel I have a responsibility to share what I know." For John, part of his love of words was his connection to others through words. In retirement, he gained the most satisfaction from sharing words, rather than keeping them to himself.

Dorothy, a widow and avid reader, also felt alone with her books. She decided to volunteer her time at the local hospital. At first she ran the hospital gift shop, but found herself yearning for more personal contact. "I suggested they start a program of reading to elders," she relates. "I found it fun, and so did my patients. Their taste in books

Unless someone like you cares a whole awful lot, nothing is going to get better. It's not.

—DR. SEUSS

57

ranged from the classics to what I'd call 'trash.' To my surprise, I found myself enjoying some of the more lurid reads."

Volunteering to share our knowledge and being of service to others is an age-old concept. What might surprise us is the level of reward we receive. Retired, we too often feel that our skills are no longer needed. This is rarely the case. Usually, we can find that our skills are more needed than ever—just in places we may not have yet considered.

TASK
Volunteer, Just a Little

Where can you volunteer, even just a little, right now? Perhaps it is the gift of time in a local soup kitchen. Perhaps it is the gift of advice to one who is building a career in your area of expertise. Perhaps it is the gift of listening. We all have something to share. What could you "give away, for fun and for free," today?

Support

One of our chief needs as creative beings is support, and seldom is this more true than when we are beginning a creative endeavor. Especially if we are new to practicing our creativity, it is paramount that we consciously build relationships that can serve as support for our projects and an outlet for our own generosity. Some of these relationships may be continuations of bonds we have formed in the workplace, some may be relationships we wish to deepen now that we are possessed of more time, and others may be brand-new connections we make based on shared interests. Likely, we will want to cultivate a combination of the three, and as we pursue new interests that serve our needs during this time of our lives, it is important that we pursue relationships that also serve our needs.

Before retirement, many of us enjoyed the contact of colleagues and clients that automatically came with the job. We now need to make a special effort to find ourselves a peer group—an effort we may not have made in decades. It may take some time to reawaken our friend-making skills, but when we do, the relief is enormous.

"When I was working, I often resented my job," says Babette, a retired trucking company dispatcher. "Not working, I found I missed the camaraderie. This was my dirty little secret until I joined an exercise class for beginners at the gym. Most of the people in the class were women my age, and I was surprised by how excited I was to see that. The teacher was a contemporary of ours, too, and it was quickly evident that what got exercised were our spirits as well as our bodies. I began to form friendships with my workout buddies in class. At first, we just confided in each other about our struggles with the class, working to get into shape and keep up. We'd help each other out, grabbing a mat for another here or putting away another's weights there. It soon progressed to having a quick coffee before or after class.

"The class was such a simple thing, three times a week," Babette says, "but it really bonded us. We talked about our problems—with our partners, our children, our health—and we felt relief. We had a lot in common, but we also had different stories and we were interesting to each other. Now we get together for dinner at least once a month. We're a tight group. Sadly, one of the women is going through a health challenge right now, but we've rallied around her. We take turns bringing healthy meals to her at home and we keep the faith together. I wouldn't have thought the gym would bring me so much friendship, but I went there hoping for support and being willing to give it—and I was rewarded with more community than I've had in a while. We all know we can count on each other. There's really something to be said for women of a similar age helping each other out."

As we support others, our self-worth increases. When we see how much our support matters to others, we find it more natural to ask for support for ourselves.

Lamar was asked to retire from his long-held marketing job before

I like to listen. I have learned a great deal from listening carefully. Most people never listen.

—ERNEST HEMINGWAY

59

he had anticipated. "I'm only sixty-four," he says. "I thought I had another ten years at my job. But the company wanted to shake things up, bring in young people, and for the senior members of the team, they offered us time-sensitive retirement packages we couldn't really resist. Although I would have preferred to keep on working, it wasn't too much of an option within the new structure of the company. So here I am, and I miss my work," he says.

No act of kindness, no matter how small, is ever wasted.

—AESOP

Although nothing is officially wrong, Lamar is disturbed in his sudden new role as retiree. "I have enough money, I have a nice home and a lovely wife. I have lots of energy. So I feel guilty complaining," he says. "But I really miss my team at work. Specifically, I miss bouncing ideas off of each other. I miss brainstorming sessions and hearing other people's process." In other words, Lamar misses the creative support of his work colleagues.

When asked how he'd like to spend his time and energy, Lamar is quick with an answer. "I wouldn't mind consulting or even freelancing," he says. "But what I really want to do is start a blog I've been thinking about for a long time. It'd be a funny blog, with animation and pithy sound bites about marketing and how products sell themselves to the consumer. I have so many stories I want to tell." So, what's the problem? "I want to talk to my old colleagues about it. I want to bounce ideas off of them. Who would be better?"

When pushed to say why he couldn't just call them up, Lamar is uncomfortable. "I'm afraid they've moved on, I guess," he says. "Everything is different over there now. I'm not part of the dynamic anymore."

Lamar knew exactly the support he was lacking, but he felt like he shouldn't ask for it. He is not alone in deciding that he'd "better not bother" his old work buddies. But the truth is, they would likely be more than happy to hear from him. No, the dynamic is not the same when a company reorganizes and makes a push toward younger workers. But it does not render the elders obsolete. When Lamar finally reached out to a former associate, his colleague was thrilled to hear from him and quick to set up a rendezvous with a few of the members of the team.

"I can't tell you why it was so hard to pick up the phone," Lamar says, "and I'm ashamed to admit that it was. But once I did, it was such a relief. There were my buddies, just the same as before. We had a meal together and I told them about my idea. It was just like old times—they threw lots of ideas at me. But this time, the idea was mine to do. I left that meal knowing I would finally start my blog—and that the support I had assumed wouldn't be there would be. They also had a few questions for me about what they were working on—and I realized they missed my input, too."

Reaching out for support can feel impossibly hard, but it is almost always rewarded with a burst of energy and creativity. As we invite the help and support of another person, we experience the help and support of the universe. As we ask for guidance, we are guided. The input we receive from our friends and former colleagues often opens the door to our own intuitions and inspirations. Our bonds with others may deepen and become more joyful when we relinquish our need to be the sole authority. We allow others to expand to their full size by mentoring our dreams.

Ernest loved to read mysteries, and when he retired, he binged on his collection—reading books he had always meant to get to and books he'd loved many times over. "For the first few months it was bliss," he says. "But then it started to feel like I was just burying myself in other people's words. I was losing track of myself." So Ernest started a book club to discuss the mysteries with his friends. "I enjoyed our shared perceptions and our hard-won wisdom," he says of spending time with his reading group, "and getting together with other readers curbed my loneliness. But it didn't scratch the itch I knew I needed to scratch. You see, for years I've wanted to try my hand at writing a mystery myself."

It is true that no amount of reading will satisfy the urge for writing.

The greatest compliment that was ever paid me was when one asked me what I thought, and attended to my answer.

—HENRY DAVID
THOREAU

61

While reading dozens of mysteries certainly put Ernest in touch with the art form, he himself had never broken the seal, putting pen to page and getting his own ideas out where he could look at them.

"I'm not a writer," he said. "In grade school I used to hate those creative writing assignments—I just froze up at the sight of a blank page." I pushed Ernest to write whether he believed he was a writer or not, but he insisted that the "real" writer in his family was his daughter-in-law, a prominent lawyer. "I'll just tell her my ideas, and she can write the books," he said.

"Only you can write your books," I told Ernest. And when he approached his daughter-in-law with his idea, she agreed.

"I'm sure you can write, Ernest," she told him. "I only write legal briefs, anyway. Why would I know more about writing a mystery than you?"

Ernest's answer, of course, was that she was paid to write in her job—so she must be a better writer than him. Retirees often feel as if activities pursued for pleasure aren't as valid as activities pursued for pay, even if they're the exact same activities. But as Ernest wrote about his long-held beliefs in his Morning Pages, he realized that, writing his Morning Pages, he was writing already, and gaining confidence in expressing himself. Before long, he started to sense that he himself might be the one to tackle the mystery he had been forming in his mind over the past two decades.

"I realized I didn't need my daughter-in-law to write the book for me," he told me, to my great delight. "I just wanted her support. I see her as a writer, and I thought she might have tips for me."

When he approached his daughter-in-law asking her that very question, she demurred. "I'm not sure I have any mystery-writing tips," she said, "but I'd sure love to read anything you write. I'll be here to back you up."

Ernest realized that this simple act of support was all he needed to enthusiastically begin. "We send each other a text message every day," he says. "It's so nice to know someone else is writing too. And it's extra nice to be connecting with my daughter-in-law in such a special way. She says it helps her, too. Oh—and by the way, I've written thirty pages."

Asking for support, we open ourselves to new relationships with others. We show willingness to take action. Offering support, we tend to receive it in return. As we reach out to others, we build a true bridge between us, ripe with the promise of connection.

TASK
Strength in Numbers

Take pen in hand and list five people who have been supportive of you at different times in your life.

1. _____
2. _____
3. _____
4. _____
5. _____

Now, choose one and reach out to that person. Is this person still a potential source of support? Can you offer that person support? When you do, do you find you receive support in return?

WEEKLY CHECK-IN

1. How many days did you do your Morning Pages? How was the experience of doing them?
2. Did you do an Artist Date? What was it? Did you discover anything in your Memoir that you'd like to explore in an Artist Date?
3. Did you take your Walks? What did you notice along the way?
4. What "ahas" did you discover this week?

5. Did you experience any synchronicity this week? What was it? Did it give you a sense of connection to another person, a memory, a higher power?

6. What did you find in your memoir that you would like to explore more fully? How would you like to explore it? As always, if you have a loaded memory that you feel requires further attention but aren't yet sure what additional action to take, don't worry about it. Just keep moving forward.

Reigniting a Sense of Purpose

This week, your Memoir will focus on early impulses and ideas you followed—or ignored—as you began to form your adult identity. Many times, early clues and interests contain the answers to the question "What would make me happy?" Excavating these memories, you are likely to reconnect with a core impetus that will guide you in choosing activities that give you a sense of purpose. You will look at historical touchstones that define you and carry meaning for you. You may find yourself inspired to muse on the type of legacy you are leaving—and the type you would like to leave. Your early dreams may inspire you to support others in turn.

Callings

It is never too late to be what you might have been.

—GEORGE ELIOT

"You have a calling," I've been told. "You're a writer." It's true that I have always been called to write. But it is also true that many people who are not immediately able to identify a calling for themselves assume that they don't have one at all. This is because the "still, small voice" may speak too softly for them to hear when they are focused on worldly goals. We all have one or more callings, but sometimes we do not recognize them as such because the term "calling" has become so weighted—"a calling to join the priesthood." But a calling does not have to be a mission requiring exclusive devotion or self-sacrifice. Many worthy callings are far less dramatic, and could be simply defined as a "committed interest." This week, in your Memoir, you will look for ideas, hunches, interests, and prods that you at some time sensed within yourself—and either followed or ignored.

Many people have experienced what I call creative U-turns, which is where they were working along in an art form only to abandon it— often suddenly and completely. It might be quitting flute lessons in fourth grade. It also might be turning your back on cooking after having your first child. There might be a "reason" for the U-turn ("I didn't have time to cook anymore"), or there might not be ("I'm not sure why I stopped the flute. I don't remember making a clear decision about it."). Sometimes creative U-turns happen because we got discouraged: your unsavory chorus teacher made you sing a solo and then pointed out that you had demonstrated exactly what not to do, and you never sang again. Instead of blaming the teacher, you decided you "couldn't" sing and moved onto other interests. U-turns can also happen because of the opposite: You are showing promise in art class, and the teacher encourages you to apply to a fine-arts summer program. Nervous about leaving your family and staying in a cabin with strangers for two weeks, you miss the deadline—and stop painting. It wasn't the painting that was the problem; it was the intimidation you felt at the idea of going to sleepaway camp before you were ready. But instead of naming the real issue, which can be scary to do, you turned your back on the art form itself.

These types of examples are, sadly, extremely common, and can dampen not only our nascent artistic impulses but other aspects of our personality as well. Perhaps we're "too loud" reading aloud during history class—and then, shamed and embarrassed, are afraid to audition for a school play. Maybe we're told our personality is "too big," that we "hog the room"—and then become hesitant to make bold choices, lest we offend those around us.

This is all to say that there are many small choice points in our stories where we formed ideas about ourselves and followed—or abandoned—interests with little awareness of how or why our decision was made at the time. It is time now to look back, to revisit the opportunities we took and those we rejected, to consider ideas and passions we had early on, and to rediscover those interests that we were once called to explore.

Kendra saw in her Memoir a pattern of starting—and then quitting—various musical endeavors. As a child, she had taken clarinet lessons, but when she didn't enjoy the band director in elementary school, she stopped, "focusing on gymnastics." At the time, it seemed a logical choice, but as she continued through her Memoir, she saw the pattern repeat itself. "I sang in the high school chamber choir, and we competed at the national level, and it was thrilling," she says. "But in tenth grade I had to decide between chamber choir and speech because of the schedule, and I chose speech because the teacher was more dynamic." Again, a clear enough choice in the moment, but Kendra saw over and over that her musical interests were often abandoned because of a person she associated with them as opposed to an internal choice on her part to move away from the art form itself. "This went on and on," she recalls. "In college I dated a guitar player, and even sang with his band for a while, but when we broke up I abandoned not just him but singing altogether."

The work you do while you procrastinate is probably the work you should be doing for the rest of your life.

—JESSICA HISCHE

Now, in retirement, Kendra is seeing a clear series of attempts to be involved in music throughout her life. "I love music," she says. "It sounds so simple, and yet I couldn't have told you that before. I thought music was for other people—not for me." Kendra now senses that pursuing even the most humble of musical endeavors could be deeply satisfying for her. "I could join the choir at my church," she says. "They're very good and I've often wondered what it would be like to be a part of that." Kendra has expanded her playlist as well. "I added lots more types of music to my library, and I'm so excited about it. I thought rock music belonged to my college boyfriend, and classical choir singing belonged to my high school choir teacher. It's amazing how easily I counted myself out. But not anymore." She reports a great sense of satisfaction and fun at rediscovering musical styles that she excluded herself from in the past. "I can't believe how satisfying music is for me," she says. "It inspires me. Who knows what I'll do next—but having music as a companion will certainly make it better."

It is all too easy to dismiss creative endeavors as "just" short-lived hobbies or something that "belongs" to someone else. The truth is, we are all creative, and there is no "wrong" creative interest. Many times, one leads to the next, and playing around in whatever areas call to us brings us a sense of joy and purpose—and a connection to some benevolent *something* that feels greater than ourselves.

Eli spent much of his childhood and college years experimenting with cooking. He dreamed of being a chef and tried out new recipes for his family, roommates, and any other nearby subjects. "I was overwhelmed by the memories that were triggered by taste and smell from each era of my life," he says. "As a kid, I cooked simple things—some very unsuccessfully, I might add. From ages ten to fifteen, the smell of burnt bacon was so prevalent in my story, it was almost comical." Eli remembered cooking meals that were popular—and unpopular—with his dining companions, branching out into more difficult and exotic flavors, and ultimately, when he entered the work force at twenty-three,

If God gives you something you can do, why in God's name wouldn't you do it?

—STEPHEN KING

"abandoning cooking so completely I'm almost embarrassed." As a busy movie producer, he still enjoyed food—but from then on, it was cooked by someone else, "a real chef in a real restaurant," as he puts it. "I wined and dined people, including myself, but it was never with my own creations again. I guess I would have told you I didn't have time for it, or that my job was more important."

Living in Hollywood, Eli has now spent the better part of forty years eating at some of the world's best restaurants. "I appreciated the artistry of many, many chefs," he says, "but I lost my own." Now, with time on his hands, he finds himself drawn once again to cooking. "I'm going to be rusty," he promises, "but I think and hope I can improve." Writing about the possibilities in his Morning Pages, it occurred to him that he could plant an herb garden and cook with fresh herbs. "I live in Los Angeles," he says, "it's almost a crime to not have an herb garden. For that matter, there are plenty of fruits and vegetables I could harvest, too." Eli is slowly reconnecting with his former passion, and it is deeply fulfilling for him. "It's not just that I'm having fun doing it," he says, "but I feel closer to chefs when I go to restaurants now. I think about what they're doing and try to learn from it. I may be an amateur, but we're both trying to make something."

When we discover abandoned dreams in our Memoir, we can be quick to assume they are off-limits for us because someone else has been doing them longer or because we aren't trained professionals. However, it can be amazing to discover not only the satisfaction in trying our hand at these creative acts once again but also the connection we feel with others who are pursuing the same goals, no matter the level.

TASK
Memoir, Week Four

AGES: _____

1. Describe your major relationships in this period.
2. Where did you live?
3. What creative ideas called to you? Did you follow these callings?
4. Describe one sound from this period. What are the emotions associated with this sound?
5. Describe one taste from this period. Is there a taste you have not revisited since then? Could you? (Re-create a recipe, visit a restaurant you might not usually patronize, etc.)
6. Describe one smell from this period.
7. Were there callings that you tried and then abandoned?
8. Did you have dreams, questions, or impulses about your greater purpose in this period?
9. What was a source of joy for you during this time?
10. What other memories feel significant to you from this time?

Legacy

Beginning the new chapter of retirement, many of us begin to think about our own legacy. What do we want to leave, and for whom? For some, it is an account of memories to share with future generations. For others, it is a work—or works—of art in the form of song, painting, or poetry. While each person is called to leave something slightly different, all are possessed of interesting and rich stories that are well worth sharing.

Many of us have had the experience of losing a parent and not having asked many questions that now go forever unanswered. As we trigger our memories by working through the Memoir, we answer many of the questions held by those who follow us—our children and grandchildren, and sometimes those related to us by bonds of love, not blood. Many of us find that as we recall our stories, we discover a richer sense of meaning in our lives and a deeper sense of connection not only to those who follow us but also to those whom we have followed. Recalling the events that shaped our characters and values, we give to those who follow us a blueprint for their own maturation. Reaching back in our own histories to connect with our personal sources of inspiration, we may in turn inspire others. As we seek to recall the incidents that shaped us, we find greater and deeper understandings of our own lineage.

My grandmother raised boxer dogs, and whenever I see one my heart leaps with joy. I find myself stopping to talk with their owners, telling them, "We used to raise boxers!" An affection for the breed is something bred in the bone in my family. As I remember my grandmother, I remember the names of the dogs we so adored—Trixie, Clooney, Shawn. For all of us, our memories and histories make up the colorful fabric of the lives we live today.

Especially when we are new to the wide-open possibilities of retirement, we may be full of ideas and not sure where to start. In such cases, "begin at the beginning" is sound advice. When I wrote my memoir, *Floor Sample*, I started with a memory of childhood reading, and once started, the narrative continued to unfold. I was shocked at the level of detail that reappeared before my eyes, as if in Technicolor. I have written Morning Pages for three decades, and always saved them just in case I ever wrote a memoir. But once I began writing, one memory led to the next, and I never once looked back into my pages for clues to my past. Beginning at the beginning gives us a gentle structure. Our memories and ideas will come. There will be room enough for all of them.

As we focus on sharing the highlights of our lives, we naturally honor our own experience. As we draw on our past experiences, loves, and ideas, we are possessed of a greater sense of purpose in our present. We realize we do indeed have much to share. My love for my

No legacy is so rich as honesty.

—WILLIAM
SHAKESPEARE

71

childhood pony, Chico, gave me the nudge to take my then-toddler daughter, Domenica, on pony rides in the park. Like me, she loved this adventure. Now, with a daughter of her own, Serafina, she leads her on pony rides. Remembering my childhood love of Rodgers and Hammerstein has led me to share some of their melodies with my grandchild, Domenica's daughter. Writing about my memories of the thrill of first-time cookie baking inspired me to invite Serafina to participate in my own baking adventures. Cherishing our past enriches our present.

It is not only writing that can embody our legacy. Quilting was Ellie's chosen art form, and she created piece after piece to honor the different people and places of her past. "When my first grandchild was born," she says, "I made him a quilt with clothes that my grandmother had left. I felt I honored the past and the future in this way, and I felt like I was a part of both."

Lee, who has pursued photography in retirement, sees photographs as a way of capturing the stories of the past, present, and future. "At first, I took pictures of what I saw," he says. "I documented experiences that I was a part of, and it was satisfying for me. Then I took the photographs and gave them as gifts to the people I had shared the experiences with. We all became a little bit immortal with each one. It's a small thing, but it crystallizes our experience. For me, a photograph gives me something concrete to hold on to and remember, and the magic in it is that everyone remembers the moment and experience a little bit differently."

After several years of taking photographs regularly, Lee discovered he was drawn to older photographs as well. "Here I was, taking pictures of the present to share with the future, but what about the person who went before me?" Lee started to collect photographs taken by his father and grandfather, and began a process of digitalizing them. "I wanted to preserve them, but I also wanted to find out what the stories were behind them," he explains. "Lots of people in the pictures were people I didn't know. I started to reach out to family to ask questions and learn as much as I could about my relatives and the people in their

Are we being good ancestors?

—JONAS SALK

lives. The project brought me closer to both my living family and family members who had passed on. I felt very drawn to this project, and the personal satisfaction and sense of connection was very deep. I felt it was my mission." The project gave Lee an ongoing sense of purpose as he worked, and a lasting memento to be shared with present and future generations.

TASK
Legacy

Answer the following exploratory questions:

1. I would like to be remembered as . . .
2. I wish I could leave . . .
3. A person whose legacy inspires me is . . .
4. As a child, I dreamed of . . .
5. One way I am already leaving a legacy is . . .

Now, look back at your list. Are there clues in this list about projects you might like to begin?

Touchstones

When we retire, we lose our familiar daily touchstones: the crossing guard we waved hello to, the man at the security desk who knew our name, the cashier in the cafeteria, the midmorning coffee break routine we looked forward to. We were accustomed to friendly faces and kindly greetings. Retired, we need to generate new touchstones. I ask newly retired people to make a list of twenty-five things they love. This list, deceptively simple, often becomes a source of new—and old—touchstones. What do I love? Black beans and rice. The Beatles. Dalmatian dogs. Vintage Mercedes sedans. Blue velvet. Freshly fallen snow . . .

Here is a test to find out whether your mission in life is complete. If you're alive, it isn't.

—LAUREN BACALL

If we are feeling lonely and discouraged, reviewing our list of touchstones can provide us with a greater sense of connection. Whether it's a favorite meal, a well-loved jacket, a piece of music, or a soaring hawk—there is something in each touchstone that fuels our sense of identity.

When we make lists of what we love, we remember who we are. Our authentic self steps forward. "It is *I* who loves *that*," we declare. When we remember what we love, we remember our true values. If we have drifted away from what we love, we will see the degree of drift and be able to correct it.

If we have drifted to a considerable degree, we may need to alter our lives to encompass our loves. If we love horses but can't afford to own one, we may find a local stable and sign up for a riding lesson. If we love forests but live in the concrete world, we may find that the act of nurturing houseplants puts us in touch with our love of greenery. Taking small steps in the direction of our loves gives us a feeling of power. We are not the victims of circumstance. We are, instead, the cocreators of lives that bring us joy.

Mary saw on her list of loves that memories of her grandmother were high among them. Her grandmother, a gardener, had loved pansies, and Mary named pansies immediately when thinking of her loves. As she continued on her list, she saw that other memories of her grandmother were present—neatly stitched needlepoint pillows, toast with butter and jam, the smell of a specific fabric softener. Mary had always acknowledged with pride how much her grandmother had influenced her. But now, as her life began to look more and more the way she remembered her grandmother's life, she saw her memories in a different light. Her grandmother had been widowed when Mary was young, and she remembered her living alone in a joyful house filled with colors and flowers and smells. Now, Mary, retired and widowed herself, realized that she craved building a home that evoked the same joy.

"My grandmother was certainly an artist," Mary says, "although she might not have defined herself that way. But everything in her environment had her artful touch. I feel now a real urge to do the same thing

The invariable mark of wisdom is to see the miraculous in the common.

—RALPH WALDO
EMERSON

for myself." Incorporating her loves into her home, Mary feels a sense of guidance and comfort. "I know this is right," she says as she takes steps to fill her home with things that bring her beauty, joy, and memory, "because I feel calm as I do it. And when I finish—or finish 'for now'—I sense that I will receive ideas—I'd even call it guidance—about what to do next."

As we search for a sense of purpose in retirement, we do well to get in touch with the small things that matter to us. Many times, the larger answers that feel elusive are actually closer than we think, present before us in many small clues.

Mioi speaks of feeling ambivalent on many occasions throughout her life. "It was as if at every moment, I saw many choices before me, and I couldn't say for sure which one was right. I weighed my options, was very logical about it, but ultimately never felt like I knew what my purpose was. I was successful enough, but I always envied people who approached life with more passion and freedom than I did. I didn't know how they did it." As Mioi worked through her Memoir, she saw herself again and again at choice points that she encountered very intellectually. "I studied the violin, but I also studied science in college," she says. "It was more logical to pursue a path in science, so I did, even though I felt a pull to the violin. I watched myself make choices like that over and over. I had a career where I served others, doing scientific research, but I don't know if I ever had a real passion for it. It's always bothered me that I felt this way."

Mioi is not alone in being unsure about her path. A formidable intellectual, she may have in some ways overthought her choices, denying herself the joy and freedom that can come from following an impulse or being spontaneous. She consistently followed her head rather than her heart, and ultimately lost touch with her true wants and desires.

Mioi completed her list of touchstones and was surprised by what she found. "I've asked myself so many questions throughout my life," she says, "but I'm not sure I was asking the right ones. I had such impossible goals for myself that I think I was setting myself up to never

The most beautiful thing in the world is, of course, the world itself.

—WALLACE STEVENS

be satisfied." On her list of touchstones, her loves ranged from some she expected—violin, classical string quartet music, going to the symphony, hardcover books—to others that she had nearly forgotten about: her yellow raincoat and rain boots she'd had as a child, chocolate croissants, and camping.

Dwell on the beauty of life. Watch the stars, and see yourself running with them.

—MARCUS AURELIUS

"I couldn't believe how revelatory this list was for me. And by the way, it seemed too simple, so I almost didn't do it—but I'm so glad I did." Some of Mioi's early wardrobe memories inspired a flurry of Artist Dates. "That yellow raincoat," she remembers, "brought me so much joy. I loved it. It had a green lining and I would often hope for rain so I could wear it. The memory was so powerful for me that I actually wanted to explore it further, and so I painted a modest watercolor of a young Japanese girl in a yellow raincoat. It was very enlivening." The memory of the raincoat made her look at her wardrobe anew. "I had so many conservative work clothes. There was almost no color in my closet. I felt a sense of excitement at the idea of changing that, and, propelled by the yellow raincoat memory, I started going clothes shopping on my Artist Dates. I went to stores I thought I'd never set foot in and picked up items that I'd never look twice at. It felt a little wild—but I figured, it was an Artist Date, so why not push my comfort zone?"

Today, Mioi's wardrobe still includes the black and gray staples she is used to, but she almost always sports a bright piece or accessory. "My red reading glasses make me smile every time I see them," she says. "And I'm not going to an office, so why not carry a kelly-green purse?" And yes, Mioi is indeed waiting for rain—to wear the vintage yellow raincoat she found on an out-of-the-way Artist Date.

While Mioi's whimsical expansion of her wardrobe may appear superficial, it is anything but that. She is getting in touch with her creativity, her inner youngster, her former self, and her more vibrant future as she expands her palate in all ways. It is no surprise to see her pursuing more and more music as she brings color to her life in many small but significant ways. Joining the local community orchestra and offering her formidable writing skills as a volunteer grant writer for the symphony followed naturally one from the next. For Mioi, her "simple" early step of naming things she had loved was important in paving the way to a purposeful life. "It's not intuitive to me on the surface, but I see that when I set the bar lower for myself I am a lot more daring. I'm not reaching for an impossible perfection anymore. Looking back, I realize I didn't let myself have very much fun," she says now. "But now I'm having fun, and it's very exciting. I really think people who have fun have good ideas."

Touchstones are personal, and every person's list is different. Do not feel that you need to have lofty items on your list—what speaks to you is all you are after. Be open to memory and open to joy—and allow yourself to experiment as you reconnect with things you once enjoyed and may well enjoy again.

TASK
Touchstones

Make a list of twenty-five things you love. Then select one item you can access today. A cold winter's evening becomes cozy when we access the touchstone of a fire. An afternoon spent writing becomes friendly when a favorite CD is set to play. In naming things that we love, it can help to enumerate touchstones for each of the senses:

TASTE: green chili, rhubarb pie, rice pudding, apricot jam, cocoa

TOUCH: velvet, suede, a feather pillow, a soft cotton comforter, your dog's silky coat

SMELL: homemade vegetable soup, freshly baked bread, nag champa incense, sage, pine boughs

SOUND: the Beatles' *Rubber Soul* album, Handel's *Messiah*, Schubert's *Ave Maria*, Dolly Parton's greatest hits, the sound of waves crashing on a beach, distant thunder, cicadas

SIGHT: a soaring hawk, a snowy mountaintop, a wood-burning fire, pictures of your children, pictures of your grandchildren, a bouquet of fresh flowers

Touchstones are personal. They remind us of our own identity. They put us in touch with what brings us joy.

Mentoring

Few things bring us more of a sense of purpose than the experiences of learning and of teaching. I teach regularly—close to home, at Unity Santa Fe or the Sol Acting Academy in Albuquerque, or far away, traveling yearly from coast to coast of the United States and beyond, frequently visiting new countries through invitations to teach my creativity workshops. I often teach in London, through the lively non-profit called Alternatives, where humor abounds and my students are quick to joke and quick to laugh. I recently taught in Tel Aviv, where a translator stood in a sound booth, interpreting my teaching into the headsets of those students who did not speak English. I teach small groups and large ones, from a few dozen to a few hundred. Over and over, I watch my students dip a toe in, then submerge fully, and eventually emerge from the work refreshed and inspired. The most common sentence I hear is, "Your book changed my life," but I am quick to share my belief: "No, *you* changed your life. But I'm glad the tools were helpful." Watching students have "aha" moments in class delights me. And for those friends close to me who have worked with the tools over a lifetime, seeing their creative flourishing is an ongoing source of joy and awe for me. Teaching has brought purpose to my life, and to interact with those I can mentor is a gift that I cherish.

As we age, whether we consider ourselves teachers or not, we have the opportunity to be a sage, and acting on this opportunity does bring us a sense of purpose. We are elders, and when younger people look to us for our help, we can accept this request as a gift. One of the fruits of aging is wisdom. We know how to handle situations that once baffled us. We have discernment. Sharing our hard-earned knowledge is one of the joys of aging. Mentoring others can bring great satisfaction. As we make ourselves available to be sounding boards, we are paid handsomely with the priceless gift of gratitude.

Selena is a retired professor of poetry. As a tenured academic, she spent a career reading and sharing poems and developing a deep understanding of the art form, as only time can build. No longer teaching, she still knows which poems will capture the imagination of students. She is frequently called upon by current professors to suggest pieces, authors, and resources, and even to guest lecture. Sharing her knowledge bank gives her a feeling of usefulness, and the younger teachers are grateful for her generosity. As we share the fruits of our experience—wisdom, shortcuts, "tricks of the trade"—with those we mentor, we fulfill our purpose by passing them on.

Thomas is an appliance repairman. He has worked at his trade for forty-five years. As he mentors the young man who will take over his trade, he shows him many shortcuts for diagnosing the troubles of cranky machines.

"Thomas is generous with me. He helps me improve. Rather than be threatened by me, he sees me as an opportunity for expressing his own mastery," says the young man Thomas mentors.

Adam mentors, too. An expert on the architecture of his neighborhood, he works as a tour guide. But he voluntarily shares his knowledge with younger guides.

"The knowledge is the important thing," says Adam. "I try not to hoard it. By passing on what I know, I help ensure that my store of knowledge will not be lost. It feels like a way of valuing all that I have learned."

Mentoring is a two-way street. We not only help others, but we help ourselves. By sharing what we value, we validate ourselves. Mentoring

Love is when you meet someone who tells you something new about yourself.

—ANDRÉ BRETON

keeps us young at heart. For those we mentor, we are a source of valuable knowledge. For us, our mentees are a source of inspiration. There is a spiritual element to sharing hard-earned wisdom, which, paradoxically, is often the most simple wisdom of all.

"When I was young," Cecily, a novelist, says, "I tried to write from my ego. I had to go through a long, arduous process of trial and error to learn to set my ego aside. That's what I'm trying to teach Beth, a young writer working on her first novel."

Beth's relief at Cecily's words is palpable. "I think I've overcomplicated things for myself by trying to seem 'smart'—but I'm learning to stop thinking that way. It's so much more enjoyable to work from my heart and not from my head—I never knew writing could be so easy," Beth marvels.

"Ease is what we're after," says Cecily. "There is an ease that comes when we let go and allow what we want to write to write through us. It just takes some focus to get used to doing that." Cecily notices that when she works with Beth, her own writing flows more easily, as well. "Maybe it's about 'practice what you preach,'" she says, "but it feels more spiritual than that. I'm showing her something very intimate in my process, and sharing it seems to reignite it in myself."

There is much to be said for being older and wiser. But there is also much that we gain by being friends with people who are younger—and being open to learning from them. Those younger than ourselves are in their prime. They are alive to new ideas. They have the energy to carry things out. Their zeal inspires us, reminding us of a real and still thriving part of ourselves.

I enjoy a lively friendship with Ezra, twenty-five years my junior. A mentor to him as a moviemaker, he is a mentor to me on a frequent basis as I learn to use new technology in my work. Raised on this new technology, Ezra is a whiz at all things technological—a self-proclaimed lover of "gadgets." "You'll love the iPad," he tells me, showing me how to text my daughter. To my delight, I immediately receive a real-time picture of my granddaughter in return.

If I have seen further it is by standing on the shoulders of giants.

—ISAAC NEWTON

I am mentored not only by younger souls but by older souls as well. Three of my best friends are well into their eighties. We have been friends for thirty years. They are twenty years older than I—an age difference that grows more acute with the passing years. My friend Julianna recently had a knee replaced. I found myself worrying about the surgery, the dangers of general anesthesia to an elderly patient. My friend Elberta is on her third pacemaker. She assures me the device makes her life livable. My friend Jessica has no pacemaker and no life-threatening surgeries. She bemoans her lack of stamina, although she seems full of energy.

The meeting of two personalities is like the contact of two chemical substances: if there is any reaction, both are transformed.

—CARL JUNG

All three of my friends live daily with the recognition of their impending deaths. "I'm going to die soon," says Julianna; yet she had her knee surgery to make the most of the time she has remaining.

"I have to think about life, not death," states Elberta, who runs a horse farm and a paving empire.

Jessica, too, focuses on life—attending plays, concerts, and openings.

"You're just a spring chicken," Elberta tells me. And to an eighty-five-year-old, I do seem young.

Julianna and Jessica are both actors, still auditioning. Elberta is still energetically in charge of her large business. All of my closest friends consistently pursue their creativity, regardless of their age. As I take daily steps on behalf of my own creativity, I appreciate the lessons I have learned from each of my friends.

TASK
Mentoring

Writing freely, explore your memories of a mentor who influenced you. Who was this person? What did you learn from them? How did their lessons change you? Now, look around at your current life. Who could you pass some of these lessons on to?

Next, take a few minutes to reach out in appreciation to a friend who is older and a friend who is younger. It can be a handwritten note, an e-mail, a text, a call. Connecting ourselves to those who have gone before and those who follow us, we become part of a larger whole. Reaching out to those who influence us, we remind them—and ourselves—of their importance in our lives.

WEEKLY CHECK-IN

1. How many days did you do your Morning Pages? How was the experience of doing them?
2. Did you do an Artist Date? What was it? Did you discover anything in your Memoir that you'd like to explore in an Artist Date?
3. Did you take your Walks? What did you notice along the way?
4. What "ahas" did you discover this week?
5. Did you experience any synchronicity this week? What was it? Did you have any new ideas about what you might like to contribute to your immediate—or larger—circles?
6. What did you find in your Memoir that you would like to explore more fully? How would you like to explore it? Did anything come up repeatedly that you suspect might bring you a sense of purpose? How could you examine this in more depth?

Reigniting a Sense of Honesty

At this point in the process, you are likely to remember a time when the structure of your prior life (living at home, going to school) disappeared and you were suddenly faced with creating a new life for yourself. The same challenges apply to retirement. The essays and tools this week will help you live more honestly by resisting the impulse to please others or do what is expected of you. Perhaps in your work or family life up until now, you've had to toe the line in order to fit in at your job or be a good parent, but now that the kids and job are gone, you can get in touch with what you really think. If you were honest, what would you say you are sad about? Angry about? Stating the honest truth in your Morning Pages and exercises, and ultimately (with discernment) in your life, is liberating and enlightening. As you come to know yourself, the light you have to see by increases, and you present to yourself— and the world—a more complete, authentic, and unique persona.

The Truth Is . . .

One of the most empowering things we can do is know—and own—our opinions. It is easy, in the workplace and in our lives, to get into habits, perhaps subtle, where we censor ourselves to some degree. We want to be nice people, good people, cooperative people. We want to be good colleagues, good collaborators, good friends and relatives. This is all well and good, unless—or until—we act this way at the expense of our own truth.

Your life does not get better by chance, it gets better by change.

—JIM ROHN

"But of course I'm an honest person," you may be thinking, and that may well be true. We are not talking here about dishonesty in a large-scale ethical sense. We are looking closely at the small ways we may have ignored our own small voice, when our honest opinion of a situation was squelched in favor of a less complicated consensus.

Let's say, for example, that you are in a business meeting where a decision begins to be made "by committee." You may sense as the meeting goes on that the group is losing sight of the bigger picture. You may notice a path being abandoned that you thought was viable. But you may also sense that it will be a lot of trouble if you voice these opinions. Your insight won't be welcome, you'll "open a can of worms," so you decide to take the easier, softer way . . . you keep your mouth shut.

The problem with this choice is that slowly, over time, moments where we do not speak up for our own values start to chip away at our self-esteem. "I'm an opinionated person" slowly, sneakily morphs into "I'm an agreeable person," one small concession at a time.

Often, when we start to think about what we *really* think and how we *really* feel, we scare ourselves—and maybe our intimate others.

"I didn't know you felt that way," a sibling or partner exclaims, horrified, when you firmly refuse to wait for them to change their outfit one more time while you sit in the car, about to be late for church. "You always wait for me," they say, wide-eyed, out of breath, as you begin to pull away and they race out of the house.

"Yes," you agree, "I always do—but I don't like it. I don't want to be late."

One of the biggest hindrances to speaking with complete honesty is the fear that we will offend those we interact with and they will reject us. As we slowly move toward owning and articulating our true feelings, values, and opinions, the unexpected result is that other people, despite their initial surprise at the change, ultimately feel safer with us than they once did. When we know where we stand, so do others. And paradoxically, we then develop more secure—and honest—relationships.

As Delia worked through her Memoir, she found that in her early and midtwenties, she considered herself very opinionated. "When I finished law school," she recalls. "I couldn't wait to go into the world and show them who I was. I was impatient to prove myself." Delia discovered many parallels between that time and retirement—in both situations, she felt hungry to begin something new. "Everything that had structured my life was falling away. I felt then—and I feel now—the scary freedom of figuring out what I want to do with the rest of my life. The difference was, back then, I thought I was invincible. I was cocky, educated, smart, and naive. Now, I'm experienced—and sadly, more cautious, and more wary." After decades of practice in intellectual property law, Delia is both interested by—and nervous about— beginning writing projects of her own. "I want to try playwriting," she says. "I always have. But I've gotten very good at asking questions before I begin. I can talk myself out of anything, it seems. Yes, I've seen some really crazy things regarding authors and their work in my day. I've worked on plenty of upsetting cases. But I wish I'd stop being so lawyerly with myself. What good does it do to reason myself into inaction?"

Delia is correct, and not alone, in sensing that her own questioning is a stalling device used to avoid action.

"So you used to be opinionated, willing to take risks, and put yourself out there, but you no longer are?" I ask her, mirroring her belief back to her, while seeing as clear as day that she is still very opinionated.

Whatever is lovely, true, noble, right, pure, admirable, excellent or praiseworthy, think on such things.

—PHILIPPIANS 4:8

85

"Well, of course I'm opinionated. I just know too much now. I had beginner's luck back then when I started my practice with such a bold hand."

Beginner's luck—or good instincts? When I press Delia further, asking what she'd like to write about, she has, as I suspected, multiple ideas.

Honesty is the first chapter in the book of wisdom.

—THOMAS JEFFERSON

"I have a hundred ideas floating around," she says. "It's just that I would need to know which ones are most viable before I start."

The ones that are most viable, I tell her, are the ones that are most honest—and most honestly exciting—to her. I suggest that she search for clues in her Memoir. Are there recurring themes? What does she like to read? What did she used to like to read? What are her favorite plays? What does she think about? Looking back, she saw a common theme of betrayal and justice in her favorite books, movies, and stories—not to mention the career she spent defending justice and rectifying betrayals. By looking back, she was struck with a realization that her whole life had been quite consistently spent fighting for what was right.

"I am a fighter," she says, "and I do care about justice. I think as a proud recent grad, I felt I deserved the world. I fought to create a successful practice, and I did eventually do it. I fought for my clients. I fought for their work. And now, I still have that energy. I want to write plays about people—yes, opinionated people—who are strong enough to stand up for what they believe in. I realize I have been—and can be—that person myself."

By getting in touch with the honest themes in her own life, Delia discovered deep truths about herself that were important to her to express. When I last saw her, I was thrilled to hear that she had begun writing a play about a former lawyer.

It is equally important for us to express our truths in our art and in our lives, and both expressions can feel intimidating. Morning Pages are a safe place to vent and explore. It is essential that we keep the pages to ourselves, for "our eyes only," and that we feel free to write what we choose, no matter what that is. Morning Pages are uncensored. This is both why they work so well and why some people choose to shred, burn, or recycle them almost immediately. Morning Pages open their arms to us. "What do you honestly think?" they ask. "What do you want? What are you angry about? Why are you scared?" Writing freely, we learn what and why. Writing freely, we may learn that we are very angry at our neighbor for making noise late at night—and then, writing more, we may learn how we want to deal with that in an appropriate way.

"I had to learn to speak up to my brother," says Bill. "We own a piece of property together, and I've always done most of the work of maintaining it. I don't mind that, per se, but I get tired of him just assuming I'll take care of—and pay for—all of the repairs. It's not about the work or the money, but it's about the chronic nature of the situation. I've always been pretty agreeable about it, so I see that I'm at fault here. But I want to make a change. It's bothering me to pretend I'm fine with it when I'm not."

For Bill, his Memoir yielded a perspective on a longstanding dynamic between him and his brother. Three years his junior, his brother had looked up to him throughout his life. With the loss of their father when they both were children, Bill had taken on a protective, if not paternal role with his brother. "These things I knew," he says, "but it took my writing about them with my own hand to see that the way to actually help my brother was to stop taking care of him." For Bill, his newfound clarity would require honesty going forward. "I'm going to talk to him about it," he tells me. "And the thing is, because I can now see our relationship in the context of our lives, I'm going to be a lot gentler with him than I might have been. I'm not just annoyed about the house. It's a lot more layered than that. I want him to be okay, I want to protect him, and I want him to stand on his own feet."

Bill's revelation that the honest truth is more complex, and thus more gentle, than the unexamined emotion, is a powerful one. As we understand our own truth, we also understand how best to share it with others. And as my friend Jane has often said, "Doing the right thing for ourselves is doing the right thing for everyone." It is up to us to look closely and honestly to find that "right thing."

Morning Pages compel us toward honesty. They encourage us to admit how we really feel. Before Morning Pages, we may just say, "I feel okay about that" without examining what "okay" really means. "I feel okay" may mean, "I feel resigned." It may mean, "I feel hopeless." Or, by way of contrast, the same four letter word may mean, "I feel optimistic, pleased, resolute." With Morning Pages we are encouraged to be specific. When we catch ourselves saying we feel "okay," we must delve a little deeper. If we are honest in our pages, we find we have a great variety of feelings, some of them masquerading as others. Anxiety and excitement are one such pair of twins. Worried and afraid are another. As we strive to be accurate in naming our feelings, we often feel a sense of relief. The act of naming something accurately helps lead us to the right action we seek.

I often call Morning Pages the "greased slide" to honesty. On the page, we record our bold truth. We answer the sometimes difficult question: how do I feel about that? They say that the truth will set us free, and, telling the truth, in our pages and then in person—however difficult—is a step toward freedom.

Mimi went to dinner each Friday night with a group of friends from her acting class. Intellectually, she thought the dining expeditions were a good thing, giving her a chance to bond with her classmates, but she frequently went home afterward feeling depressed. I suggested she explore her experience in her Morning Pages, and when she did, she discovered that she found many of the people from her class to be quite pretentious. She didn't enjoy their company and she doubted that they enjoyed hers. There was one woman Mimi considered deeply fascinating, however. Mimi cornered her before class and asked if she would consider dining alone together rather than with the group. "That would be just great!" the woman exclaimed. She went on to confide, "When we're in a big group, I never feel I can have a meaningful conversation."

Mimi felt much the same way. Bowing out of dinner with the group felt somewhat tactless but authentic. But ultimately, her honesty yielded a new, deep friendship.

Often, the truth may surprise us. We think we feel one way—and "officially," we do—but unofficially, we may feel something quite different. Officially, we might be fine with the fact that we always do the dishes. What's the big deal? We like a clean sink, don't mind cleaning up, it doesn't take long . . . but what do we actually feel when our husband habitually leaves dirty dishes behind with the assumption—no, knowledge—that they will magically be done for him? Officially, "no big deal." Unofficially, we may be annoyed, even resentful. We might feel taken advantage of, and that feeling may be subtly poisoning our relationship. The difference between our official and unofficial positions may be quite vast. Honestly facing the difference empowers us.

TASK
Honesty

Getting in touch with our true feelings is one of the great benefits of Morning Pages. We often find that there are areas in our lives where our official feeling about something is very different from our actual one.

Allow yourself to be honest:

1. When it comes to _____, I officially feel _____ but I actually feel _____.
2. When it comes to _____, I officially feel _____ but I actually feel _____.
3. When it comes to _____, I officially feel _____ but I actually feel _____.
4. When it comes to _____, I officially feel _____ but I actually feel _____.
5. When it comes to _____, I officially feel _____ but I actually feel _____.

TASK
Memoir, Week Five

AGES: _____

1. Describe your major relationships in this period.
2. Where did you live? Did you live in more than one place?
3. What was your driving force during this time?
4. Describe one sound that "rings true" to you from this period. Does it still touch you today?
5. Describe one taste from this period. Is there a taste you have not revisited since then? Could you? (Re-create a recipe, visit a restaurant you might not usually, etc.)
6. Describe one strong opinion you held during this period.
7. Were there parts of your personality that were more pronounced during this period?
8. In what ways did you effortlessly express yourself during this period? In what ways did you struggle to express your truth?
9. What was a source of frustration for you during this time?
10. What other memories feel significant to you from this time?

The Drought of Doubt

One of the most terrifying places we can find ourselves is in a state of self-doubt. While self-doubt often stems from past injuries or insecurities, its power in the present can be both convincing and unsettling. Self-doubt can hit us all at once in a wave of horror—"I can't do that!" "I should just forget the idea of trying to be creative!"—or it can sneak up on us in subtle, seemingly legitimate justifications: "You probably shouldn't try painting. Aunt Joan was the real painter in the family," or "Are you really going to wear red? Didn't someone once say it made you look washed out?"

Self-doubt is a formidable foe, because when we doubt ourselves, we have only ourselves to fight back against. Self-doubt is often a very skillful adversary; it knows our Achilles' heel better than we do. It is very important that we learn to dismantle this voice and understand that just because our self-doubt might doubt us does not mean it is right.

"When in doubt, don't," the old saying goes, and this is a dangerous saying for creative endeavors. In fact, the opposite might be more true. Or, more accurately, "It doesn't matter if you have doubt; try it anyway." Doubts can come from within us or can be voiced—for our own best interest, of course—by those nearest and dearest, either historically or in the present. Either way, latching on to doubt tends to stall, frustrate, and confuse us.

"Everyone has a trigger," says my friend Conrad. "And everyone's trigger is different." For one person, the idea of speaking in public might trigger a torrent of doubt—even grief—and a life-or-death sense that they need to avoid the situation at all costs. For another, speaking in public is a breeze, but the thought of showing early work to a critical relative makes them defensive, unsettled, and prone to trying to anticipate (and answer) all the critical questions in a theoretical conversation that is all happening in their mind. No matter the trigger, self-doubt can make us feel—and act—desperate. When we engage with fears regarding our own limitations rather than trying our hand at that which entices us, we risk falling into a deep, dark hole.

For recent retirees considering—or starting—new creative endeavors, self-doubt is a very real pitfall to avoid. Working, there may have been less time for doubt. The work itself was probably an area in which we were experienced and had a hard-earned confidence in our abilities. Suddenly, with novel endeavors and long bolts of unstructured time unfurling before us, self-doubt can creep in. It may appear as a blanket rejection of a category of ideas or as the tiniest small voice doubting our own capacities.

One of the main benefits of Morning Pages is that they inevitably

The greatest mistake you can make in life is to be continually fearing you will make one.

—ELBERT HUBBARD

move us into action. Self-doubt festers in inaction. In the face of action, it has a significantly slimmer chance of derailing us.

Peter always had an interest in drawing cartoons and a father who thought his doodles were a "waste of time." Peter grew up on a ranch, and his tough and weathered cowboy father could see nothing more useless than "sitting around with a pencil when there are horses to work and fields to maintain." But Peter loved to draw. With time, though, his father's voice crept into his mind, and he began to hide his drawings.

One day, there was a message from Peter's school asking a parent to call in. His father laid into him: "What did you do wrong?"

"Nothing," Peter thought.

"Think harder! What did you do today that they're calling us at home? You must have done something!" Peter racked his brain, becoming more and more undone as he tried to imagine why he would be in trouble. He dug deep into the fearful corners of his mind. Did someone not like him and lie about him to try to hurt him? Who? Why? What could they have said? Had he turned in all of his homework? Yes, he thought he had. As his father made the call, Peter was shaking and near tears. He watched his father listen, somewhat confused, to the voice on the other line. When he hung up the phone, his father told him that it had been his art teacher calling. The teacher had chosen Peter to draw a cartoon for the logo of the upcoming state fair. Peter hadn't done anything wrong. He'd done something right.

He was so nervous from swimming in his own active self-doubt, and so discouraged by his father's disparagement of his cartooning, that he stuffed his excitement deep down inside him and pretended the assignment wasn't of much interest to him. His father moved on to doing something else, the moment passed, and Peter was left to try to get his bearings after a deeply fretful afternoon. The next day at school, Peter drew and redrew the cartoon, erasing until the paper tore. His cartoon was widely enjoyed and celebrated, but Peter never lost his discontented feeling.

Believe you can and you're halfway there.

–THEODORE ROOSEVELT

"I'm still so scared of my father's disapproval, even though he has now passed," Peter said, "that I worry and worry before I do anything at all. I don't know if it's because of that one incident or because of a million smaller ones—and maybe it doesn't matter. But I'd say my own self-doubt, wherever it originated, is the most crippling part of my personality."

"Don't pick up the first doubt," says my friend Julianna, adding that "the first doubt starts a chain reaction of further doubts." This is sound creative—and spiritual—advice. Every new undertaking involves some element of doubt. And those who do great things—or small things—are those who do them despite their doubts.

Doubt is a pain too lonely to know that faith is his twin brother.

—KAHLIL GIBRAN

I have written forty books, and yet, I still have doubt when I begin a new one. I pray to be useful, lighthearted. I pray to be of service. I pray to be guided. Embarking on a creative endeavor, whether it is a large one or a small one—a book of cartoons or a doodle on the edge of an envelope—we allow ourselves to exercise a very real and sometimes very vulnerable part of ourselves. "I see it this way," our art, whatever it may be, says. "I think this." In short, the act of creating—and I mean creating anything at all—is the opposite of self-doubt.

Peter began doing Morning Pages, and, meticulous by nature, committed to them fully. "At first I doubted I'd have anything to say," he tells me. "There it is again—self-doubt. Then I worried in my pages—worry after worry after worry. I worried about my kids, my pets, my house, my wife, my brother, what I said to the neighbor, what I didn't say to the plumber . . . but the more I put on the page, the less it seemed to be in my mind all day. I almost didn't know what to do with myself, having so much less worry and self-doubt clouding my mind." To the outside observer, Peter appears to have plenty of confidence—he was at the forefront of the advertising industry for years. "But," he admits, "my work was very separate somehow. I almost had a 'work persona' who acted very sure of himself. But secretly, I was doubting—watching my every move like a hawk—or like my now-deceased father."

Peter slowly saw marked improvements in his retired life as he started his days with Morning Pages. "I subscribed to *The New Yorker*," he says, grinning. "It sounds like a very small deal, but for me, the cartoons are a huge treat. I'm finally allowing myself to enjoy them." Peter tells me he plans to head to the bookstore to buy a blank notebook he can carry. "I think I'll start sketching what I see," he tells me. "It sounds simple, but I feel like by doing Morning Pages, I happen to the day instead of the day happening to me."

Sometimes our self-doubt is triggered by more recent—or present—situations that challenge us. A friend of mine is being threatened by a former business partner. The idea of a legal battle has been tossed around, and my friend is, understandably, deeply distressed by the thought. From the outside, I see that he's being bullied, and I don't sense that a legal course of action will ultimately come to pass. But he's distracted and disturbed, projecting what-ifs about the future. "What if this person ruins me financially? I've worked my whole career to be able to retire now, to end up here?" I have a lot of compassion for my friend's worries. But looking at "just the facts," we both know he did nothing wrong. The thought of financial or other ruin does not look possible, and his lawyer has assured him of the same. But still, he's been thrown into doubt. His trigger has been pulled.

It is important to remember, when we are suffering, that we are not alone. Every person experiences self-doubt at one time or another. In the throes of it, the prospects look dismal. We are in what feels like a drought, crawling forward, hoping for water, seeing nothing promising on the horizon. If we give in to our skepticism, we may start to convince ourselves that nothing will ever be on the horizon. But giving in to our skepticism is actually giving in to our intellect, not our heart, which is limiting because the intellect tends to focus on facts and logic, and alone, it can block our progress. We reject the smaller, quieter information offered to us by our spiritual tools: the hint in our Morning Pages of an idea, the inspiration of an Artist Date, the exhilaration of making a connection to a memory in our Memoir, the creeping optimism we feel as we consistently walk.

Giving in to our skepticism, we say, "I can't do that," and become negative and fearful. Fear and negativity conspire to create self-doubt, which, in turn, becomes this drought, sapping us of the sustenance necessary for creativity. Droughts feel agonizing, as if they will never end. This is where tenacity enters the picture. We must be brave enough—and stubborn enough—to use our spiritual tools despite our skepticism. During a creative drought, Artist Dates feel especially futile and foolish. "I have nothing to say," we wail, "and so I'm going out to play?"

But the key word here is "feel." Artist Dates are not futile. They are not foolish. What they are is brave and filled with grace, which will all reveal itself as we keep moving forward. During a drought, what is called for is courage: the humility to inch ahead despite our reservations. The courage to write our pages.

When we are in the drought of self-doubt, it is hard for us to believe that the drought will ever end. But droughts do end—and we often contain the antidote to our own episodes of doubt. With a little willingness to look, it is easier than we may think to find the silver lining we suspect must be there.

TASK
Dismantling Doubt

It is important to give yourself the dignity of grieving your wounds—creative and otherwise. Many times people will acknowledge their wounds but feel they should somehow be beyond them. You cannot move beyond your wounds until you fully acknowledge them.

When we experience self-doubt, it is often triggered by the present but rooted in the past. We may find that kernels of the emotions we are feeling now are familiar, reminding us of old pain. Acknowledging these past injuries helps us to avoid the pitfalls of self-doubt they may create.

Complete the following sentences:

1. As a child, I felt discouraged when . . .
2. I felt at a loss about . . .
3. I wish I hadn't . . .
4. A person who I suspect damaged me creatively was . . .
5. I wonder if . . .

Shadow Artists

A "Shadow Artist" is a term I devised for a person who spends their time and energy near an art form but somehow on the sidelines of that art form. Shadow Artists are often interested in this art form, probably accurately sensing a gift they have in this area, but feel safer not participating directly. Rather than making an attempt to participate in their dream, they find themselves standing close to the dream instead. Shadow Artists are common and may have successful "shadow careers" as they enable and facilitate the art form they are drawn to. Retired, these hidden artists may find that their passion for the art form they shadowed is actually a long-buried desire they have harbored themselves.

What precisely is a shadow career? It is a career near the dream but not in it. Would-be novelists settle for careers as literary agents or advertising copywriters. Would-be fine artists settle for careers as gallery owners or commercial artists. Their dreams hover nearby but remain unfulfilled. Typically, Shadow Artists beat themselves up. "If only I had more courage," they say to themselves. The concept of "more" courage may be a mirage that is perpetually out of reach. All anyone ever really needs is *enough* courage to take the first small step, and then that step leads to another, and another, and another. Before long, Shadow Artists often find they are succeeding at their game of catch-up ball—the years on the sidelines have made them acutely aware of just what is necessary to fulfill their dreams. Using this knowledge, they find themselves taking shortcuts, and the shortcuts do pay off. Once convinced they lacked an edge, they may discover they, in fact, have one.

Gene holds a master's degree in fine arts. "I studied painting with amazing people," he says. "I took my art and my training very seriously. But when I learned how much money I could make as a photographers' rep, I went in that direction instead. My knowledge of art helped me make the photographers successful, and I was successful in a material way. But I wasn't happy. I just bought things; I didn't make things—except deals, I guess." Retired, Gene looks back on his "brilliant career" and feels frustrated—and a yearning to paint.

"I think a part of me always wondered if I'd ever be here," he says, "approaching the brushes and easel again, after all this time. I did always wonder if I'd regret my decision to turn my back on what I had invested so much of myself in." Uncertain of what would come, but called to try, he found that he kept writing the phrase "It's now or never" in his Morning Pages.

Gene decided to vote for the now. He found himself rusty—it had been thirty-five years since he'd finished his master's. "Just keep trying," he told himself, as painting after painting flowed from his brush. "If I'm one thing, it's disciplined," he says. "I work. I like to stay in motion. That's probably my best trait—and it's a lucky thing for me."

While Gene considers himself disciplined—and he, by all accounts, is—it is enthusiasm even more than discipline that brings creativity forward. With just the slightest encouragement, our creativity responds to our taps, as if it has been lying in wait. I would argue that it has—everyone has a wellspring of creativity flowing beneath the surface, just waiting to be released.

Gene held himself to very high standards, as his classical training had taught him to. He kept on painting, gradually building up a body of work. "On my twenty-second painting, I felt like I was getting back in shape," he tells me. And what a good lesson! There is no magic, overnight success, but there is marked improvement as we work, day

As soon as you trust yourself, you will know how to live.

—JOHANN WOLFGANG VON GOETHE

97

in and day out. Art takes practice—and when we practice, we make progress.

"I was so happy when I felt like I had a painting that was 'there,'" Gene says. He reached out to a gallery owner friend, who suggested a list of places to visit.

This above all; to thine own self be true.

—WILLIAM
SHAKESPEARE

Gene set out to visit the galleries—and the first twelve were discouraging. He was told his work was old-fashioned. He was told there wasn't room for another artist. He was told he couldn't submit unsolicited work. He was told, again and again, "Sorry."

But on he plodded, and at the thirteenth gallery, he struck pay dirt.

"You're just what we're looking for," he was told. "Classical oil." With the incentive of having a gallery to show his work, Gene painted in a near frenzy. He produced thirty-two more paintings. The gallery owner rewarded his efforts with a one-man show. Imagine Gene's delight when two of his paintings were sold on opening night. "You're a painterly painter," one of the buyers told him enthusiastically. "Where have you been?"

Many people retiring from shadow careers harbor a dream and the admonition "now or never." Like Gene, they may decide to doggedly move forward despite any misgivings they may have. "A day at a time," Gene says. "That's all we have and all we need. Just do the day's work and then do it again tomorrow." When a Shadow Artist steps toward the light, the potential for both knowledge and satisfaction is bright.

It is common for Shadow Artists to feel critical of other people's work in the art form they desire to be a part of. A blocked screenwriter may have a rewrite for every movie she sees. A blocked singer might have stronger-than-average opinions on every current pop star. What I have found, over and over, in myself and in my students, is that when we dare to try, we are suddenly no longer a critic. We are now an artist, doing the same thing as our fellow artists: making art.

I do not believe that art has to be famous, or sold, or even shared to count as "real" art or to make us "real" artists. Stories abound of artists whose work outlived them and who never sold a piece during their lifetime. Van Gogh wasn't known well until after his death. Edgar Allan Poe published only two books in his lifetime, and they were *self-published*. Had these artists, and countless others, decided that to be a "real" artist meant only that they be known or popular, and thus given up making their art, we would have far less art in the world. Shadow Artists, who have spent careers next to—and often helping—people they would call "real" artists, need to especially remember this fact: In the act of making art, we are artists.

Sometimes artistic ambitions may be driven into the shadows after an initial disappointment. Dan had always wished to write short stories and dreamed of a life in a cabin on a lake where he could earn his living through his pen. But during his freshman year of college, he encountered a discouraging creative writing teacher who loved to talk about "the odds" of making it as a writer. Dan was sliced to the core by the words of this teacher and, after his freshman year, changed his major to premed, going on to become a research psychiatrist.

"I have written," he says now, "but only psychiatric research. It was a more stable kind of writing job, I guess. But it was nothing like what I once dreamed of. It was all very dry and clinical." Undertaking Morning Pages, he soon found that he was comfortable on the page, where his thoughts could run free. He noticed that he wanted to write beyond the pages, that he was more comfortable writing than not writing. When a friend of his self-published a short-story collection, it lit a match under Dan's ambition. "If he can do it, I can do it," he caught himself thinking. And at the urging of his wife, he decided to give it a try.

At first, when he sat down to write, he watched himself create excuses instead of characters: it's too late; he's too old; it will take too long; what if it isn't good . . . but, consistently writing Morning Pages, he knew what he had to do—what he *wanted* to do—and he saw through his own efforts at procrastination. And so, one sunny after-

Be who you were created to be, and you will set the world on fire.

—SAINT CATHERINE OF SIENA

noon, he started his first short story. Soon he had a routine: Morning Pages and housework in the morning, calls and e-mails during lunch, working on his stories in the afternoon. The pages piled up. The characters kept speaking. The stories kept unfolding.

When he finished his first short story, he felt a sense of elation. When he finished his second short story, he found a steely resolve. "I bet I can do an entire book," he thought to himself, as his third, fourth, and fifth stories flowed from his pen. In six months, he had twenty short stories. No longer content to inhabit the sidelines, he decided to self-publish as his friend had. When he reached out to his friend for advice, he received both advice and support.

Artists frequently love other artists. Accomplished artists often enjoy mentoring beginners. Beginning to actually practice creativity, Shadow Artists often find their dreams are closer than they think.

TASK
Imaginary Lives

Name five imaginary lives. What would it be fun to do or be? When you are finished, choose one of your imaginary lives and see if there is a step in your current life that you could take toward this imaginary life. For example, if your imaginary life is to be a fashion designer, you might have fun visiting a fabric store. Allow your step to be small and your list to include delights, not duties!

Crazymakers in Our Midst

In *The Artist's Way* I introduced the concept of crazymakers. Crazymakers are people who thwart the creativity of those they purportedly love. If you are involved with a crazymaker, you probably know it. All crazymakers share certain qualities:

Crazymakers break deals and ignore schedules.

Crazymakers expect the world to cater to their whims.

Crazymakers discount your perceptions.

Crazymakers spend your time and your money.

Crazymakers triangulate those they deal with.

Crazymakers are superior blamers.

Crazymakers create drama—but seldom where it belongs.

Crazymakers hate schedules—except their own.

Crazymakers love chaos.

Crazymakers deny that they are crazymakers.

Everything that irritates us about others can lead us to an understanding of ourselves.

—CARL JUNG

Crazymakers can show up anywhere: they may be your former boss, your sister, your brother-in-law, your neighbor, your golfing buddy. You may be related to them by birth, by marriage, or by choice. You might have worked with them. You may share a living space with them. You might never see them—and yet they drive you crazy through the Internet and the phone. They may be dead but still alive and well in your mind, second-guessing your every thought. Or you may realize—*gasp*—that you are the crazymaker.

Crazymakers thwart dreams and plans. They create drama and confusion. Often they have an air of superiority. They cause their hapless victims to doubt themselves. They are known to capsize the best and most carefully laid plans. Particularly when it comes to money, crazymakers cause chaos. There is always some new agenda requiring cash. Crazymakers demand that others go along with their schemes. They deny common sense. Crazymakers enlist mysterious others in favor of their antics. The beleaguered victim feels isolated and abandoned. The crazymaker demands, "Agree with me," and, all too often, the other caves in, convinced by the crazymaker to go against his own good instinct. Life with a crazymaker is debilitating. It becomes a battleground with many skirmishes. Sarcasm and scorn are weapons the crazymaker employs with abandon. "It's just so stupid," the crazymaker may rail when faced with a sensible plan. The crazymaker undermines modest and steady growth, often preferring to chase the fantasy "big deal"—the phantom idea that will prove the crazymaker right.

Crazymakers flourish with a lack of structure, and recent retirees with crazymakers in their personal lives are often shocked to see the extent of the toxicity in the relationship. Until now, their job and routine had served as a defense, but now the crazymaker has a field day, often going for the jugular, attacking the character of the hapless partner.

Few things are more distracting than constant drama in an intimate relationship, and yet, when we can pull back and see where our power and responsibility lie, we can act with courage and discernment, and we can rebuild our life—with or without that person in it—in a way that supports us.

I have received many letters and had many students ask how to defeat, destroy, or escape their crazymakers over the years. I have seen many crazymakers leave, mellow, and even heal through the use of creativity tools—either when they use the tools themselves or when their intimate other uses the tools and thus changes the dynamic of the relationship.

It is unlikely that you can change your crazymaker. But you can come to understand why the connection to this person is so strong for you, and you can slowly expand, soothe, and mend yourself. You can distance yourself physically, emotionally, or spiritually. You can pull away—pull back into your own power and your own right to make decisions for yourself. When you change, you change the situation. Any intense relationship works like a mobile: you cannot move one

Other people may be there to help us, teach us, guide us along our path. But the lesson to be learned is always ours.

—MELODY BEATTIE

piece without affecting the rest. So while the situation may feel dire and you may feel powerless, you do hold the potential to alter it.

One of the key elements in understanding our relationship to our crazymakers is to understand what we are getting out of it. A crazymaker is a giant distraction, but the unvarnished truth is this: most of the time, we use our relationship with our crazymakers to block our own next creative or positive actions.

Simon, a designer, married a very controlling person who worked in finance and was quick to dismiss Simon's art as a "frivolous" career that was only as valuable as the money it made. Because Simon's income was very erratic and his spouse's was very steady, Simon found himself in the position again and again of feeling "less than"—and his spouse was happy to point out why this was true. Simon had long wanted to try costume design, moving from his comfort zone of men's mass market into the very technical and very whimsical theatrical world. But when he spoke of this, his spouse rattled off a list of logical— and toxic—questions. How will you do that? You aren't that kind of designer. You'd have to learn a lot to do that. How will that ever make money? On and on, until Simon felt it was easier to ignore the whole idea than to talk about it. As I watched Simon, who was deeply creative and wildly talented, move more and more into a passive state, I felt devastated. His crazymaking spouse was a baffling choice for him on the surface. What did they possibly have in common? But beneath the surface, I saw that Simon had a deep fear of risk. Though his dreams and desires were large, he was afraid to make a step toward them. And though his spouse was a crazymaker and he felt that he was "shrinking" in the relationship, she let him solidly off the hook. If he wanted to stay blocked, there was scarcely a surer way than to spend his life with a person who would knock his ideas down faster than he could.

Simon needed to do a lot of work to first see, and then, eventually, escape the situation he was in. Simon stubbornly stayed in his marriage, and when he finally retired at sixty and left the freelance design

Things do not change; we change.

—HENRY DAVID
THOREAU

world, he was hit hard with the thoughts of the life he hadn't lived. His spouse had never changed, he realized, and neither had he. He had learned to balance the relationship; although it was toxic, if he stayed quiet, "things" stayed mostly quiet. He had become a master of walking on eggshells but was an amateur at respecting himself.

Working on his Memoir, Simon was pained to remember a young version of himself drawing intricate costumes that he never tried to make. Today, he credits illuminating his own story and writing daily Morning Pages with eventually giving him the strength to ask for a divorce. Today, at seventy, he has designed two shows for his local community theater. He has a twinkle in his eye that has finally returned from the young man he left behind long ago. "I stayed in my marriage for thirty years too long," he says. "I know that's a really depressing thing to hear, but I also feel so much hope today. It took a lot of courage for me to finally speak up for myself and then stand my ground. My spouse huffed and puffed, and the legal battle was horrendous and demoralizing—not to mention expensive. But I got out. The truth is, as hard as the divorce was, not being divorced was harder."

Not every crazymaker needs to be left in a legal battle in such a dramatic fashion. I have had students who, working with the tools themselves, became more autonomous, and the crazymakers' grips naturally seemed to lessen. "My mother-in-law just seemed less threatening to me when I began taking charge of my life." Likewise, crazymakers sometimes take on the tools themselves, and, turning inward, have less desire to stir up trouble around them. I have had students leave their crazymaking relationships and I have seen the relationships heal. I have seen family members get back in touch after years apart. I have seen friendships drift that needed to drift. I have seen legal, final separations made that saved the people stuck in the relationships. No two crazymakers are the same—although in some ways they are all the same—and every escape from a crazymaker is unique, although all escapes involve slow, courageous, honest steps toward self-respect.

As painful and scary as it is to live with a crazymaker, it often feels more painful to face what we want to avoid. Crazymakers thrive on doubt, and it is our self-doubt that causes us to align with crazymakers in the first place. Each new volley of disparagement engenders more self-doubt. "Maybe they're right. Maybe I am stupid," we think. The poisonous barbs do their trick. Life with a crazymaker may feel daring. It is a life lived on the brink. And yet it prevents authentic risk taking and true daring from happening. It is important to reassure ourselves that we do have hope, though. Morning Pages are a potent defense against the crazymaker's wiles. They create a bulwark of consistency. They prevent confusion and point out contradictions. They are a safe place to vent and to plan. Their clarity undoes the crazymaker's tangled schemes.

One clue that may tell us that *we* are the crazymaker is if most—or all—of our intimate relationships are volatile. Lynn discovered in her Memoir that she had consistently fought with the people closest to her throughout her life. "It started with my mother and continued on from there," she says. "I think I believed that fighting was the way to show strength. But the truth is I have been terrified my whole life." Lynn would consistently stir up trouble with those around her. A recently retired librarian, she recalls childhood dramas among her friends and family, and then very similar relationships all the way to today. "My colleagues at work were happy when I retired, I think," she says. "Only a few came to my retirement party. They said it was a busy time of year, which it was, but I noticed that all the people I fought with the most just didn't bother to come. I wonder if it wasn't a coincidence." Lynn started to do Morning Pages when she retired and was surprised to find a lot of grief underneath her anger.

"I complained and complained," she says. "I wrote about all the terrible people who didn't treat me well. I included my colleagues, family, and husband high on the list. But when I read about the crazymakers, I stopped in my tracks. For all my complaints, the crazymaker traits described me." Lynn realized she had always had a habit of doing things at the last minute, requiring her work colleagues to drop everything to help her. "I *was* dramatic with them," she says. "I thought whatever I was doing was more important. I felt like whenever I had an emergency—which was usually a result of my own procrastination—I was the victim. I thought they owed me the help." For Lynn to see her part in the toxic dynamic is a very large step, and one that has taken many Morning Pages. Behind anger is usually fear—fear that we're not enough, that we won't get what we need, or that someone else has what we want or deserve. And facing fear is difficult.

"I am mourning in these Morning Pages," she says. "I did the same thing to my husband—dumping projects all over the house and then complaining that I couldn't find anything. He'd help me look for whatever I had lost, but he always had this pain and hurt in his eyes. And he'd get frustrated, too. It's like I always push people around me to fight. The truth is, I'm afraid of people not liking me. I think I figured I'd better push them away first, so they couldn't hurt me. But guess what? They also didn't like me. I didn't like me too much, either."

Realizing that she has been a crazymaker is the first step for Lynn, and continuing to demystify her patterns empowers her. There is room for change, I tell her, and there is room to make amends. The last I heard from Lynn, she was trying to take very small steps, starting with putting her own belongings in order at home. "Just that one thing will help my husband, I know," she says. It will help her, too.

It is common for recent retirees to find themselves surprised to be suddenly faced with relationship issues at home—patterns they took for granted no longer hold up when they are now in the house much of the time. Before retirement, their lives may have been bedeviled by difficult personalities at work. After retirement, the bedevilment may be found closer to home.

When we are involved with a crazymaker—or are acting as one ourselves—we are almost always doing this as a stalling device. Few distractions are as powerful as someone in our immediate circle voicing doubt and casting wrenches into our path. But once we begin to act in our own best interest, the crazymaker's grip—or the urge to make others crazy—lessens. It takes deep honesty and great courage to break this cycle, but one page at a time, one conversation at a time, we pry loose the crazymaker's grip on us. As we record our own perceptions, we are no longer victimized by the crazymaker's *crazy* version of reality.

TASK

Crazymakers in Our Midst

1. Have you ever known a crazymaker?
2. Are you involved with a crazymaker now?
3. What creative action do you suspect you are blocking with this involvement?
4. Do you suspect that you yourself might be a crazymaker?
5. Crazymakers are experts at using energy incorrectly. One of the best defenses is positive action. What positive action, however small, can you take, right now, on your own behalf?
6. Take this action.

TASK

Anger

Complete the following:

1. If I let myself admit it, I'm angry that . . .
2. If I let myself admit it, I'm angry that . . .
3. If I let myself admit it, I'm angry that . . .
4. If I let myself admit it, I'm angry that . . .
5. If I let myself admit it, I'm angry that . . .

Now, looking at your list, choose the thing you are most angry about. Allow yourself to write honestly about it in depth for twenty minutes. See if you find yourself in a place of more clarity when you are done.

WEEKLY CHECK-IN

1. How many days did you do your Morning Pages? How was the experience of doing them?

2. Did you do an Artist Date? What was it? Did you discover anything in your Memoir that you'd like to explore in an Artist Date?

3. Did you take your Walks? What did you notice along the way?

4. What "ahas" did you discover this week?

5. Did you experience any synchronicity this week? What was it? Did it give you a sense of connection?

6. Did you find yourself being more honest this week, in your Morning Pages or in relationships?

7. What did you find in your Memoir that you would like to explore more fully? How would you like to explore it? As always, if you have a loaded memory that you feel requires further attention but aren't yet sure what additional action to take, don't worry about it. Just keep moving forward.

Reigniting a Sense of Humility

By now, you may be uncovering memories of a time when true humility was a lesson still to come. In the Memoir, it is common at this point for people to feel like they have "figured it all out"—maybe settling into a career, receiving a promotion or two, having an apartment and a friend group and maybe even a relationship. Looking back on this time, you will have the opportunity to examine which decisions were made by your ego, and which were more authentic. Are there ways your ego may be hindering your forward motion today? As you learn to set the ego aside, you will find that your dreams become bigger—and your steps to achieve them become more humble. Ironically, it is when we act from a place of humility that we become larger. It is when we stop trying to be perfect that we start to make strides. It is when we are willing to ask for help that we move ahead—and, paradoxically, inspire others with our strength. As our more authentic self emerges through our pages, we find ourselves feeling more comfortable in our own skins. No longer needing to pose, we

find ourselves willing to be beginners. In place of grandiosity, we elect humility. We are willing to try with no guarantee of success. We are willing to take risks because expansion is good for our souls. We undertake paths that are new to us. We find ourselves prospering in small ways and large.

Humility

When I am asked what is the biggest block to creativity, I find myself answering, "A lack of humility." Dreams remain dreams, nothing more, when we insist on their being fulfilled instantly and perfectly. We measure ourselves against masters and we tell ourselves that we will never achieve our dreams. But masters began as beginners, and their willingness to risk appearing foolish is a form of courage that is often invisible. Let us say we dream of being filmmakers. Rather than enroll in a beginners' course, we look at the polished masterpieces we so admire, and we say to ourselves, "I could never do *that*." We are right, too, that we could never do "that," but, with humility as a starting point, we could do original work that is very fine indeed.

So let us imagine that we have signed up for our beginners' course in film. If our teacher is wise, he will direct our focus to the beginning works of those we wish to emulate. George Lucas directed *Star Wars*, but long before he undertook his masterwork he made early films that might best be described as "bumpy." Perhaps we cannot duplicate *Star Wars*, but we can make our own beginners' films, and those baby steps will often lead us further.

When I was in my late thirties, and a veteran of Hollywood, I decided I wanted to make films, not just sell them. I enrolled in a class called Sight and Sound. I was a decade-plus older than my classmates. They seemed to me to be so young, and filled with enthusiasm and energy. Surely, I thought, they would make great films. Drawing on my own life experience, I made several short films. Imagine my surprise when our teacher singled them out, saying they were fine examples of storytelling. While my own experiences had challenged me, I now had them to draw on in the name of art.

Moving through the Memoir, it is likely that you have already uncovered interests, patterns, and delights. Insights bubble to the surface as you write—and as you drive, cook, walk, shower. You are in a powerful process. You are asking questions, and receiving answers. Sometimes the answers are ones you expect. But many times our answers surprise us. At this point in your Memoir you may be visiting a period where you were establishing more structure in your life. You were solidifying your independence and starting to form an identity that may well have a strong resemblance to the identity you still have today. You had dreams for yourself, and you were starting to act on them. You had established yourself to some degree, and were working to fill in the gaps where you felt unsatisfied. You may have felt confident—even expert—in some areas. In others, you may have still felt naive. Similarly to today, you have, at this point in the course, made great progress forward. You have reconnected to yourself in small ways and large, and you are having thoughts of areas you'd consider pursuing. Perhaps you have too many thoughts, or fear you have more ideas than you can accomplish. But one small step at a time, you will move forward. Satisfaction is possible, and you do have time.

There is no such thing as a time that is "too late" to begin a creative endeavor. Creativity is a part of our spiritual DNA—nothing that lessens or fades or disappears. No, it is a fire that we must stoke, and it is a place where we will find joy, a source that connects us to our purpose. If the antidote to fear is action, the way to take action—and to thus outsmart, outrun, or avoid our fear—is to make the action small enough, humble enough, that we are able to take it.

Many retirees, having reached closure in their working lives, long to make their personal mark on the world. Many harbor a dream of making art. There may have been a rock drummer left behind, a novel waiting in the wings, a desire to paint or act left untouched. We must be gentle with ourselves as we gather the courage to name our dreams.

The best thing you can do is the right thing; the next best thing you can do is the wrong thing; the worst thing you can do is nothing.

—THEODORE
ROOSEVELT

111

It is common for a barrage of blocks to attempt to scare us out of trying at this early point in the process. "What if you never achieve distinction in this art form?" the fear asks us. But often distinction comes through humility, not grandiosity. "What if your art is irrelevant?" "What if you do all that work, only to find that your art is beside the point?" But these questions are grandiosity masquerading as logic, and grandiosity asks the wrong questions. Making art makes self-esteem, and in the act of making something—anything at all—we make something of ourselves. And, by the way, no art is irrelevant.

Courage is resistance to fear, mastery of fear—not absence of fear.

—MARK TWAIN

When my father was nearing the end of his life, he decided he would build a house. He designed, planned for, and began the house. It was a red house on a lake, a tall and narrow structure reaching for the trees, almost like a tree house with views of birds at eye level. "Nest level," one could say. He drew and thought and built. He was excited by the house as he watched it begin to come to form. He felt a sense of pride and purpose as his creation came to be. He looked forward to his daily work. He was invigorated by each small step of the process.

My father did not live to see this house at completion. He did not climb the tall staircase to live in the trees with the birds. But this house brought him joy, and this house now stands, finished, on a lake in Libertyville, Illinois. It makes me smile to think that someone is looking out the window at the trees. I believe this makes my father smile, too.

My father may have wondered if he would live to experience its views and cozy rooms. If he did, he didn't mention it. If he did, I suspect that his active pursuing of his vision outweighed any misgivings he may have had of the future. Our creativity does not diminish with age. Our creativity lives at least as long as we do. I would say, much longer.

It does take humility to begin a project, not knowing how or where the project will end. Nonetheless, it is worth it to begin. It is satisfying to create. It is satisfying to allow ourselves our process.

Our ego is loath to admit it, but it is our ego that is afraid of failure. Our artist isn't thinking that way. Our artist naturally acts in humility; small steps beget further steps as we have stories to tell, delights to share, ideas to try without a focus on "success" or "failure." Our ego fails to realize that failure may be a necessary stepping-stone on the path to success. What is failure, after all, but an invitation to begin again? It has been said that success can be boiled down to two simple rules: 1. Start something. 2. Keep going.

I believe it is human nature to desire growth. I believe that all growth is thrilling. The truth is that the more humble our steps, the larger and more courageous our actions. Taking the time and effort and care to discover our authentic interests, we move forward in the direction of our authentic dreams.

"I long to accomplish a great and noble task, but it is my chief duty to accomplish humble tasks as though they were great and noble," said Helen Keller. When we are willing to take a small step forward, we open a door to something far greater. So often we are blocked because the dream in our mind seems out of reach. Humility reminds us that there is always a way to move ahead, and that every great accomplishment involves many small, ordinary steps.

We can easily forgive a child who is afraid of the dark; the real tragedy of life is when men are afraid of the light.

—PLATO

TASK
Practicing Humility

Name a dream that sounds out of reach. Now, allow yourself to name—and take—the most gentle step toward it. This step should be tiny; the smaller the better. Taking one small step will always inspire another.

TASK
Memoir, Week Six

AGES: _____

1. Describe your major relationships in this period.
2. Where did you live? Did you live in more than one place?
3. What was the role of your ego in your life during this time?

4. Describe one sound that brings you back to this period.
5. Describe one taste from this period.
6. Describe one fear you held during this period.
7. What dream did you harbor during this period?
8. What was your greatest challenge during this period? Do you relate to this challenge today?
9. What did you have to learn? What did you feel you already knew?
10. What other memories feel significant to you from this time?

The Defense of (and Defensive) Ego

The ego doesn't want us to be a humble beginner. The ego wants us to be an expert. This demand often freezes us and keeps us from pursuing new interests. In order to move into new territory, we must dismantle the ego's need for perfection. We must be willing to have humility. Humility grants us the grace to be a beginner. Humility grants us the courage to take the first small step—which will lead to the step after that.

Our ego demands that we be perfect, admonishing us when we suggest that our practice attempts are worth something, too. Ego is a very narrow-gauge track. It insists that we be faultless, achieving an icy perfection with no thought for how goals and dreams are actually achieved.

When we retire, many of us find that we had an identity grounded in our work. But often, when we look at it squarely, our ego was tied up in this identity as well. Yes, we took pride in our work, and it was natural to enjoy and celebrate our successes. But if our ego was too involved, feeding off our successes alone, we may be in for a shock. Retiring, we may feel ourselves at a loss. Our identity feels wobbly. Our ego is simply shattered. "Who am I without my job?" we wonder.

Edward had a distinguished career as an orthopedic surgeon. When he retired, he found himself bereft of his working identity. Taking pen in hand—although he made a point of telling me how stupid the exercise felt—he listed ten interests, from any point in his life. High on the list was the simple word: fish.

"Explore fish," I urged him. And, feeling idiotic, Edward made an expedition to an aquarium store in his neighborhood. He admired a tank full of shy swordtails and another tank housing aggressive angelfish. He found himself spending the better part of an hour with a tank full of tiny neon tetras.

"Can I help you, sir?" the clerk inquired. "Are you starting up a tank?" The question brought a thrill to Edward's heart. He *could* start a tank, he realized.

"Yes," he answered, "but I've never done this before. I don't know what goes with what."

"I can help you," the clerk volunteered. "Perhaps you'd like to buy a beginner's pamphlet?"

"Yes," Edward agreed. "That seems like a good place to start." And so, he purchased the modest pamphlet. Feeling a sense of glee, he took it home. The pamphlet was chock-full of tips for a first tank. Edward read it avidly. "What next?" he wondered. And it came to him: Take an expedition to Sea World. Putting his pamphlet aside, he googled Sea World. It was a scant hour's drive south. "I could take my grandchildren," Edward realized, but then he thought, "No, this trip is for me alone." Arriving at Sea World, he was faced with many choices. What should it be? The dolphins? Stingrays? Killer whales? Edward chose the dolphins. Their handler explained, "We know they're very smart—we just don't know how smart." As Edward leaned toward the tank, a dolphin came to the lip and appeared to observe Edward with lively curiosity. He could almost hear the dolphin thinking about him, "We know they're smart—we just don't know how smart."

Back in his car on the way home, Edward found himself planning his tank. It would be modest, but he knew he would find real excite-

I can accept failure. Everyone fails at something. But I can't accept not trying.

—MICHAEL JORDAN

ment in owning it. He had to admit that his two simple—even childish—treks to explore his interest, fish, had been deeply enjoyable. Already he could feel his personality expanding.

A bright mischief now in his eyes, Edward reported back to me: "Maybe the exercise isn't so dumb after all."

There is nothing noble in being superior to your fellow man; true nobility is being superior to your former self.

—ERNEST HEMINGWAY

Maybe not. And maybe the ideas we might dismiss as "dumb" because they seem so simple—something we would "just" enjoy— actually hold keys to our own growth and happiness. We just have to have the humility to ask ourselves what we might enjoy, and listen for the answer.

Tracy, a former art director at an advertising agency, had once had a passion for pottery, but she had long ago left it behind. "I used to have a kick wheel and a kiln in my basement," she says, "but I sold them years ago. I think about them sometimes—how much I used to use them." When Tracy retired, she wanted to revisit pottery—perhaps, she thought, there would be a beginners' course. But when she inquired at her local rec center, she learned that they had no such course: they were missing a teacher. "But it's so easy," she caught herself thinking, and then realized that teaching a beginners' course might help herself and others.

"I went in a few days before and played with the clay," she says. "I was a little rusty, but I could get people started—and get back into it myself." She discovered that she enjoyed teaching, something she had never done before. "I was the boss in my career, but teaching is a very different type of leadership. I hadn't thought about other people or what I could offer them for a long time. I didn't know if teaching would be enjoyable for me or not—or if I'd be good at it or not." But Tracy found it wonderful to think about the work of others. Setting her own ego aside, she found herself enjoying being in service to them. And teaching others about potting only heightened her memory of what had originally attracted her to it. "Watching my students reminds me of potting for the first time," she says. "It rekindles my love for it."

Tracy is not alone in finding increased pleasure from diminished ego. Teaching naturally pushes the ego at least somewhat to the side. At her job, Tracy was used to giving orders, instructing others about how to carry out her vision. Now, she is responding to the visions of her students and her role is to help them carry out their ideas successfully. "I am surprised by how many ideas I have to offer," Tracy says. "I also seem to be having more ideas for projects I'd like to start. My students are inspiring me." Many of us find that as we set aside our egos, we experience a blossoming of creativity. Taking ourselves more lightly, we are able to create more freely.

Comparison is the thief of joy.

—THEODORE
ROOSEVELT

TASK
Dismantling the Ego

For many of us, the quickest route to a more authentic and well-rounded identity is through pen and paper. List ten interests that delight you. Some of them may surprise you. Some of them may give you a glow of satisfaction just thinking about them. These ten interests that you note point you in the direction of your authentic self. You can then proceed to take steps in the directions of your buried dreams. Often, our interests appeal to a childlike part of ourselves. They may or may not be heady intellectual pursuits, may or may not be ideas that our egos would deem impressive. Allow yourself to put your ego aside as you complete this task.

Perfectionism

Perfectionism is the enemy, not the friend of creativity. When we try to get something "right"—meaning perfect—we create a debilitating loop. We focus only on fixing what we see as wrong, while remaining blind to what is right. The perfectionist redraws the chin line until there is a hole in the paper. The perfectionist rewrites a sentence until it makes no sense. The perfectionist edits a musical passage over and over, losing sight of the whole. For the perfectionist, nothing is ever quite good enough. Obsessed with the idea that something must be perfect, we lose sight of the joy of creation.

Perfectionism is the ego's wicked demand. It denies us the pleasure of process. We are told by the ego that we must have instantaneous success—and our perfectionism believes it. Perfectionism tells us that to move ahead, we must first be perfect. And yet, it is often perfectionism that stalls us and keeps us from moving ahead at all. Perfectionism is the opposite of humility, which allows us to move slowly and steadily forward, making and learning from our mistakes. Perfectionism says do it "right"—or not at all.

Use what talents you possess: the woods would be very silent if no birds sang there except those that sang best.

—HENRY VAN DYKE

During our work life, we were often rewarded for our perfectionism. We defended it as "attention to detail" and "having high standards." But perfectionism is neither of these things. Now that we are retired, perfectionism is a creative block, not a building block. It frequently stops us in our tracks. Instead of creating freely, we are stymied. Instead of moving easily in new directions, we are paralyzed.

Arthur retired from a long and successful career as an editor. He was a perfectionist, and as an editor, that trait had, in some ways, served him well. His editing was meticulous, and many writers relied on him. Retired, Arthur planned to do some writing himself. But when he took to the page he found himself blocked. There were so many ways to begin, and he wanted to choose the "best" one. But which one was it? The more he thought, the more he spiraled into obsession, thinking endlessly but not writing a word. He knew what he wanted to write about, but how best to write it?

"I want you to experiment with Morning Pages," I told Arthur. "If your inner editor protests—and it will—simply say, 'Thank you for sharing,' and keep on writing." Skeptical but desperate, Arthur undertook Morning Pages. At first, they were difficult for him. He wanted them to be brilliant. He wanted them to be perfect. "Brilliant and perfect are not the aim," I told him. "The aim is simply to fill three pages." About his third week in, Arthur began to experience freedom. He realized he was trying to edit his Morning Pages, and began to see the almost cartoonish humor in that.

"Now go ahead and start your book," I urged Arthur. He did so, and to his surprise, the piece flowed smoothly. "Tell your inner editor you'll let him have his licks on your second draft," I told him, "just like you edited other people's work." Arthur did as directed.

And now that you don't have to be perfect, you can be good.

—JOHN STEINBECK

"I realized that I had been trying to edit an idea I hadn't fully formed," he says now. "It was like I was hovering over the shoulder of a writer I would edit, questioning them as they tried to build a first draft. How horrible that would be! But yet, I was doing it to myself. No wonder I wasn't writing anything. Thinking of it that way helped me tame my own perfectionist—at least enough to be free to write."

In order to forge a creative recovery, we need to let go of our perfectionism. We will not recover "perfectly," but we will recover if we allow ourselves the latitude to make mistakes. There is no wrong way to do Morning Pages. They are intended for our eyes only. Pursuing our Artist Dates, we may find that some leave us feeling fulfilled, while others are less successful. It is important that we not beat ourselves up over the dates that fall short. The point is to be willing to try. The knowledge that we are willing to try may be all the reward we receive—and all the encouragement we need to try again. Do not underestimate the thrill of trying.

As I work on a manuscript, knowing that I intend it to be read, my perfectionism may rear its head. But, as I continue writing anyway, without editing, I have discovered an interesting phenomenon. In retrospect, revisiting what I have produced at a later date, I often find there is very little substantive difference between what my inner perfectionist deemed "good writing" and "bad writing." In reality, my perfectionist isn't actually an authority on what I'm doing.

It is essential to learn the trick of evading our perfectionists. I recently wrote a book in which I felt so bullied by my own perfectionist throughout the first draft that I nearly abandoned it. When the book was published, I tried to read it with an open mind. It read smoothly and thoughtfully. I wondered how many other books my perfectionist had talked me out of. The perfectionist is a bully. It wants us to doubt ourselves. But saying no to bullies does often make them go away.

If you wait for perfect conditions, you will never get anything done.

—ECCLESIASTES 11:4

Over the years, I have learned that a perfectionist will also magnify any criticism. My good reviews go in one ear and out the other. My bad reviews are amplified and repeated. All of us have an inner perfectionist whose greatest wish is to take us out of the game. All of us have the capacity to learn to ignore the perfectionist and work anyway.

Make no mistake: the perfectionist is a formidable foe; yet we do well to try to defeat it. One of the most effective ways to dismantle the perfectionist is to enlist the help of a believing mirror. When my friend Sonia Choquette was writing her first book, befuddled by perfectionism, I was a believing mirror for her, reading chunks of her writing and encouraging her to continue. My publisher of seventeen years, Joel Fotinos, was—and is—a believing mirror for me on every book I write.

Perfectionism is a common and tragic blocking device for many retirees. "I'm old," they may decide, "so what I do had better be good. There's no time for practice shots." Creativity is an awkward process; two steps forward, one step back. As we work with our tools, we find ourselves growing. But that growth is sporadic. What is required now is patience and tenacity. We must be gentle with ourselves and have reasonable expectations, lest the perfectionist try to take us out of the game. With humble forward motion we are strong—stronger than the perfectionist.

TASK
Name a Believing Mirror

A person who mirrors us back to ourselves as creative, capable, and expansive is one of the best allies in fighting the perfectionist. Who in your life is a believing mirror? Who in your life would say it is more important to try than to be perfect? Is there more than one person? Allow yourself to enlist a believing mirror's support in your endeavor.

Asking for Help

You must do the thing you think you cannot do.

—ELEANOR ROOSEVELT

Many of us were highly accomplished in our careers. We made partner in our law firms; we made CEO in our corporations; we were granted tenure by our universities. In retirement, these stamps of approval can actually become a trap. They prevent us from moving into new territory because they tell us we are too accomplished to ask for help—even if we do need help. In this way, the accolades we have achieved in our careers can sometimes become blocks to further accomplishment. It is for this reason that the spiritual tool kit I prescribe is purposefully uncomplicated. The tools, deceptively simple, spur us in new directions, and they suggest what we need help with—and the steps we can take to reach out for that help.

Most blocked creatives have an active addiction to anxiety. They play the game of "What if . . ." "What if I commit creativity and it is ill-received?" Note that this thinking indulges only in negative fantasy. It does not fantasize, "What if I commit creativity and it is well-received?"

"I'll look like a fool," the beginning artist fears. Ashamed before they begin, blocked creatives do not realize that the dream they are trying to turn away from will continue to haunt them.

Many of us harbor a youthful dream that we bury and tell ourselves we have outgrown. But we do not really outgrow our dreams, and when we work with Morning Pages, we often find our dreams come rushing back. The good news is that with our dreams also often comes the power to accomplish them.

Sometimes our dreams seem so far out of reach that we discount them before we begin. But if we are willing to look for supportive mentors and are able to recognize them when we meet them, we will move ahead. We just have to find the courage to speak up and ask for help.

"It doesn't matter how we speak up," my friend Jean says, "it just matters that we do it. We might be scared to ask for help, but we just have to get the words out somehow. It doesn't matter how. It certainly doesn't have to be perfect."

The more passionate we are about our dream, the more pressure we may put on it. My friend Damien, a retired architect, has long had a dream of being a filmmaker, but it seems out of reach, even precious to him. Because he has put the idea on such a pedestal, he has struggled to ever make a move toward it, leaving it there, pristine, untouched, and theoretical. Damien isn't comfortable asking for what he really needs, which is help—he is only comfortable *thinking* about his dream. But art does not happen in theory. Art only happens in action. Many, like Damien, can get so caught in heady concerns that they barely notice that they've actually just been standing still.

"I don't see how I could ever really make a film," Damien told me when I first met him. "I didn't go to film school; I don't know anyone in the business. Don't I need A-list actors? Do I need to move to Hollywood?" Damien had scared himself silly with the long and unattainable list of "needs"—that he had invented himself based on his own self-proclaimed ignorance. I listened thoughtfully and then urged Damien to undertake the basic tools—writing Morning Pages, taking Walks and Artist Dates, and gently exploring his Memoir. Skeptical—what did these tools have to do with his goal?—but ultimately willing, Damien began writing his Morning Pages. And barely two months in, he found himself at a dinner party seated next to a filmmaker.

"I would have ignored this," Damien told me, "but I had started to train myself to look for synchronicity. I was terrified, but I knew I had to talk to the guy. I just opened my mouth and asked him to tell me about his work. He was a humble guy, very friendly, and he made it all seem pretty uncomplicated. Before I knew it, I told him I'd been an architect dreaming of filmmaking. It just came out. I just said it. After I did, I couldn't believe I had—but even more amazing was his response."

"I'm going to be teaching a beginning filmmakers' course at the community college," the filmmaker told Damien over dessert.

"I'd love to take it," Damien responded. "But I'm sure the class will be filled with youngsters."

"Probably true," said the filmmaker. "But it would be nice for me to have a peer."

The next morning, Damien woke up to his Morning Pages urging him to sign up. He phoned the registrar and learned that the filmmaker had already enrolled him. He phoned the filmmaker to thank him, but his thanks were brushed aside.

"I told you I'd enjoy teaching a peer," the filmmaker said.

On the first day of classes, Damien found himself to indeed be several decades older than the other students. He complained the next day in his Morning Pages only to realize as he wrote that his life experience might prove to be an asset. As the class unfurled, this proved to be the case. Every time he entertained a negative view of himself, the Morning Pages countered with a positive. At course's end, he had completed a fifteen-minute short. He also received an A– from the filmmaker.

"The minus gives you something to grow toward," the filmmaker explained. "But offhand I'd say you're a natural."

"So now I'm not so much of a skeptic," Damien told me. "I am so glad that I asked him for help that night. I can't believe how different my life is today because I did. Now I am an optimist—not a pessimist."

All of us have things we would like to learn more about. And all of us can find, with a little effort, someone who can help us learn. Although we might want to claim self-sufficiency, the secret truth is this: rarely do we feel more connected to a higher power than when we ask for help. We must reject the thought that it is better to pose as a creative loner than ask for help—and then we must ask for help.

There is a crack in everything. That's how the light gets in.

—LEONARD COHEN

TASK
Asking for Help

Too often, as accomplished individuals, we feel we shouldn't need to ask for help. "I should be able to figure it out," we protest. "I've done harder, haven't I?" The truth is, there are many things we can figure out—and many that are much more easily and efficiently accomplished when we allow ourselves to turn to another's expertise.

Name one area where you could use assistance or advice. Who do you know who possesses the information you desire and is willing to share it? Choose one small step—one question, one piece of information you'd like to acquire—and reach out to this person. Often, our peers are thrilled that we have reached out and are more than willing to share their knowledge. They may even have a question or two in return, allowing us to help them, as well.

WEEKLY CHECK-IN

1. How many days did you do your Morning Pages? How was the experience of doing them?
2. Did you do an Artist Date? What was it? Did you discover anything in your Memoir that you'd like to explore in an Artist Date?
3. Did you take your Walks? What did you notice along the way?
4. What "ahas" did you discover this week?
5. Did you experience any synchronicity this week? What was it? Did it give you a sense of humility, a sense of being somehow guided by a higher power?
6. What did you find in your Memoir that you would like to explore more fully? How would you like to explore it? As always, if you have a loaded memory that you feel requires further attention but aren't yet sure what additional action to take, don't worry about it. Just keep moving forward.

Reigniting a Sense of Resilience

This week we delve into held beliefs about a higher power and explore simple paths to spiritual alignment. Do not worry: you need not believe in a traditional God to discover a sense of companionship from a benevolent something greater than yourself. This benevolent something may come to you as guidance, as inspiration, as synchronicity. It may appear as a lucky break or a "chance" encounter. In your work with your Memoir, you may find that you explore a period when you grappled with spiritual questions about your place in the world. How many of these questions remain with you today? What were your answers then and now? Practicing self-care, moving ourselves forward but not too quickly, counting on ourselves but not overburdening ourselves, we are resilient.

The Scientific Method: Experiment and Record the Results

The important thing is not to stop questioning; curiosity has its own reason for existing.

—ALBERT EINSTEIN

At this point in the Memoir, people often recall settling into situations and discovering patterns that would become long-term for them. Perhaps they married or had children; perhaps they made decisions based on the locations of their parents or other family members—whether to move closer or farther away. Some of these plans and patterns may have indeed been lifelong. Others may have changed—subtly or drastically—by now. By this point in most of our memoirs, we can see that we had sufficient life experience to sense what we believed would work for us and start to build a life that reflected those discoveries. We experimented and, based on our results, we made decisions. Looking back now, half a lifetime later, we have perspective on these decisions. Some might have been spot-on, even putting our life on course toward some of our greatest moments of success and happiness. Others might have been learning experiences, where we would ultimately need to change course.

Maggie looks back on this period of her memoir when she was aged thirty to thirty-five. "I had lived in many different places by this point," she says. "I had moved as I went through school and found my way to what would become my long-term job, but I had also moved while working at this large company, being transferred from one city to another. I grew up in a small town in Texas, I lived for the first part of my work life in San Francisco, and I ended up in New York—with a few places in between." As she moved from place to place, Maggie had the opportunity to experiment with different lifestyles—urban and rural, west coast and east coast. "I ultimately wanted to live in New York," Maggie says, "and I bought an apartment there almost thirty years ago. I still live there today. It's an example of something I did very consciously. I remember moving in—how expensive it was, how little I had, but I owned something, and it was defining for me. I have never regretted buying this apartment, and I know it is because I tried living so many other ways and places before I made this move."

Maggie is proud of the choice she made and how it is still bringing her satisfaction and joy today—not to mention an excellent return on her investment. "When I bought the apartment, it was just barely within my reach. The neighborhood was safe, but not fancy. Today, I own a prime piece of real estate and my investment has paid off handsomely." Maggie is grateful to her younger self for this decision, and she looks back on it with interest. "Sometimes I discounted it as dumb luck, but I see that it actually wasn't dumb—or luck. I was very willing to experiment, living almost anywhere, in my twenties. Because of this easygoing attitude, I learned what I liked. I knew that I would be happy in a New York apartment. But I figured it out by trial and error. Yes, I knew I was home when I got here—but it was because I had lived in so many other places that weren't home before that."

Maggie's willingness to experiment and weigh the results in making her decision provides her with great insight today.

"Now that I'm retired, I have an open schedule for the first time in decades," she muses. "A part of me is very focused on 'not messing it up.' But looking back at my own actions, I'm actually a little inspired by myself. Back when I was starting out, I wasn't trying to 'get it right' on the first try. I was willing to try anything. I've never been a religious person, but I look back and am impressed by my own faith and ability to listen to—and follow—my own instincts. I was moved around a lot by my company, but I was resilient. I'd set my life up; I'd see how I liked it. Some places spoke to me and some didn't, but I always tried again to make my life work—and I did." Maggie can take a cue from her younger self as she tries different paths that may be satisfying for her now. "When I first retired, I was pretty stressed out about what to do next. I'm realizing I can cool it a little, do one thing at a time. Looking back on my younger self is actually giving me patience with my current self."

Today, Maggie is discovering ideas around every corner that might

Dreams are today's answers to tomorrow's questions.

—EDGAR CAYCE

interest her. "I keep thinking that I want to be more active," she tells me. "So far, that's all I know. But I have a park nearby, so that's a start. I'm also thinking of trying a spinning class. And I wonder about karate—I noticed on a recent walk that there's a new gym just a few blocks from me. Hmm . . . how long would it take me to become a black belt? I'm going to give them all a college try, like I would have when I was younger. I'll see what speaks to me." Maggie is hopeful, beginning to trust that she can find her own way. I have seen many, many students discover this same thing: the ability to change their own lives, to find their own passions, to properly adapt to stress and adversity, and ultimately, to thrive in their own handmade life.

For those who are skeptical, the scientific method of "experiment and record the results" often yields faith and optimism.

Catherine found herself drawn to visual arts. She had an itch to try sketching, but she told herself, "If I had any talent, I would know it by now." But her Morning Pages were insistent: "Try sketching." Feeling a little foolish, Catherine decided she would try. It might or might not end up being fun for her, but there was only one way to find out. She bought herself a sketchpad—an 8.5-by-11 sheaf of blank pages. Waiting at her eye doctor's, she found herself sketching her surroundings. The act of sketching was enjoyable, and it also helped kill time. Her eye doctor kept her waiting thirty minutes. Ordinarily she'd have been annoyed, but with her sketchpad for company she found that time passed quickly. "That was fun," she caught herself thinking. "So far so good . . ." Leaving the optometrist, she made her way to a toy store. She intended to buy her grandchild a birthday present. The toy store was busy, and she found herself one more time waiting for service. Taking out her sketchpad, she drew a teddy bear. When it was her turn to be waited on, she selected the same teddy bear as a gift. With two drawings to her credit, she realized she had a hunger to draw more. That night, she sketched her cat asleep on the living room sofa. The next morning her Morning Pages announced, "You see? Aren't you glad you tried it?" Out for her morning walk, buoyed by the optimism her sketching was bringing her, she took herself to an art supply store. There, she purchased a set of forty-eight colored pencils. "Sketching makes me happy," she recorded in her next day's Morning Pages. "I'm so glad I had the nerve to find that out."

Alan undertook the tool kit with great reluctance. Trained as a scientist, he venerated objectivity. But he thought the tool kit sounded "woo-woo."

"Just try it," I urged, "and record the results. In other words, experiment and have an open mind, just as you did in your scientific career."

This advice spoke to him, and so, against his better judgment, Alan began the pages. Six weeks in, he had to admit that the tools showed results.

"I realized that I was the one with the closed mind. I was like the scientist who refused to perform a certain experiment, lest it prove his pet theory wrong. I don't know that I'd call it God—yet—but there is definitely a higher something that seems to speak to me through the pages."

It's now ten years since Alan undertook the tools.

"Do you still do them?" I recently asked him.

"Yes, I do, whenever I get in trouble," Alan responded. I had to laugh. If he wanted to avoid "trouble" he'd do well to use the tools consistently.

"I suppose that's true," Alan chuckled. "I do know that every time I use them, my life takes a turn for the better." Alan has to admit that his results speak for themselves . . . and seeing *is* believing.

TASK
The Scientific Method

By now, you have experimented with many of the tools. What results have you noticed so far? What tool or task have you avoided, or felt most resistant to? We often resist the thing that would give us the greatest payoff.

Do that thing and record the results.

TASK
Memoir, Week Seven

AGES: _____

1. Describe your major relationships in this period.
2. Where did you live? Did you live in more than one place?
3. What was a source of humor in your life during this time?
4. Describe one sound that brings you back to this period.
5. Describe one taste from this period.
6. Describe one way you were resilient during this period.
7. What was your concept of God during this period? Did you have one?
8. Were there experiences or decisions made during this period that are still part of your life today?
9. What was your relationship to exercise during this time? How does it compare to today?
10. What other memories feel significant to you from this time?

Our Unique Concept of God

Before you cry out—"God? Is this a religious book now?"—let me explain what I mean by God. Yes—it may be a religious god, if you have a relationship with one that you are happy with. But it may be a more generalized sense of spiritual guidance or "instinct." I like to think of God as "good orderly direction." I think of God as a benevolent force, a cocreator, a guide and protector. Every day I pray in my Morning Pages to be "guided and guarded." I feel, looking back each day, that indeed I am.

I was raised Catholic; my schooling involved the Sisters of Mercy, the Sisters of Charity, the Carmelites, and finally the Jesuits when I got to Georgetown. I was taught, mentored, and scolded by nuns. I sometimes call this upbringing "the greased slide to agnosticism." But when

I got sober in 1978, I was told that to stay sober, I would need to find a higher power I could believe in.

I was, at the time, very resistant to such an idea. I couldn't imagine talking about—much less believing in—God. I'd had enough, and I hadn't seen much evidence of a higher power working in my life up till then. I rejected the advice of my sober friends until I started to understand I was not so alone in my position on spiritual matters. Did I believe in an all-powerful, religious god? I once had, but I was not sure I could now. But did I believe that *something* was there—a force of goodness, you might say, something benevolent, ubiquitous . . . well, maybe. I had had enough moments of feeling inspiration, or guidance, or luck, in my life to explore the idea further. When one of my friends told me that the god she could believe in was the sunspots on her windowsill, I started to understand that maybe I, too, could name a "god" that I was comfortable with. I eventually found a line from a Dylan Thomas poem that summed it up for me: "The force that through the green fuse drives the flower." Yes, this I could believe in. Yes, there was a greater life force, and yes, I wanted to have a relationship with it.

At this point in my journey, I had to learn to write sober after a period of doing the opposite. I was told by a mentor of mine that I should "let the higher power write through me." At first this sounded crazy, but when I imagined the force through the green fuse, it was easier for me to imagine that this force could, perhaps, flow through me as well and "drive the flower" of my writing. In these early experiments of my own, I began to develop the set of tools I would not only teach but also live by. I learned by practice that my creativity flourished when I set my ego aside and allowed myself to write as if I were "taking something down," rather than "thinking something up." My writing flowed more smoothly. My ideas bubbled up gently and steadily. I was, for the first time, writing as if in partnership with a higher self—with my best self. I learned to ask myself what kind of God I would *like* to collaborate with. I immediately thought, "funny, lighthearted, full of ideas." After all, whatever created not just one

I know nothing with any certainty, but the sight of the stars makes me dream.

—VINCENT VAN GOGH

131

flower but thousands of flowers, snowflakes, and fingerprints with no two the same—whatever that force was, it seemed like a pretty good creative collaborator to me.

I have worked with atheists and with people who practice an organized religion. I have worked with people who are "spiritual but not religious" and with people who haven't given the question of religion or spirituality much thought before. For all of my students, Morning Pages do connect them to something—perhaps a sense of guidance, perhaps a greater understanding of themselves. Many times, it is both. Some resist trying, saying they just don't have time, that they don't see the point. To them, I say, the point of Morning Pages is connection. When we do Morning Pages, we connect to a higher power, to our best selves, or, if you will, to God. It's important to realize that Morning Pages are sacred time spent communing with the universe.

And those who were seen dancing were thought to be insane by those who could not hear the music.

—FRIEDRICH NIETZSCHE

"Oh, Julia, don't be so airy fairy," I hear some complain. These resistant ones are actually those most likely to benefit. I don't ask them to believe anything. Instead, I ask them to try it. Practically without exception, they speak of heightened awareness, higher intuition, and increased synchronicity. Although they may be reluctant to speak of God, they find themselves speaking of a higher something that is helping them change the way they live.

Many retirees, faced with the prospect of defining—or redefining—a spiritual path, find that they think of God in childish ways. Often they have not revamped their God concept since childhood. I tell these people that it's time for a spiritual overhaul. What kind of God would they like to believe in? Many times, they spent their life believing in an adversarial God. I tell them to try believing in a friendly God instead. What if they espoused a God concept that was friendly to them and their goals? What if this God was supportive?

"But Julia, such a God sounds like wishful thinking."

"Just try it," I urge. "Try believing God is on your side."

Ethan had been raised in a religious home, but when he recalled his upbringing in his Memoir, he noted that the religious environment in his home had filled him with fear. "I believed God was always watching," he tells me. "I felt nervous to make a wrong move." Now retired, he wanted to try songwriting but was afraid his ideas were stale and unworkable. "I never would have connected my fear of creating to my concept of God," he tells me. "The music I loved was pop, not spiritual. I wasn't yearning to write hymns, and so I thought God might disapprove. I think it's possible that's what is stopping me."

Yes, it is possible, and it is also very common. Creating art is an intimate act, and if we do indeed feel someone—or something—is "always watching," we may censor ourselves before we begin. As Ethan began to redesign his own notion of God, thinking more of a general positive source than the negative, fearful God he had once tiptoed around, he started to feel excited to try songwriting for the first time. He sat at the piano daily, listening for melodies and writing down what he heard.

Be faithful in small things because it is in them that your strength lies.

—MOTHER TERESA

"Maybe my ideas *are* good," he wrote one day in his Morning Pages. "Maybe they *do* come from some higher place—whether it's within me or outside of me. Maybe it doesn't matter where they come from." Trusting in a divine source, whatever that might be, Ethan found himself composing more freely.

Writing Morning Pages is a form of prayer. We are telling the universe—or God, or a higher power, or the force, or the Dao, name it what you will—exactly what we like, what we dislike, what we want more of, what we want less of. We are contacting an inner resource that guides us carefully and well. Many of us would shy away from prayer. But writing our pages, we may discover ourselves doing something that resembles praying. We contact an unsuspected inner resource. It doesn't matter what name we give to this force. What does matter is that we listen to it. And this listening, done daily, brings startling results. "Please guide me," we pray, and soon we receive guidance. It may come as a hunch or intuition. It may come as a conversation with a stranger. The point is that guidance does come, and if we are open to listening, we hear it.

At first, this idea of guidance may seem like wishful thinking or coincidence. But as we practice being receptive, it comes to be a relied-upon part of life. "What should I do about my partner's negativity?" we may query. The answer may be, "Just love him. Don't try to fix him." All prayers are heard, and all prayers are answered, although sometimes the answers are subtle. We may be guided in an unexpected direction. "Call X," we may be told, an unlikely answer, we think, and so we pray again. "Call X," our intuition persists. So we pray yet again. "Call X," we hear, until finally, obediently, we do call X, who unexpectedly opens a door for us. Through Morning Pages, we practice tuning our receptors. It's as if we have built a spiritual radio kit able to pick up messages from what we might call "the source." Again, it doesn't matter what you call this helping energy. It only matters that you give it a chance to help you.

Veronica was battling depression and a number of life stressors. I suggested that she ask for guidance in the areas that baffled her, but she was deeply uncomfortable with the idea. "I'm an atheist," she told me. I assured her that this was okay. She didn't need to change her beliefs or call what she heard "guidance" if she wasn't comfortable with that language. She needed only to ask a question in her pages, and listen for an answer.

"Well, I'm in pain," she told me, "so I'll try it."

Listening after she posed a question in her Morning Pages, she often heard wisdom coming from somewhere beyond herself. "What should I do about my son-in-law?" she asked of a troublesome relationship. "Be generous with him," the answer came back. "What should I do about my chronic overspending?" she inquired. "Keep a log of money in and money out," she was advised. No matter what the question, her pages held an answer—or they pointed the way toward one. "Try walking," the pages advised her when she complained about being overweight. "Try walking," they advised her again when she complained that her ideas seemed flat. Her pages continued, "As you become more active, your ideas will come into focus. You have many ideas; you just need to access them."

And so Veronica, obedient to her pages, undertook a habit of walking. Sure enough, she found herself feeling more alert, more vibrant and alive. Her depression lifted as she found herself tapping an "unsuspected inner resource," as she called it. "Whatever it is," she says now, "I appreciate it."

This huge shift in perspective was not lost on Veronica. Although she wouldn't phrase it this way, she is truly experiencing a spiritual awakening—a large psychic change from the negative to the positive.

Often, we explore our God concept in a spirit of skepticism. This is fine. It just matters that we explore it. In our secular, workaday lives, the boss was our higher power—or we were. Pages demand that we surrender control. We pose questions and answers seem to come from nowhere—or somewhere—but not from us. We come to rely upon our newfound discernment. We sense a higher hand than our own guiding us as we write. Seeking guidance, we find it comes to us from all directions. Sometimes it is a quiet inner knowing. Other times it is a coincidence, the words of a stranger overheard. Gradually we recognize that we are always led, always guided. We need only ask for help and then listen, expecting it to arrive.

TASK
God Concept

Our childhood God may be very different from the God we now believe in—or wish to believe in. Working quickly, list ten traits of your childhood God.

My childhood God was:

1. Male
2. Judgmental

3. Catholic

4. All-seeing

5. Etc. . . .

Then, list ten traits of a creativity God that you would design yourself.

I would love my God to be:

1. Creative

2. Lighthearted

3. Guiding

4. Accessible

5. Etc. . . .

TASK
Ask and You Shall Receive

Now that you have designed your creativity God, try asking for its help. Some like to write out a question at night and then listen for an answer in the morning. Some go out on a walk with a question in mind. Perhaps you enjoy writing your question in your Morning Pages and listening back for the answer. Perhaps you will try all three. The point is to experiment with open-mindedness. The answers that you "hear" may surprise and enlighten you.

The Exercise Investment

Too often, we tell ourselves it's "too late" to exercise. We resign ourselves to a body that is not fit. But doctors tell us it is never too late to begin to exercise. Many communities offer Pilates and yoga classes for all ages. Almost all of us can walk, and walking also leads to fitness. I have a puppy that loves to walk. When I put on my gym shoes, she pirouettes with excitement. When I retrieve her leash, she nears ecstasy. She is a young dog, and exercise brings her joy. I alternate walking and jogging. One day as I jogged, a raven swooped low over the road ahead. "Come on," it seemed to be saying, "you can go faster." But I did not want to go faster. I wanted to set a gentle, easy pace, one that I would not become discouraged by. And so, we walked ten paces and then jogged twenty. And then we walked ten more paces and then jogged twenty again. My trail is a dirt road that stretches through the piñons. Already, the puppy knows to follow the road. When it veers left, so does she—and so do I. A gentle pace is all that's called for. I tell myself it's fine to be a fitness beginner.

The other night at the health food store, I bought fresh strawberries and a magazine on running. The magazine was inspirational; it contained tips on how to gently increase your pace and fitness. I read the magazine eagerly. Even though I was a beginner, I already identified myself as a runner. I thought of calling my friend Dick and telling him I had launched into a gentle regime. Dick is seventy-two years old and has run six marathons since the age of fifty. He often lopes six or seven miles "just to get the kinks out." Once upon a time, I was a more serious runner. Then, for reasons I can't explain, I stopped running. Maybe it was because I lived in Manhattan. Whatever the case, I was ready now to resume. Santa Fe is a runners' town. Runners travel the many dirt roads. Runners climb the hills—some even tackle the long hill that leads to the ski valley. I watch them, impressed and inspired.

Exercise "raises our vibration" as my friend Sonia Choquette would say. It clears our minds and connects us to a source of spiritual support. Going outside, breathing fresh air, and allowing our heart rate to be elevated brings us optimism and a sense of accomplishment that we carry through our day. Some of us, like Dick, are lifelong athletes. Others, like myself, have gone in and out of a routine.

Earleen retired from a long career as a music professor at a university. "I've gone years without exercising," she says. "I had short stints with gym memberships—once in my twenties and once in my forties—but

Physical fitness is not only one of the most important keys to a healthy body; it is the basis of dynamic and creative intellectual activity.

—JOHN F. KENNEDY

137

now, in my sixties, I'm basically a total beginner." At a recent visit, Earleen's doctor told her that her cholesterol was slightly high—"on the verge of needing medicine."

"This scared me," Earleen explained. "I have had relatively good health all this time, but the idea that I'm almost at a point that I'd need cholesterol medicine really woke me up. All of a sudden it wasn't about wanting to lose twenty pounds out of vanity. It was my health, and I realized I only get one body to take care of. I know I can make some changes in my diet, but I think, for me, the bigger thing is exercise." Knowing she needed to begin at the beginning, Earleen decided to tour the local gyms and see what they had to offer. When she did, she was met with welcome arms and a wealth of information.

If we could give every individual the right amount of nourishment and exercise, not too little and not too much, we would have found the safest way to health.

—HIPPOCRATES

"I've never stayed at a gym for long, and I told them this up front," she says. "They were all so encouraging. I never stuck around long enough to figure out that people who exercise a lot tend to be optimists. It's fun. They're very friendly."

Weighing her local gym options, Earleen decided to join the nicest gym in her town. "It was a little bit more per month," she says, "but I walked in and knew I would want to return there. It smelled like eucalyptus, it had a pool and lots of classes, the locker rooms were beautiful, and I'll admit that the steam room and sauna caught my attention." Earleen has hit on a great piece of wisdom here: she has chosen the gym where she would *like* to go. When we choose an activity that calls to us—whether it is a class, a walk in nature, or the environment of a full-service gym—we are much more inclined to return and embrace the habit into our lives.

"I've been going for a month," Earleen tells me now. "I take two classes a week and then I try to walk—either on the indoor track or outdoors, if the weather is good—a few times a week. I'll try to increase as time goes on, but for now, I'm exercising more than I ever have and I feel really, really different. My aqua-fit class is hard for me, but I do enjoy it, and I tell myself I can go sit in the steam room when it's over. Sometimes it's the promise of the steam room that gets me to the class. But I think that's okay."

Yes, it certainly is okay. Bringing joy, comfort, and yes, even a little luxury, into our exercise habits keeps us coming back—and keeps us taking productive—and proactive—actions on behalf of our health. As Michelle May, MD, writes in her book *Eat What You Love, Love What You Eat,* the benefits of exercise are enormous, and incorporating an exercise routine into your life is "one of the most powerful prescriptions you can write for yourself." The many well-documented health benefits range from the physical to emotional, from lowered stress, cholesterol, and blood pressure to increased optimism, energy, and longevity. As she puts it, "If you could buy all that in a pill, everyone would want a prescription." When we exercise, we become resilient in body, mind, and spirit.

An early-morning walk is a blessing for the whole day.

—HENRY DAVID THOREAU

Back in my routine, I enjoy the excitement of progress. The scale drops as my endurance rises. My dog Lily continues to be an excellent companion and enthusiastic workout buddy, always ready and hoping to go for our walk/jog. Making an appointment to meet a friend for a hike or a game of tennis can help us to keep our exercise commitment. As we choose the form of exercise that works for us, we must be careful to allow ourselves baby steps toward our goal. Five minutes a day from zero is an infinite improvement; ten minutes from five is a 100 percent increase. Those who have never exercised will quickly learn that "just a little" is much more than nothing.

TASK
Exercise, Just for Today

The key to any sustained program lies in doing it one day at a time. Rather than create grandiose goals beyond our reach, it behooves us to commit to one discrete, feasible action. What small amount of exercise could you do, just for today? Do that thing.

Nature's Gifts

Live in the sunshine.
Swim the sea. Drink the
wild air's salubrity.

—RALPH WALDO
EMERSON

Forging a connection with nature can be a shortcut to an increased conscious contact with your higher power. For me, a starry night with moonrise over the mountains leads me to exclaim, "I love you!" Nature seems to exclaim right back, "I love you, too." Wild roses alongside a country road, sunflowers and hollyhocks blooming by a wooden fence, tiny violets garlanding a tree trunk—each detail of creation inspires my own creations. The puppy basking in the sun, the horse grazing in the field, the kitten batting its ball of yarn—all fill me with wonder. On a city street, the Brittany spaniel tugging at its owner's leash, the sharpei with its clown's frown, and the pit bull tracking by its neighbor's side enchant me with the earth's glories. The pink froth of a cherry tree, the glistening green of a willow, and the gorgeous gold of an aspen catching fire remind me that each day, as I strive to connect to the world, I am gifted with a great bounty.

This world is beautiful, and we are intended to love its many delights.

Brendalyn, my minister friend, recently undertook an eight-day vision quest involving four days alone in the wilderness with no food, only water. "I wasn't frightened at all," she reports gleefully. "Instead, I felt a heightened sense of divinity."

We need not spend eight days alone in nature to connect to its wonders, although Brendalyn's insight after her bold endeavor is enlightening. "My spiritual awareness was heightened by my time in nature," she says. As we strive to make contact with the natural world, we inevitably make contact with the force that helped to create it, however we define that force for ourselves.

Helen had a long and successful career as an accountant. She advised many high-powered businesspeople. When she retired, she found she missed the stress-filled days as a problem solver. To fill her time, she began a practice of daily walking. "Oh my goodness!" she exclaimed to herself as she spotted a great blue heron. "How beautiful," she breathed, seeing a red-winged blackbird. She walked a mile into the village. It was a mile she had often whizzed past. But now, walking, she cherished the beauty that was there for the looking. A month into her daily walks, she bought herself a pair of high-powered binoculars. She began scanning her surroundings as she walked. She spotted the blue heron's nest and she spotted some mallards, busy in the rushes. In her Morning Pages, she cataloged the beauty she found in the natural world. "All this beauty was always all around me," she told me when I phoned to see how she was doing in her retirement. "Now I have time to notice it."

Look deep into nature, and then you will understand everything better.

—ALBERT EINSTEIN

The more Helen walked, the more she yearned for more time in nature. She began a practice of taking small adventures—a trip to the ski valley before the snow when the aspens were ablaze, a drive up a nearby canyon to revel in the mountain asters, a drive alongside the Rio Grande River. These expeditions filled her heart.

"I saw a hawk yesterday," Helen told me with wonder. "It was riding the thermals, and just spotting it, I felt my own spirit soar. Last week I drove north to the junction of two rivers. Even from my car, I could see the power of the current. It gave me the resolution to write a blog. My forays into nature give me something to share."

When we connect with nature, we have something to share. When we connect with nature, we forge further connections, to those around us, to our higher self, to our past and our future. Our world expands.

An activity in nature that rewards time well spent—in your own backyard, at that—is gardening. Often undertaken by retirees who suddenly have time on their hands, gardening is fertile with beauty and satisfaction. When Isabel retired from teaching, she filled her backyard with flowers and spent many happy hours tending to, and cherishing, her crop. Granny's Garden, as the grandchildren knew it, was magical, filled with pansies and roses. She taught her grandchildren to press flowers and plant new blossoms. To this day, show any of her now-grown grandchildren a pansy, and they will be transported immediately to that enchanted backyard on a small street in Indiana.

Thomas Berry wrote that "gardening is an active participation in the deepest mysteries of the universe." Many a gardener will agree that this is true. Connecting, literally and directly, with the earth brings a certain peace and perspective that may otherwise seem elusive.

Frank knew he wanted to garden, but could not decide whether to plant flowers or vegetables.

There are always flowers for those who want to see them.

—HENRI MATISSE

"Why not plant both?" his wife suggested, and that is precisely what Frank did. He planted zinnias and tomatoes, hollyhocks and zucchini, sunflowers and squash. His afternoons spent gardening gave him a deep satisfaction. He took pride in his pastime, and his wife enjoyed the many fresh bouquets his garden yielded. The vegetables he grew were fresh and delicious. There was simply no comparison between his homegrown produce and store-bought. The first year he gardened, Frank excavated a modest plot; yet its yield seemed to him to be prodigious. The second year, Frank expanded both his flowers and his vegetables, adding carrots and cauliflower, lettuce and radishes. It became a point of pride for him that all the vegetables they ate were homegrown. The third year Frank gardened, he grew glossy eggplant and cucumbers. He began cooking special vegetable dishes, discovering he enjoyed cooking nearly as much as gardening.

Zucchini bread became his specialty. He gave family and friends his freshly baked loaves. Homemade vegetable soup was a close runner-up, with every single vegetable plucked fresh from the garden.

"Before I retired, I had the desire but not the time for my pastimes. The combination of time and desire came with retirement. Next year I'm going to double my tomato patch."

Whether your lifestyle allows you to explore the forest, plant a garden, walk along a beach, or simply visit a local park or greenhouse, it is worth a foray into nature, and worth noting what this foray elicits in you. The answers may surprise you.

TASK
Discovering Nature

What can you do in your current environment to appreciate or explore nature? When I lived in the city, collecting pinecones in the park or having fresh flowers in the apartment brought me a sense of connection to nature. When I lived in Los Angeles, walks along the ocean provided a "wash" of cleansing air. In New Mexico, I love the long dusty roads that I explore with my dog Lily. Some people like to collect leaves or stones. Others like to sit outside, soaking in the sounds of wind and birds. Choose one action you can take and note whether actively connecting to nature makes you feel more in touch with a higher source.

But in every walk with nature one receives far more than he seeks.

—JOHN MUIR

Synchronicity

The late, great mythologist and teacher Joseph Campbell advised his students to "follow their bliss." He told them to expect synchronicity, which he defined as "helping hands." "Follow your bliss," he taught, "and the universe will open doors for you." An octogenarian when he became famed as a teacher, he had decades of teaching experience with which to back up his theories. Over and over again, he had seen doors swing open. His life had taught him to be a firm believer in the advice offered to us by Johann Wolfgang von Goethe: "Whatever you think you can do, or believe you can do, begin it. Because action has magic, grace, and power in it."

Synchronicity is an ever present reality for those who have eyes to see.

—CARL JUNG

Another quote comes to mind, this from the Scottish explorer Joseph Murray: "There is one elemental fact, the ignorance of which has scuttled many a grand design. That is this: when you are committed, the universe moves, too."

When we write Morning Pages, we are contacting the universe. We are telling a benevolent something our precise needs, goals, and desires.

It is as if we are in a life raft, bobbing in the sea. When we write our pages we send out a signal that tells our precise location and allows us to be rescued. Within a short period of time after we contact the universe, the universe contacts us back. We begin to have the experience of synchronicity. We find ourselves increasingly in the right time and place for our wishes to be fulfilled. When I teach and I explain to my students the concept of synchronicity, they may at first protest that such a concept seems too good to be true. Not wanting to be gullible, they exclaim, "Julia! Do you really believe the universe opens doors for us?" I tell them yes, and I ask them not to believe me, but to keep track themselves of the instances of synchronicity they now encounter.

The universe is full of magic things patiently waiting for our senses to grow sharper.

—EDEN PHILLPOTTS

For Eva, looking for synchronicity became a game. In her Morning Pages, she listed the arenas in which she needed help. Some of them seemed important. Others seemed almost petty. She had recently moved to a new city and needed to find a hairdresser she could trust. Attending an evening lecture on minimalist art, she found herself sitting next to an attractive man who was full of sympathy for her position as a newcomer to town. Feeling silly, Eva confessed that her biggest worry was finding a hairdresser. The man chuckled. "I am a hairdresser," he told her. Eva took his number and the next day called for an appointment. She needed a specific type of help with her curly hair.

"That's my specialty," the handsome hairdresser told her. He gave her an appointment the very next day, and although she had her doubts—it all seemed too easy—Eva emerged from his salon with beautiful, softly curling hair.

"It really makes me so happy to have found him," she says. "I know it seems very frivolous, worrying about my hair, but I do—and it's the type of thing I would have considered a nonspiritual request. But maybe all requests are just fine. I'm learning that there's no wrong way to write Morning Pages and no wrong thing to ask for help with. I'm more humble and more faithful. I'm thinking about what to ask for help with next, and I'm excited to see what happens."

WEEKLY CHECK-IN

1. How many days did you do your Morning Pages? How was the experience of doing them?

2. Did you do an Artist Date? What was it? Did you discover anything in your Memoir that you'd like to explore in an Artist Date?

3. Did you take your Walks? What did you notice along the way?

4. What "ahas" did you discover this week?

5. Did you experience any synchronicity this week? What was it? Did it give you a sense of humility, a sense of being somehow guided by a higher power?

6. What did you find in your Memoir that you would like to explore more fully? How would you like to explore it? As always, if you have a loaded memory that you feel requires further attention but aren't yet sure what additional action to take, don't worry about it. Just keep moving forward.

The world is all gates, all opportunities, strings of tension waiting to be struck.

—RALPH WALDO EMERSON

Reigniting a Sense of Joy

This week you will explore—and act on—the simple but often profound question: "What brings you true joy?" Looking back in your Memoir, you may find that this was a period of creating a family or household for the first time. For some, the present will parallel that time as the "second time around" with the arrival of grandchildren or great-nieces or -nephews. Others may look back on this period as a time when career was in the forefront and beginning to blossom. Today, second careers—or simply fresh endeavors—may be beginning. In deciding how to move forward, laying the foundation for tomorrow, it is important to consider what delights us. What is your relationship to the natural world? What is your experience of having—or having had— pets? This week, you will illuminate those things that are joyful for you, exploring the whimsical and childlike as well as those totems and experiences that speak to you of luxury. With a light heart, you will uncover many of your *true values, and it is acting within our true values that brings us a sense of abiding joy.*

True Joy

What brings us true joy? Have you discovered sources of joy in your Memoir? What were you doing when you experienced joy? Were you exploring passions and interests? Which ones were they? Or did you have ideas of passions and interests that you abandoned during this time in the name of work, family, or something else? Many people abandon interests in the name of logic or reason. "I'd like to write songs," we might think, "but that's not very sensible. How can I support myself / my wife / my kids / my lifestyle on a hobby?" The truth is, songwriting might bring us immense joy. This has been true for me. All of us have ideas that speak to us, and whether we have abandoned them in the past or not, now is an excellent time to revisit these passions—these sparks—that, if we are willing to scratch the surface, may very well contain true joy for us.

Many times, a negative emotion may color what was once a dream born of joy. Just the thought of it may trigger a torrent of emotion: regret, jealousy of those who are pursuing it, a sense that the moment has passed, sadness, anger. I ask you to not be scared off by your knee-jerk reaction. Underneath this negative emotional overlay may exist something much more gentle: a sense of simplicity, an innocence, an interest. Allowing the childlike part of ourselves to play in the field of this dream, we are likely to discover a near-gleeful sense of freedom and excitement. So, while we may fear that revisiting our lost dreams will cause us only pain, the opposite may be true. These dreams may well contain our healing.

It is important to remember to set very small goals for ourselves. We must venture slowly and gently into the healing of creative wounds, lest we create new ones. It is also good to keep in mind that it is common for people to leave dreams behind. Leaving a dream behind does not equal a grand mistake or an irreparable loss. Rather, the opposite: when we gently explore these dreams, joy awaits. At times in our life we must make choices, and those choices sometimes involve abandoning a creative dream. Two roads may diverge, as Robert Frost noted, but we have choices again. The beauty of retirement is that it provides us with the opportunity to travel back in time and explore the paths we didn't take. The painter who was left behind in the name of supporting a family may still be excited to clean his brushes and approach a blank canvas today. The storyteller who spun tales on the playground may have tried to make further attempts to speak, only to be pushed aside in the name of earning a good living or being a doting spouse. But that storyteller is still alive and well, and with a little nudge, would love to speak again. The Memoir reveals our lost dreams to us. It shows us when those dreams knocked at our consciousness—and we did or did not answer. But dreams do not die.

It is a happiness to wonder; it is a happiness to dream.

—EDGAR ALLAN POE

Jake is a musician. His early career was highly successful. But now, at sixty, he is stalled. "I'm afraid I've lost it," he tells me. "I look back on my thirties and I was so much more confident then. I'd write because I wanted to, because it was fun. Those were some of my best songs. Some of those songs still pay my bills today." Jake is pressuring himself to re-create his greatest hits, when, in fact, all he needs to do is sit at the keys—even if for just a few minutes.

"Just try the tools," I coaxed him. Skeptical, Jake did as I asked. He wrote Morning Pages, he took Artist Dates. He took Walks. He worked with his Memoir, even though he was afraid it would be too painful to face. Within weeks, his lost creativity began to reappear. New songs began piping through his system. "I was so afraid to look back on what I considered my 'peak years,'" he says, "because I thought it was a time that was lost forever. I thought I'd be steeped in regret. The truth is, I've always known exactly what brings me joy. Songwriting. But I had taken such a hiatus, it was like it was off-limits to me now."

Jake had to admit to himself that he both knew what his passion

149

was, and also knew that it was there, waiting for him to reconnect to it. "I was scared to do the Memoir, because I thought I'd left myself behind. But instead, I felt inspired. The attitude of my younger self reminded me that it's just about writing. Everything comes from that. And now, here I am. Writing again, I'm elated."

A year later, rounding up fellow musicians, many of whom believed themselves to be similarly blocked, Jake went back into the studio and recorded his first album in fifteen years.

Find a place inside where there's joy, and the joy will burn out the pain.

—JOSEPH CAMPBELL

"I believe in the tools now," Jake recently told me a bit sheepishly. "I had to see it to believe it. But my new album is the proof in the pudding. I'd say to people, it's easier to create than not create." Seeing Jake today, surrounded in music, he is not just joyful—he is truly himself.

Clarence's pages repeatedly turned to the question, "What will make me happy?" At first, the answer seemed simple. "I finally have time to read!" But as he kept on with his pages, Clarence found a deeper answer. "I can read to those who can't read." He contacted a literacy program and offered his services. Throughout the week, he read to a variety of people, and he discovered that these people had a variety of interests. One man loved Dick Francis novels. Another man loved historical novels. A woman, housebound and blind, found great pleasure in travel books. Clarence found great pleasure in all his reading. A retired minister asked Clarence to read scripture. Doing so, Clarence found his deep-seated restlessness coming to calm.

"Reading to others has become the most important thing in my life," Clarence tells me now. "It does make me happy."

TASK
Plan an Extended Artist Date

Set aside more time than usual for your Artist Date—allow yourself a half or even full day to enchant and delight yourself. Perhaps you will plan multiple activities, revisit memories from multiple eras of your Memoir, or simply go on a longer and more extravagant excursion than you would usually plan. Look out for synchronicity: an extended Artist Date promises to include it!

Grandchildren

Grandchildren—or great-nieces and -nephews—can be an important source of joy for retirees. They want to play, and we may find, to our delight, that they liberate our inner playfulness. Grandparents make great playmates—we are available for trips to the park or the zoo. We have the patience to read—and reread—a favorite book. We often catch ourselves laughing at our grandchildren's antics. We may buy them frivolous and delightful baby clothes. Stuffed animals may suddenly strike us as necessary companions.

Stephen finds himself feeling guilty at the ease he feels with his grandsons. "My son asks me if I was as patient with him as I am with his sons, and I did try to be. But I was at a different point in my life then. I was so concerned with earning money, and everything was so new. I am more relaxed now than I was then, and my relationship with my grandsons is more joyful than it was with my own son."

Many of us, like Stephen, find that when we retire we are caught up in regret. Suddenly having the time for introspection, we find ourselves criticizing the choices that we have made. Retirement allows us the time to revisit those choices in a new context. Many of us are now grandparents and we find ourselves paying closer attention to our grandchildren than we paid to our children. It is as if we are given a second chance to be the kind of parent we dreamed about.

Frida explored her late thirties and early forties in her Memoir from the perspective of her midsixties. "I was very focused, during that time, on my work, which was in fashion design," she remembers. "It was also a painful time for me, in that I was struggling to accept that I probably would not have children. I felt my last chance was upon me, but I had not met the right partner, and I wasn't comfortable with the

151

idea of having kids on my own. Ultimately I did not have children, and, looking back, I see that I still had a wonderful life. I followed my passions, which, for me, were work-related. I have many creations to show for myself—just not human ones." Frida is aware, now, of her peers having grandchildren. "I didn't know if this time in my life would feel like the first time around, but I can look back on my own choices now and appreciate the wisdom in them. I can find compassion for that younger self that struggled so much with her decision. I wish I could go back and tell her, 'It's all going to work out.' I've loved my career. I've been able to help people. I might have a great-niece or -nephew one day, and I've been able to share my life with lots of children. I brought my nephew to my studio many times, and I'd like to believe that it influenced his decision to become a designer in his own right. His journey—and my chance to help him on it—has been fulfilling—actually thrilling—for me."

As we express our love through caring actions toward others, we must also be loving toward ourselves. We must learn to forgive our inadequacies. After all, many of us were single parents, and as much as we loved our children, we may have found our focus was largely financial as we struggled to keep afloat. We may now be seized by regret that we didn't show our love for our children in more concrete ways. But what could be more concrete than dinner on the table? We must learn to forgive ourselves and give credit where credit is due. We sometimes had no choice but to work extra hours rather than attend to our child's activities. Retired, we may now be a ready audience. As we appreciate our grandchildren's many gifts, attending choir practice, speech tournaments, and theatrical performances, we give ourselves a second chance. Supporting our children through supporting their children, we build a bridge of generosity and healing. And we may find it all quite fun.

There's something to be said for aging, and that something, paradoxically, is youth. Aging seems to awaken the latent inner child. A grandparent's patience often seems to be a match for the grandchild's energy. As our grandchildren learn to use language, we delight in their newfound expression. In some ways, as we now reinvent ourselves, it parallels our own newfound expression.

Roger found himself tempted to sculpt. "It's childish," his inner Censor protested. But, urged by his pages, Roger bought clay. For his first model, he used his cocker spaniel. "That was fun," he recorded in his Morning Pages. Next, he sculpted from a photo of his granddaughter, rendering it three-dimensional, right down to her curls. "It doesn't really matter what it looks like, it's about the joy of doing it," he surprised himself by thinking. And when his granddaughter came to visit, he proudly showed her his bust.

"It's me!" she exclaimed, delighted.

"Yes," he said. "I'm sculpting my favorite things." He showed her the cocker spaniel.

"It's Scruffy!" she exclaimed. "Grandpa, it looks just like her."

Roger found himself delighted with his granddaughter's response. He took her by the hand and led her to the kitchen counter where a lump of clay waited.

"You see?" he said, "It starts out like this, a round ball. Then I pinch it and pull it until it looks right."

"It does look right, Grandpa," his granddaughter exclaimed.

"I'll make more things for you," Roger promised. "And on your next visit, I'll give you some clay."

"That's great, Grandpa," his granddaughter piped up. Roger caught himself thinking, "Now that I have a hobby, I'm joyful. And now that I'm joyful, I'm fascinating."

My daughter is the mother of a baby girl, Serafina, who is both very bright and very willful. At sixteen months she had a small working vocabulary: "Mama," "Dada," and "no." I am told that my first sentence was, "Me do it self." My mother was ill and a nurse was called in to help. She tried to put a sweater on me and I pronounced my defiant rebellion with the sentence that would go down in family history.

When I visit my daughter, I marvel at her patience. She reads and sings to Serafina, who greets her efforts to put her to bed or to change a diaper with a firm shriek: "No!"

Serafina resembles my baby pictures: bright, alert, and stubborn. I find myself eagerly waiting for her to "really" talk. She certainly has the temperament to pronounce "Me do it self." Serafina loves to be read to, and my daughter, Domenica, obliges her by reading aloud many children's books. She loves taking pony rides, and I wonder if her love of horses may be genetic.

"Don't you love being a grandmother? Isn't it the best?" I am asked. There is great joy in watching Serafina's growth. It is fascinating to spend time with a person I relate to in so many ways before we are really able to communicate. But truth be told, being a grandmother makes me feel closer to my daughter. Every day, over the long-distance wire, Domenica relates some new achievement. Serafina now dances and sings. She loves the Beatles. I tell Domenica that she loved the Rolling Stones. Domenica is eager for any tidbit I remember. "Did I do X?" Domenica will ask. "Did you?"

I find myself wishing my own mother had lived longer, to tell us more tales. Instead, she died at fifty-nine, six years younger than I am now. I want Serafina to know all she can of her mother's history. I put pen to page with a sense of mission. Writing, I feel the joy of right action.

TASK
Forgiveness

Do you have children, grandchildren, or relationships with those younger than you who have been important in your life? What do you feel you need to forgive yourself for in relation to these people? Quickly jot down three past situations. Which one of them pains you the most? Allow yourself to take pen to page and explore this topic. Can you extend compassion to your former self?

TASK
Memoir, Week Eight

AGES: _____

1. Describe your major relationships in this period.
2. Where did you live? Did you live in more than one place?
3. What brought you happiness during this time?
4. Describe one sound that brings you back to this period.
5. Describe one smell from this period.
6. Did you have any pets?
7. What passions or interests did you explore during this time? What passions or interests did you ignore?
8. What was your greatest challenge during this period? Do you relate to this challenge today?
9. What was the prevailing mood of this time? How does that relate to today?
10. What other memories feel significant to you from this time?

The Power of Whimsy

In decades of teaching my tool kit, I have often seen resistance, but there is seldom more resistance than to the thought of taking an Artist Date. I believe it is because we are raised in a culture where we understand work, and the Morning Pages look and feel like "work." Taking walks, answering questions, and doing tasks may also feel like work. But the Artist Date is assigned play. It is very clearly not "work," and that leaves many of us—myself included—hesitant in the face of embarking on conscious fun. However, the power of whimsy is great— very great. The whimsical paperweight on my writing desk, catching the light in shades of pink, reminds me of the Artist Date I took to a glassblower's studio where I made the paperweight myself. Under the glassblower's careful eye, the glass went into the inferno, shaping itself as it melted into its current design. "Just" whimsy, "just" play—but the excursion left me optimistic, enchanted, and with a beautiful totem to remind me of that sense of mystery, frivolity, and fun. It intrigues and inspires me as I write. Its many angles fill me with wonder as I examine its depths, working out a sentence or a plot point.

We have the expression "the play of ideas," but we seldom realize that this is a literal phrase. Literal—and potent. Playing, we trigger our imagination. We are free to make improbable connections that our serious, logical brain might not see. And those improbable thoughts can become the germs of creative invention.

Lucy, a retired teacher, missed her job. "I'm depressed," she told me. "I feel like I've lost my purpose. I'm lonely, I'm gaining weight, I'm . . ."

"Let yourself play a little," I suggested to her. She was aghast.

"Play? It's work that I miss."

"Oh, come on," I coaxed. "There must be something you like to do for fun."

Lucy thought for a moment. "Well," she said finally, "I do like dancing."

"So dance," I told her.

"We'll see," Lucy said dubiously. A few weeks later, I heard from Lucy again, and was thrilled to hear that she had taken not one, but two Artist Dates to woo her inner dancer.

"I'm having a blast," she announced. "I took two dance classes and signed up for a third. I can't believe how good they made me feel. And is it a coincidence? I met a very nice man who happened to take the same two classes that I did. We have a date to go dancing this Saturday. I always said I wanted to learn to dance."

That was six months ago. Lucy's dancing man is now her steady companion. She dances three times a week and has lost the fifteen extra pounds she put on during retirement. She is effortlessly committed to enjoying what sounds fun and whimsical to her, and has even signed up for a dancing cruise.

The child is in me still . . . and sometimes not so still.

—FRED ROGERS

It's easy to dismiss ideas as "too whimsical" before we even give them a chance to show us where they might lead. I would encourage you to try following your most whimsical leanings anyway—even if they seem pointless at first glance.

Allowing ourselves to be whimsical is an exercise in setting aside our intellectualism in favor of what might simply make us happy. This can be, in theory, quite daunting, but in practice, quite delightful.

Michael has a master's degree in education from Harvard. When he called me, he said, "I use my education to help others, but I don't seem able to help myself."

"Are you taking Artist Dates?" I asked him.

"I do Morning Pages," he replied defensively. "But as far as Artist Dates go, I assign them to my students, to my clients, but I don't assign them to myself."

"Michael," I said, "it sounds to me like you're long on duty and short on delight. Try Artist Dates for several weeks and then call me back."

Skeptical and reluctant, Michael let me know that I was oversimplifying a very complicated issue and that he didn't believe it would work. Ever the diligent student, however, he undertook his assignment. I wasn't surprised that when he called me back a few weeks later, he sounded like a different man.

"I owe you an apology," he began. "I was pretty hostile." But no apology was necessary, I assured him. I understand that it is threatening to try something "just" for fun. Especially when one's identity is wrapped up in heady intellectual pursuits, as Michael's is, the idea of play may seem foolhardy.

"I went to a historical library I hadn't visited in years," he told me. "That was something I could reason would be a good use of time. But I was so surprised by my experience of being there. It brought me back to my early studies, my academic father, and memories of many of the professors who inspired me early on. I actually reached out to one of them, and thanked him for the educational values he instilled in me. We had a great conversation. I even told him about the reason that I

Sometimes the heart sees what is invisible to the eye.

—H. JACKSON BROWN JR.

157

went to the library in the first place—that I was trying to add 'play' to my life and be okay with that. He was incredibly open. We had a long talk about the snobbery that can exist in academia. I left that call—and my Artist Date—inspired to do it again. I don't know what exactly my assumption had been, but I realized that play isn't dumb—it's almost miraculous! I'll be a better teacher for being a happier man. Since then I've taken myself to see movies, try new restaurants, tour galleries. I'm thinking for my next Artist Date, I might visit a local ice cream factory. What could be more delightful than that?"

You'll never find rainbows if you're looking down.

—CHARLES CHAPLIN

Artist Dates are an exercise in delight. One of their first fruits is joy, and that was what Michael had been missing. I told him the truth as I have come to see it: the quality of our lives is in proportion, always, to our capacity for delight.

When we allow ourselves to play, we allow ourselves to connect with a youthful part of ourselves. Often, this youthful, whimsical persona has very good ideas for our adult self. "Why don't you try that?" it asks us. "What's wrong with a little fun?"

What's wrong with a little fun, indeed?

TASK
The Power of Whimsy

Many of us have difficulty having fun. We take ourselves—and life—too seriously. Sometimes we need to trick ourselves into enjoying life. Take pen in hand and list ten fun things you currently are not allowing yourself to do. They can range from the small to the large.

1. Get a manicure.
2. Get a pedicure.
3. Read a tabloid magazine.
4. Ride a bicycle.
5. Take a bubble bath.
6. Buy patterned socks.

7. Wear a faux fur coat.
8. Eat a banana split.
9. Go dancing.
10. Buy red leather gloves.

The Balm of Humor

*Laughter is the sun
which drives winter
from the human face.*

—VICTOR HUGO

My mother kept a poem posted above her kitchen workspace. It read:

*If your nose is down to the grindstone rough
And you hold it down there long enough
Soon you'll say there's no such thing
As brooks that babble and birds that sing
Three things will all your world compose
Just you, the grindstone and your darned old nose.*

This was my mother's reminder to lighten up. With seven children, there was always some worthy task that needed doing. But no matter how important a duty might loom, a little humor was always welcome. My father and mother relied on laugher as they approached the daunting task of raising a large family. They shared with each other a taste for cartoons. They loved the humor of James Thurber and Chon Day. My mother taught us how to cook, and each recipe she shared called for a "pinch of humor." Outside the kitchen window, on what we came to call the "big oak tree," my father hung a bird feeder to amuse my mother with aviary antics. One winter, he built an iceboat, daring to skim across the ice of Liberty Lake. The iceboat brought with it hoots of laughter. We clung to its scaffolding as we sped, inches above the ice. "Now, Jimmy," my mother scolded, "they could scrape their faces off." Chastened but still proud of the mischief he'd elicited, my father took us tobogganing instead on the next snowy Saturday.

One of my oldest and dearest friends is a man named Gerard Hackett. We met as freshmen at Georgetown, and I was drawn to the twinkle in his eye as a teenager—a twinkle that still sparkles today, when we are, as he puts it, geezers. He often chuckles at his own joke. "I'm a geezer," he tells me, "and you're a geezer, too." He enjoys poking fun at our seniority, among other things. When I was recovering in a hospital several years ago, he visited me with a bouquet of flowers and a large dose of humor. "Hey, Toots," he greeted me. "This place isn't so bad. Let's brighten it up with these flowers. And in the meantime, I'm going to go talk to someone and see how soon we can get you out of here." Gerard has been a protective friend to me—watching out for my health, finances, and, without question, my spirit. But it is his humor as much as his protective nature that brings levity and hope in times of fear and sadness. I am very lucky to have a friend in Gerard, who is as quick to catch my hand as he is to make me laugh. He brings me strength and laughter, and, with this strength and laughter, I am resilient.

Many retirees are aware of the strength in humor but are unsure where to find it. One friend of mine loves to watch stand-up comedy, both live and on late-night talk shows. Another subscribes to *The New Yorker*—"Not for the articles," he says, "but for the cartoons." An occasional laugh at our own expense is healthy, and *The Complete Cartoons of "The New Yorker"* provides an encyclopedic view of the foibles of adult life. A third friend rents comic movies, both classic and new. "I appreciate humor," he says, "and the older I get, the more I find to chuckle at." Chuckling along with the comedians, the cartoonists, and the moviemakers goes a long way toward curing our all-too-common sense of isolation. Most retirees—or should I say, geezers—can use a booster shot of humor. Whether it's what we read or what we watch, humor leavens the day.

Candice, retired for six years, enjoys a steady diet of romance novels. "They're sheer fantasy," she tells me, "and I love them." Nancy is seventy-one and newly married to a man ten years her junior. "We found we laughed at the same things," she says. "Our shared humor

At the height of laughter, the universe is flung into a kaleidoscope of new possibilities.

—JEAN HOUSTON

was our first bond. Then one thing led to another, and . . ." She giggles girlishly. "We find the world humorous and we enjoy a good laugh at the difference in our ages."

Finding people who bring humor into our lives—and bring humor out in us—is a worthy pursuit. It is often a sense of humor that makes us resilient in times of change or hardship. Humor naturally brings us perspective and a balm of hope. Not all of life needs to be taken so seriously. In our lives and in our daily writing, we come to feel a light-ness of heart. Things aren't nearly as bad as we at first think they are. In fact, they might not be bad at all.

Even the gods love jokes.

—PLATO

TASK
Humor

What makes you laugh? Treat yourself to a comedy, a cartoon book, or a cup of tea with someone you find hilarious. What—or whom—you find humorous is very personal. All that matters is that you find it so. Indulge yourself, and allow yourself to delight in what tickles you alone.

Pets

A sign in a Manhattan veterinarian's office reads, "Be the person your dog thinks you are." Pets bring unconditional love into our lives. They love us wholeheartedly, despite our occasional fits of temper, and can bring us a profound sense of joy. My own life has been immeasurably enhanced by a large and varied parade of animal companions.

My main pet growing up was a hackney pony named Chico. To-gether, we won many blue ribbons. Chico performed for me but balked for everyone else. He was a one-person pony and I appreciated his loy-alty and talent, jumping fences high enough for horses. When Chico died, a part of me died with him. Nowadays, my West Highland white terrier, Lily, follows me from room to room, her brown button eyes filled with love. Every morning I say a prayer for Lily and for Tiger Lily, my cocker spaniel recently deceased. I ask that both dogs be given merriment, and Lily's joyous mood throughout the day assures me that my prayers are answered.

I wish I could write as mysterious as a cat.

—EDGAR ALLAN POE

Not everyone can be lucky enough to have a pony or even a dog, but most households can make space for a cat, bird, or fish. For those who wish to enjoy animals outside the home, visiting a zoo or even a friend's pet can be a joyful excursion.

My friend Scotty acquired her first pet in retirement. Weighing in at seven and a half pounds, her teacup schnauzer, Moxie, has the bark of a much larger dog.

"Who could believe that such a small dog could hold such a large place in my heart?" says Scotty. She walks her pet three times daily and cuts short her own social engagements "to get home to Moxie."

I turned sixty-five just as my Tiger Lily turned fifteen. We were both aging, needing naps and a careful diet so as not to put on weight. I had a teaching trip scheduled and I dropped Tiger Lily, as usual, at what I called "the spa"—a high-end kennel that featured play and dog bones. Tiger Lily loved "the spa," and would return from her stay there clean and fluffy. But this time, she did not come home. Instead, I received a phone call during my travels.

"Your dog is dying," the person who called said.

Take her to the vet, I instructed. They did take her to the vet, who ran a series of tests and came to the sad conclusion that her systems were all failing.

"If it were my dog, I would put her down today," he said. I told the vet to put her down rather than have her wait, suffering, until I could get home. There, she was peacefully and gently put to sleep. I finished my teaching and returned home. I stopped at the spa to pay Tiger Lily's bill. They had taken a picture of Tiger Lily, and I was glad that they had. In the picture, she looked old, tired, and sick. It reinforced my sense that I had made the right decision, but I found myself bursting into tears when I retrieved her collar and leash. I went home to an empty house sad that I had not had a chance to say good-bye. But I admitted to myself that it might have been for the best, as I might have fallen completely to pieces had I been present. Surely my grief would have made Tiger Lily's transition more difficult.

For several weeks I could not adjust to Tiger Lily's absence. It was a full month before the vet called to say they had received Tiger Lily's ashes. I stopped to retrieve them and once more found myself overwhelmed by grief. Everyone at the clinic was very understanding, but I was inconsolable. A tiny tin contained all of Tiger Lily's remains.

Without her to care for, my life felt empty.

"Are you going to get another dog?" friends asked me.

"Not right away," I told them.

I found myself thinking of dogs I had known, dogs that made me happy. Emma's West Highland white terrier, Charlotte, kept coming to mind. Charlotte lives in an apartment with Emma and her friend Tyler. When I talk to Emma on the phone, Charlotte hovers near her lap. If she wants to go out for her walk, she gives Emma a baleful look, which Emma has come to translate as: "Walk me or else."

Yes, I decided, if I get another dog, it should be a Westie.

Seeing my sorrow, my friend Robert began searching the Internet for Westies. He found a Westie rescue in Arizona and I quickly got in touch and filled out a lengthy questionnaire.

After laboring over an essay on why I wanted to adopt a Westie, I sent off my application. A week passed and I heard nothing. Then the agency sent me a picture of the Westie they had available for adoption. She was beautiful, three years old and housebroken—just what the doctor ordered. But then fate struck. "You don't live in Arizona. We're not placing our dogs anywhere except Arizona." I was devastated. Why couldn't they have told me at the beginning? For weeks I mulled over my loss. Then, one day, I got out Robert's list of Westie breeders and,

Until one has loved an animal, a part of one's soul remains unawakened.

—ANATOLE FRANCE

163

to my great delight, found a breeder in Colorado who was willing to place a dog in New Mexico. The holding fee was $100. I dashed off and mailed it to the woman I'd talked to on the phone.

"What I'm looking for is a smart, outgoing puppy," I told her.

"Well," she said, "I'll see what I can do."

Our perfect companions never have fewer than four feet.

—COLETTE

The puppies were born on July seventeenth. They would be ready for adoption midway through September. I added a prayer to my nightly prayers: please, God, send me the right puppy. Every night I prayed. As the due date arrived I prayed harder. My friend Pamela, an artist, volunteered to make the drive from Santa Fe with me. Colorado had flooded the week before, and we postponed our trip. Finally it was time to go. Colorado was once again dry. We drove through the mountains, passing horses, cattle, and even a herd of elk on our travels. We arrived in Aurora, Colorado, a half hour from the breeder. We had chosen, sight unseen, a Holiday Inn Express. We walked in and blinked our eyes in disbelief. The carpet was brightly striped blue, gold, and green. We looked at each other and said, "I hope this isn't a preview." Our rooms were garish, too, with orange metallic walls and green-and-gold leaf-print carpeting.

"Dear God, please let the puppy be better than her introduction," I prayed. We went out to eat at a restaurant called Sweet Tomatoes, featuring salads and soups. Then we headed back to the hotel where we found, to our relief, that the beds were comfortable and the pillows fine.

Early the next morning, we set out to meet the breeder. She had agreed to drive the puppy halfway to where we were staying. "I have a gold Blazer," she told us, and we agreed to meet her in the parking lot of a truck stop. When we got there, there was no gold Blazer. I hoped we had the instructions right. I was nervous. But when the Blazer pulled into a parking place adjacent to our own, there was the breeder with a puppy cradled in her arms.

"Oh, look, she's beautiful!" I exclaimed to Pamela.

"She's very playful," the breeder warned us. "You may want to hold her on your lap for a while at first." And so I wrote a check for the balance due and Pamela swung into the driver's seat. "Boy, this puppy seems perfect," I found myself thinking as I stroked the tiny white puppy, who promptly kissed my face. I was immediately in love.

I slid on her new collar with the name tag: Lily. Yes, Lily was going to be her name, and it did suit her. As we drove back through the Rockies, Lily curled into a fluffy white ball on my lap. She seemed smart as well as beautiful. God had answered my prayer. It was indeed the perfect puppy.

My house once again had a merry canine companion. The trainer I hired said to me, "You've got the dog with all the personality. Your hands are really going to be full with this one." True to her word, Lily was rambunctious and outgoing. When I threw a party to "meet the puppy," she was eager to greet our guests.

Our animal companions bring us joy. Their unconditional love helps soften the blow of retirement. Training them gives us a joyous project. In my morning prayers, I ask that the spirit of Tiger Lily guide Lily. I remember that when I adopted Tiger Lily, she was so wild I nearly gave up on her. As she aged, her temperament sweetened. Watching my puppy run crazily through the house, I trust I can expect the same from Lily.

TASK
Pets

Take the time to connect with a pet that enchants you. If you have a pet already, perhaps it is the day for an extra-long walk and a special treat. Perhaps you offer to visit a neighbor's dog, or perhaps you have dreamed of buying a fish tank and today is the day you will begin your research. The youthful joy of pets brings lightness. What pet can you interact with today?

Luxury

Many times, people reach retirement feeling fatigued. They have worked long years and have looked forward to a future that now seems suddenly empty. Very often, they need a dose of luxury to jump-start their motor. But what constitutes luxury? Authentic luxury may be different from what we imagine. Contrary to what we might assume, what actually speaks of luxury to us may not be expensive. For me, raspberries are an authentic luxury. At Sprouts, our natural food grocer, raspberries are two pints for five dollars. I allow myself to indulge in raspberries throughout the season. "You always smell so good," I am frequently told. A thank you is in order to my perfume, another luxury I choose to afford. Like the juniper logs I burn in my fireplace, yet another luxury, my perfume casts a gentle spell.

My friend Rhonda doesn't buy raspberries or perfume or juniper logs. Instead, she buys seven-day candles. Their flame and scent give her a feeling of luxury. My friend Brendalyn buys the makings for ratatouille. She makes up a week's supply and has a feeling of luxury whenever she spoons a portion onto her plate.

My friend Scotty enjoys the daily luxury of sandalwood incense.

"They say that incense carries prayers straight to the heavens," she explains. And so she lights a fragrant stick and then sits down to meditate. Her meditation is another form of luxury, the luxury of time spent wisely. In the morning, I practice the luxury of my own meditation by writing out my prayers. For the better part of an hour, I list my friends and my intentions for their well-beings. The sense of connection with my higher power is a potent luxury.

Many of us have strong reservations, old ideas that keep us from actualizing our desire to practice creativity. One of the most effective ways to dismantle our resistance is to give ourselves permission to enjoy small luxuries. As simple as this may sound, it is both highly productive and, sometimes, a bit challenging. In order to pinpoint what indulgence will relax our guard, we must first honestly answer the query, "What truly gives me joy?" Although we often think luxury is a monetary issue, the deeper truth is that luxury is an issue of authenticity. A luxury is something that gives you pleasure purely for its own sake, not because it performs any kind of useful function. Sometimes the cost of a luxury is very small. It's important to note that luxury is highly individualistic. When we treat ourselves to some authentic luxury, we are taking a positive action on our own behalf. We are saying, "This matters to me. I am willing to spend my hard-earned money on it simply because I like it and it makes me feel good." These small risks lead to larger ones. In no time, we are investing not just money, but our time, energy, and faith on our artist's behalf, allowing ourselves to act on our creative dreams and ideas.

Beauty is whatever gives joy.

—EDNA ST. VINCENT MILLAY

Karen reached retirement age and felt exhausted. I suggested she try spoiling herself a little.

"Spoiling myself?" she said. "I wouldn't know where to begin. And I am on a limited budget now—I don't have my work income any longer."

I suggested that she start by making a list of twenty-five things she loved. Skeptical, Karen nonetheless wrote the list. High on the list was a painting of Monet's water lilies. Karen lived in Chicago, where the Art Institute had a fine collection of impressionists and featured Monet prominently.

"So go," I told her. Karen hadn't been to the Art Institute in years. She undertook a half-day expedition and returned from her outing charged up. For her, authentic luxury centered on beauty. She was so excited by her excursion that she planned a second trip to the Art Institute, this time focusing on Van Gogh. Once again, Karen emerged from her outing rejuvenated.

"I had an incredible memory when I was there this time," she tells me. "My mother had lots of art history books in the house, and I was suddenly transported back to a time when, as a child, I dreamed of painting like these masters. The attention to detail in their work inspired me so much. I never did make any art myself, but now I wonder if I'd like to try. I think I'm going to buy a bunch of postcards at the Art Institute—images of the paintings I remember most clearly from the books, and anything that just speaks to me. I'm going to make a collage with them and see what I learn or feel. And then, who knows—maybe I'll pick up some kids' watercolors and fool around a little."

Think of all the beauty that's still left in and around you and be happy!

—ANNE FRANK

What constitutes luxury for each of us varies. Thad, an animation artist, loves to cook, and for him, choosing several ripe avocados and creating a bowl of guacamole from scratch brings him a sense of abundance—and often a creative idea or two. "For me, there's luxury in a home-cooked meal," he says. "My work projects go on for years, and to have a creative project that can begin and be finished in less than an hour is very satisfying." Last I heard, Thad had moved on from guacamole to creating the perfect homemade macaroni and cheese. The price of ingredients is well within his budget, and the sense of joy it brings to him is priceless.

Angela also found food high on her list of twenty-five loves. Used to cooking at home, she indulged by taking herself out to a new Thai restaurant. To her delight, the food was delicious and the atmosphere calm.

"I'm a vegan," Angela tells me, "so I tend to cook for myself. But I asked if they could prepare my meal without animal products. They were very cooperative and my meal was wonderful. For me, dining out while remaining inside my food plan was an authentic luxury."

Alice, who lived in New York, found her list of twenty-five loves centering on flora and fauna. For her, luxury was a trip to the country. A short train trip undertaken once a month, even just for a day, gave her a sense of well-being.

Stanley, a photographer, spent long hours on his feet in the darkroom and suffered from back pain. For him, a weekly deep-tissue massage was truly luxurious. An hour-long treatment obliterated his discomfort and allowed him to return to his darkroom refreshed and inspired.

No matter what form our authentic luxury takes, it bestows on us a gift of renewed creativity. Vibrant ideas flow to us. New and innovative ways of thinking become ours. Our inner artist responds to small acts of luxury. Rather than flogging our artist forward, we would do better to think of small bribes that lure us in the desired direction. Remember, treating yourself like a precious object makes you strong.

TASK
Luxury

Many of us find we experience depression as we enter the free fall of retirement. We have lost our jobs and our identities. We don't know who we are, and happiness feels elusive. But a sense of joy, of faith and optimism, is available to all of us. We need only ask the proper questions to arrive at an abiding sense of joy. And what are those questions? First we must ask, "What brings me happiness?"

Looking back into your Memoir to date, list several things that brought you happiness at different points in your life. Which one is filled with the most vivid memories? How can you bring it into your life today?

WEEKLY CHECK-IN

1. How many days did you do your Morning Pages? How was the experience of doing them?
2. Did you do an Artist Date? What was it? Did you discover anything in your Memoir that you'd like to explore in an Artist Date?
3. Did you take your Walks? What did you notice along the way?
4. What "ahas" did you discover this week?
5. Did you experience any synchronicity this week? What was it? Did it give you a sense of humility, a sense of being somehow guided by a higher power?

6. What did you find in your Memoir that you would like to explore more fully? How would you like to explore it? As always, if you have a loaded memory that you feel requires further attention but aren't yet sure what additional action to take, don't worry about it. Just keep moving forward.

Reigniting a Sense of Motion

Often, we feel stuck not because we don't know what to do next but because we do know what to do next—we just don't feel like doing it. This week, you will examine your gentle "next right steps" and how to allow yourself to take them. Looking back in your Memoir, you may be able to identify a highly active or productive time in your life. Where did it lead you, personally, creatively, financially? How did that period impact your life today? Does recalling how you spent your energy then influence how you want to spend it now? Your life today can be dynamic, not stagnant. Are you finding you have more a sense of what to do, and how and when to do it? Are tangled or complex situations becoming less so? There is always a way to move forward in productivity.

Redefining Productivity

Many retirees face a two-pronged problem: what can they do to feel productive, and how can they learn to feel productive without working? Commonly, when working at a job or career, productivity is defined in terms of other people's expectations: the company's, the boss's, or the client's. We received a paycheck for our efforts on behalf of an external goal set by someone else. Retired, we find ourselves needing to redefine productivity and, in some cases, to set our own goals. We need to ask ourselves, "How am I doing?" and answer by our own lights.

Rest is not idleness, and to lie sometimes on the grass under the trees on a summer's day, listening to the murmur of water, or watching the clouds float across the blue sky, is hardly a waste of time.

—SIR J. LUBBOCK

At age sixty-five, Bernice retired from a forty-year career as a teacher. For four decades, she had considered herself "productive" because she made it through each year in faithful adherence to a scholastic lesson plan. Retired, she found her days long and empty. That is, she did until she learned to redefine productivity for herself.

She loved to sing, and singing was the first activity that came to mind when she sought to be productive in a non-scholastic way. With winter came carols, and Bernice joined her church choir. As a young woman she had played the piano. Now she took up the instrument again, taking a weekly piano lesson and filling her long afternoons with practice.

"Christmas is over, but winter is not," she caroled, taking scissors to paper and crafting beautiful snowflakes, which she taped to her windows—just as she had in her classroom year after year—and distributed to her friends.

"They're beautiful, Bernice," her friends exclaimed, and Bernice soon arranged to spend a long winter's evening with her friends, enjoying the simple art of snowflake making with hot chocolate by the fire.

"Many of them hadn't done this in years, and what fun it was," she smiled. Valentine's Day found Bernice laboring with red construction paper and lacy doilies. Her handmade valentines were cherished by their recipients. At Easter time, she dyed eggs and invited her snowflake-making friends to craft Easter baskets. Shortly after that, Bernice joined a book club. Her hours spent reading felt productive to her, as had her many hours making crafts.

Bernice was my aunt, and I learned a lot from her productivity. Making crafts is a hobby that we commonly leave behind during the working years, and it is very often a great starting point when the next project feels elusive. The satisfaction of starting—and finishing—something, however small, inevitably provides a burst of energy and forward motion.

Jerry made a rule for himself to say "yes" to all invitations in early retirement. He noticed he felt productive—and open-minded—when he went along willingly with other people's agendas. Lunches, dinners, plays, concerts—he readily did them all. "I found myself busier than when I was working," he says. The problem was, how to reciprocate?

"I found a clue in my Memoir and ran with it," he relays. "My mother always baked brownies for special occasions. Looking back, I see that it was a way she connected with people. It was a very strong memory for me, and I knew I wanted to dig deeper into it. I thought, I have her recipe, so why not make it? As soon as I started on the batter, the smell overwhelmed me with memory. I was flooded with so many clear images—the way she'd wrap the brownies in wax paper for our lunch boxes, the time our cat was stuck in a tree and she brought a batch to the firemen who rescued him, the holiday gifts and the school parties." Jerry spent an emotional afternoon baking brownies, then wrapped them up and gave them to the friends whose invitations he had recently accepted, as well as to friends he hadn't seen in a while. "I connected to so many people this way," he says. "It's a very simple thing, but it's really very powerful. The brownies seem to say 'hello,' or 'thank you,' or 'I missed you,' or 'I appreciate you.' I felt so good doing it, felt such a sense of purpose, and I also felt close to my mom. Doing

We can do no great things, only small things with great love.

—MOTHER TERESA

it myself made me understand what she had done. I appreciated her efforts anew." This simple act of "running with" a memory connected Jerry to people from both his past and his present.

Before retirement, Daryl had been a recreation director for more than thirty years. Every day when he went to work he knew that he was doing something productive: helping his community. In the first days of retirement, when asked what he was up to, he'd always answer woefully, "I haven't done anything productive." As time passed, Daryl began to wonder, "Who am I without my job?"

He first found his answer in relationships: I am a friend; I am a father; I am a grandfather. "Working, I was too busy to savor my many roles. Retired, I noticed myself really cherishing all my connections." Daryl had always been a very active person, and while he was busy some days visiting with friends or taking care of his grandchildren, other days would go by where he noticed—with some horror—that time had passed "with nothing to show for it." As time went on, Daryl considered his daily productivity more. "I used to feel guilty about hours or days where I didn't 'do' anything, until I finally realized that what I was actually doing was 'self-care.' Now I think of those days more simply as 'decompression days.' And they really do seem to help a lot!"

Daryl shared his concept of decompression days with friends who had also retired, and they encouraged him to take them, warning, "Don't expect anything much of yourself for a year." Daryl listened to their advice, and allowed himself to enjoy these decompression days. "I know they won't last forever. I trust myself—and that this downtime will somehow lead to my next activity. I think there's an adjustment period here, and I can be patient with that."

Taking the pressure off of himself, and working through the memories he elicited in his Memoir, it wasn't long before it occurred to Daryl that he might like to take a woodworking class. He had always enjoyed the visual arts, and been known to draw caricatures of his family and friends as a boy. He had excelled in art class, and even got-

Happiness lies not in the mere possession of money; it lies in the joy of achievement, in the thrill of creative effort.

—FRANKLIN D. ROOSEVELT

ten in trouble for marking up his math and science books with cartoonish renditions of his teachers. It was a source of fun and humor for him, but he hadn't made art in many years—not since he reached "responsible adulthood." The proud father of artistic children, he had deferred his own creativity. But now, he realized, the time had come to defer no longer. Woodworking had always interested him, he realized. He had spent his parenting years pouring his own creativity into encouraging the creative lives of his children.

"I think it's great that Dad's going to take a class," states Piper, his middle child. "When I said I wanted to be an actor, he said go for it, backing me to the hilt." Piper feels the time has come for her to return the favor. She encourages her father's creative exploration. "When Dad says he hasn't done anything productive in three months, I feel he's being too harsh. I hope he considers the woodworking class productive. I know I do."

Daryl has patience—and the backing of his family—to thank for his new choice. In the early days of his woodworking class, he has already started to feel a deep excitement for his fresh endeavor. He has felt a new sense of productivity in woodworking. "I like to keep busy—but not just for the sake of keeping busy. This is something for me," he says. It can take courage to find that activity that will feed us, and not just "get busy with busyness."

Productivity means different things at different times in our lives. Goals we set in retirement may be very different from goals we set when we are working. They may seem "too small" or "too big." The freedom that they can be anything might be overwhelming to the point of paralyzing. I have found that there are simple tricks to jump-start productivity, though, and once a project has begun, it tends to take on an energy of its own.

Liza wanted to begin a large project of organizing and creating albums of all of the family photos she had both taken and inherited. "I felt a strong pull in working on my Memoir to connect to the past," she says, "and this is how I wanted to do it—creating volumes of this visual history. But I just couldn't get started." Day after day, week after week, she scolded herself for procrastinating. Like so many of us embarking on a large task, she was overwhelmed by the scope of the task, but beating herself up for procrastinating, then feeling guilty and inert, and thereby extending the cycle of staying stuck. I suggested to Liza that she try bribing herself. She protested. "That sounds silly."

"It is silly," I replied. "Silly is what works."

And so, against her better judgment—still believing that all-or-nothing was the way to go—Liza tried baby steps and bribery. "If you start," she told her inner artist, "I'll buy you a new pair of slacks." She had been wearing the same pair, day in and day out, for a year. To her surprise, Liza did start, and it took a lot less time and effort than she had feared. "I just had to start, so I cleared a large table in my office and deemed it my work table. I spent some time collecting photos from all over the house and putting them on the table. That was it—but I had started." She also kept her promise of the new pair of slacks. Next, she offered her inner artist another bribe at my urging. This bribe was more extravagant. "If you sort for two hours," she told her artist, "I will buy you a new winter coat." She did sort, and she did buy the coat.

"I can't afford to keep bribing myself," she exclaimed, although she was greatly relieved to be working on her long dreamed-of project.

"Try a little bribe," I urged her. "It doesn't have to be something grand."

This time, Liza told her inner artist, "When you've collected every photo in the house and reached out to anyone you can think of who might have photos you are missing, I'll take you for a fancy cup of cocoa at the chocolate factory." Again she began, digging into boxes, climbing into the attic, opening drawers, and e-mailing relatives with a cup of cocoa dancing in her consciousness. "I was so excited about it," she says. "I was looking forward to the cocoa but I was also getting momentum on the project. I was finally feeling productive. I have to admit, this really works for me." Now she had established a pattern: offer a bribe and then work. "Work and you can see the new Woody

Allen movie," she offered herself. Sure enough, eventually, she had a shelf full of photo albums, sorted by date and labeled with care.

"I have such a sense of accomplishment. I'm thinking of what my next project will be—and I know how I'll get myself to begin it. The bribes made me much happier. And happier, I was productive."

Remember, our inner artist—the part of us who creates—is an inner child. The bribes we offer it must be playful. The new slacks, the winter coat, were sensible but delightful. The cup of cocoa appealed equally to Liza's inner child.

I tried the same bribe-equals-performance technique on Kaden, who was blocked, wanting to paint but unable to begin. Likewise, he found himself responding gleefully. Kaden's bribes tended to be adventures. "If you paint," he promised his inner artist, "I'll let you see the Vermeer exhibit." "If you paint," he promised, "I'll let you take the Circle Line cruise, seeing Manhattan from the water." To Kaden's delight, he began painting steadily. And whenever he felt stymied, he knew to devise a bribe.

Whether the bribe is material or psychological, the important point is that the inner artist feels seen. It is often enticement more than demand that lures our inner artist out of hiding and renders it curious, and, therefore, willing to begin.

TASK
Productivity

Answer the following questions:

1. I used to feel productive when . . .
2. I now feel productive when . . .
3. I suspect I would feel productive if . . .
4. I'd secretly like to . . .
5. A small bribe that would entice me to begin is . . .

TASK
Memoir, Week Nine

AGES: _____

1. Describe your major relationships in this period.
2. Where did you live? Did you live in more than one place?
3. How were you productive in your life during this time?
4. Describe one smell that brings you back to this period.
5. Describe one taste from this period.
6. Describe one way you were moving ahead during this period.
7. In what ways did you feel stuck or stymied during this period? Do these relate to any sense of feeling stuck that you have today?
8. Who or what do you miss from this time? Is there some way to connect to this person or feeling today?
9. What was your relationship to money during this time? How does it compare to today?
10. What other memories feel significant to you from this time?

Taking Action

Many of us have spent years dreaming of what we want to create, but dreaming and doing are two different things. When we dream of what to create, yet take no actions, we find ourselves flagellating ourselves for our laziness. But it is not really laziness that stops us. We need to call things by their right names. What stops us is fear. But the inability to get started is not an uncorrectable character defect that renders us useless. It is a common human condition requiring gentleness and nurturing.

We can ask for guidance for the first small step toward overcoming the pain of feeling stuck. I like to ask in writing: "What do I need to do?" I am always surprised, but I always "hear" a response, and it is always small and doable. Taking that step moves me from stasis into action. It is true that when we take a step, we then desire to take another step, then another. When we move into action, we gain self-esteem. We value our actions and we value ourselves for taking those actions. We feel a sense of our own power. We find ourselves guided and guarded. As we act in the direction of our dreams, we are given strength and courage. The first brush stroke leads to the second. The first word leads to the next. Our capacity to create is tied to our capacity for the faith and optimism it takes to begin. Our faith and optimism grow with every positive action, however small.

Nothing diminishes anxiety faster than action.

—WALTER ANDERSON

Bonnie spent her working years as an advertising copywriter. Her secret passion was romance novels. She devoured them on the train on her commute to and from work. Dreaming of writing one herself, she knew just how she would begin, but somehow never got started. Retirement came and brought with it great swaths of time. Now, she realized, she had no excuse for not writing. She started writing Morning Pages, and a few weeks into them, a character strolled into her consciousness.

"What should I do?" she called me to ask.

"You should write," I replied. "Keep your Morning Pages intact and write later in the day." I have seen many ideas born in Morning Pages. The trick is to remember that the Morning Pages themselves are helping these ideas enter the world. So, as tempting as it may be to abandon the pages, believing they've served their purpose, don't. They will continue to support and guide you as you create.

Bonnie did begin to write, suspecting—and then realizing—that this was her long-awaited romance novel.

I didn't hear from Bonnie again until she called me to ask, "What do I do now? I'm finished."

"I'd love to read it," I replied. "In the meanwhile, it's time to start on novel number two."

Taking action—and then taking more actions—is the key to our progress. It's easy to forget the simple fact that when we are working on our project, our project is in motion. Our project is alive. It is up to us to nurture and sustain it.

Judith is retired from a long career as an accountant. When her days were jammed with clients and clients' problems, she looked forward to retirement and the free time it would bring her to work on projects of her own. But her free time did not bring her what she had anticipated. Instead of working busily and productively on her planned projects, she couldn't seem to get started. Retirement became a license to procrastinate. She had a kitchen-remodeling project that she had half-finished during her busy years of working. Now, she found she couldn't seem to gather enough steam to go forward.

Judith's procrastination filled her with self-loathing. "Why can't I just start?" she wondered, and spent her days pondering the cause of her procrastination rather than working on the project itself.

"How's the kitchen coming?" was a question that Judith's friends learned not to ask. The kitchen was going nowhere fast, and Judith's self-image was going to hell in a handbasket as she ate her meals amid half-painted walls and scraps of granite and tile.

"I can't seem to get myself to make even the smallest decisions on this stupid kitchen," she told me. "I think, because I am not sure what else to do with my time, I'm leaving this unfinished so I always have 'something' to do. But it's sad. Especially now that I'm at home more, I'm face-to-face with this mess every day."

"If you want something done, give it to a busy person" was a phrase Judith used to quote while working, priding herself on her ability to accomplish beyond her list of tasks on any given day. She now realized that her once-favorite saying was bitterly apt. She missed her busy days and the sense of satisfaction she would get from solving her clients' problems. Finally, feeling desperate, she started seeing a few clients through freelance work. Immediately, her mood turned to the better, and she began working again on her long-delayed project. Within three

The most certain way to succeed is always to try just one more time.

—THOMAS A. EDISON

months, she was as busy as she had ever been and her kitchen was finished in cheerful tiles.

"Maybe some people aren't meant to retire," Judith postulated. Busy and happy, she is seeing that, for her, the time wasn't right. "I couldn't have found it out any other way," she says. She's now undertaking a redesign of her bedroom, resolving to work on it in her free hours as she continues her now part-time profession as an accountant.

Judith's story is not unique. Many retirees find themselves unable to be self-starting. Not all of them can pick up the reins of the career they had set aside, like Judith could. For those who have a problem with self-starting, Morning Pages are the place to begin. They are a daily, consistent, productive action. Doing them, in conjunction with the other tools, changes our trajectory and sets us in motion.

Those who are newly retired may find themselves impatient with their new life. The tools raise questions as well as answer them. In the words of Rainer Maria Rilke, "Be patient toward all that is unsolved in your heart. And try to love the questions themselves." For many, the questions raised by pages involve a deeper level of awareness than they are accustomed to.

Janice found herself stuck. Although she lived in Santa Fe, which is a colorful city with many things to offer, she didn't avail herself of its adventures. In retirement, she was depressed because she no longer felt needed, and she found herself isolated. At the urging of a friend, she reluctantly began reading the "what's happening" pages of the Friday paper. More reluctant still, she pried herself from her self-described "boring routine" and undertook a weekly adventure, attending a lecture series on modern art. At first she was intimidated, feeling that everyone in the crowd must know more than she. "They look so cool," she complained to her friend. "They present themselves as works of art—tiny round glasses, gray monochromatic tunics and shirts and slacks, brightly dyed spiked hair. No one looks 'normal.'" It was at the third lecture that her neighbor spoke to her.

"You're coming all the time," she said.

Action expresses priorities.

—CHARLES A. GARFIELD

"Yes, yes, I am," Janice replied. "I feel like I'm playing catch-up."

"So do I," said the neighbor. "Would you like to go gallery hopping?"

"Why, yes!" Janice replied.

"There's a wonderful show by a man named Chris Richter at the Chiaroscuro gallery. We could start there."

Janice agreed to the gallery outing and found, to her surprise, that she felt unexpectedly optimistic.

"I actually felt hip," Janice remarked. And at age sixty-three, she was more active than she had been in years.

Retirement is an ideal time to increase activity. It is a time of open choices, a time of opportunity. When the possibilities feel endless, it is exciting to go ahead and try our hand at anything that inspires or calls to us.

Dave and Joan were a husband-and-wife team of dentist and hygienist. They were accustomed to working long hours. When they retired, time loomed large, and it took a great many activities to fill it. First of all, they began working as a team, carving and painting fine decoys. So good were their decoys that they won a national championship. They presented me with a specimen for Christmas.

But soon they discovered that work with the carvings was not enough for them. They volunteered their dental services at a prison. This was better, but still not enough. Joan began working out at a local gym. Soon, her fitness level surpassed many thirty-year-olds'. Not to be outdone, Dave cast about for another hobby. He found it in baking bread. When his scrumptious loaves overflowed the family larder, he gave them as gifts to friends and neighbors.

"How do you make it so delicious?" one neighbor inquired. Her question launched a bread tutorial. Dave found he loved teaching, and the loaves that he produced were loved by one and all. "The more I do, the more I want to do," Dave says. "The more I sit around, the more I want to sit around—and it's the sitting around that's hard."

Indeed. It is far harder and more painful to be a blocked artist than it is to do the work.

Blocked, we experience our dreams as grandiose, even impossible. When we actually take actions—even the smallest ones—this once-impossible daring seems easy.

The tool kit moves us out of inertia and into action. The tools themselves are active. They tell us what we want, what we don't want, what we want more of, what we want less of. They bring us clarity and they put an end to procrastination. As we remember our dreams and goals in our Memoir, our reasons for not pursuing them become transparent. We lead ourselves by our own hand into a world we may once have only dreamed of. No longer content to rest on our laurels, we begin to act—almost without realizing it—in the direction of our dreams.

TASK
Taking Action

List five large actions you dream of taking, for example:

1. Writing a novel
2. Traveling the world
3. Putting an addition on the house
4. Painting a self-portrait
5. Learning to play the drums

Now, list a tiny action you could take in the direction of each of these larger actions. For example:

1. List areas of interest
2. Go to a travel store
3. Look at architecture magazines
4. Sketch yourself quickly
5. Begin with a bongo

The smaller the action, the better; baby steps are active steps indeed!

Money Matters

Money is something all of us have to weigh and study in our decision to leave the work force. This new financial phase can take some getting used to. "I have enough money," we remind ourselves, "but what if I live to one hundred and ten? What if there is historic inflation?" We feel, understandably, a sense of instability, even when our finances are stable.

Entering retirement, it is helpful to get a grasp on how we now want to spend our money. Spending along the lines of our true values, we feel prosperous. Acting in our own best interest, we often find that unexpected funds also come our way. We do have enough. We can flourish and prosper and feel a sense of abundance. Because prosperity is a spiritual condition, the more true we are to ourselves, the more we prosper. Few things are more distressing than ambiguity; when we reach clarity about our finances, we are empowered.

Some of us worked very hard in our jobs without enjoying much more about our jobs than the paycheck they provided. In retirement, we can work at jobs "for fun" that allow us to explore our creativity. And sometimes those jobs "for fun" even bring in a paycheck. We can accept this with gratitude—and even a sense of enjoyment.

Jill is an animal lover. She is the kind of person who stops to pet dogs on the street. She knows the names of the animals on her block. Retired after thirty years as a legal secretary, she donates some of her extra time to the animal rescue league. Three days a week she spends her afternoons caring for the puppies and kittens that might otherwise go uncared for.

"I have to fight my every instinct not to take everyone home," she says, and laughs. "I have a one-bedroom apartment just big enough for me, one puppy, and one kitten that I couldn't resist. The puppy is named Harry. I think he's part Pomeranian—he has such a fluffy coat. The kitten is a little more exotic. She is a Himalayan—half Persian, half

Siamese. Her name is Meow because she talks so much, but always on the same note: meow. My friends tell me they wish they were my pet—I treat them so well. I spend my evenings happily ensconced with my pets. Harry knows half a dozen tricks. Meow holds herself aloof from training and tricks. My life is very rich with these creatures in it."

When Jill was working, she passed an exotic bird store on the way to work every day.

"I stopped by the store the other day, and now I've fallen in love with an African gray. I would love to take the little parrot home, but that would be inviting havoc. And so I must content myself with little visits, and I dread the day someone else falls in love with the African gray. I'd name him Spalding, after the great monologist Spalding Gray."

Jill dropped into the store so regularly that the store owner asked her if she wanted a job. "At first I thought, no, of course not. I'm retired. But I realized after mulling it over for several days that I could offer two days. When he told me that was just what he was looking for, I took it as a sign."

Jill is having fun with the extra "play money" she earns at the store, as she calls it, but even more fun spending time with the birds. "I'm shocked to think that I became a bird store employee. In all my years as a legal secretary, I had never thought to ask myself, what do I love? Retired, I found myself doing what I loved and getting paid for it. Why didn't I think of this sooner? Every paycheck feels like a bonus. And Spalding Gray is doing very well."

Sometimes, retired professionals feel that if a job is "too easy," they are not working to their potential, or "slumming" in some way. But asking if an endeavor is "too easy" is asking the wrong question. Artists of all stripes tend to equate ease with slumming and difficulty with virtue. The truth is that the formula should be reversed: as we embark on new ideas, we need to learn to equate ease with virtue and difficulty with slumming.

Hank is retired from a career as a Realtor. In his retirement, he turned his time to what was always "just" a hobby: glassblowing. He

Wealth is the ability to fully experience life.

—HENRY DAVID THOREAU

185

used every vacation and downtime during his work life to study and refine his craft. Now a full-time glassblower, he is loath to charge for his work, even though he has buyers offering to pay him.

Hank defends himself, saying that he doesn't need the money. "Why should I charge at all? I can afford to have this stay a hobby, you know."

In the end, it is up to Hank to decide where he will place his work in the market of other glass pieces, but he would do well to look honestly at his own effort. In underpricing our work, we run the risk of undervaluing ourselves. This isn't to say that we can't give our talents away if we choose to, but it is important to seek balance in what we give and what we receive. Just because something is fun—or easy—for us doesn't mean it isn't valuable.

Retirees are often on a tighter budget than they were when they were working, and in retirement, spending must be approached with a new awareness. What is really important to us? How do we decide what fat to trim away? There is a balance of fun-spending and prudent-spending, and there is a very simple way to find this balance: a tool I call "counting."

Counting is a tool I have used many times before. It is just what it sounds like: we count every penny in and every penny out. It is a tool of information, not of judgment. We see that we are in fact frugal at the grocery store, but when it comes to our coffee habit, we spend extra money on a daily basis, often regretting the sugary and overpriced concoctions. We may spend too much on others and not enough on ourselves, showering our friends with gifts but not replacing our own worn shoes. Maybe we feel that going to the theater is "too expensive" but in fact spend more than the price of a theater ticket in cab fares that could have been avoided. As we count, we learn where our money goes. Seeing it there in black and white, we understand what really matters to us. We learn what we want to change.

Getting in touch with our true values, and then consequently spending—and earning—in accordance with those values, our money

[M]oney is only a tool. It will take you wherever you wish, but it will not replace you as the driver.

—AYN RAND

becomes less mysterious to us. Giving ourselves the dignity of clarity, we find we have more dignity in our lives.

TASK
Counting

Try counting for one week. You may find you wish to do it for longer. Counting is simple: write down every penny in and every penny out. That includes large and small payments: buying a car, buying a newspaper, receiving an unexpected inheritance, finding a coin on the ground. Everything counts. Write it down. At the end of the week, look back at your spending. Your patterns will reveal themselves to you with clarity.

The Career Caretaker

I have seen many times in my retired students that those whose careers were ones of service have an extra hard time shifting their focus to themselves in retirement. Nurses, doctors, teachers, chefs—anyone whose "job was never done"—often have the most trouble adjusting to not working. Even when a person is ready to retire—and even when a person is exhausted—the switch to feeling like they are not "needed" causes a shock. When someone's purpose has always been to care for others, the transition to retirement and self-care can be especially difficult. No longer needed in the capacity they were used to, they may feel untethered, even resentful. This can apply to people who worked serving others, but it can also apply to parents whose children are flying the nest, people who have cared for an elderly relative, or anyone who has been a "battery" for someone else.

Dennis was an executive chef at a high-end restaurant for many years. "When I first started out," he says, "I clawed my way to the top. I was relentless, and I was filled with ambition and drive. Nothing

187

could stop me." The rough-and-tumble lifestyle of a chef worked for him. He was, as he put it, "never able to truly get ahead, and always running on adrenaline." Because his career was one in which there was no real "catching up," his to-do list was always overflowing, and he was always needed. Retiring was like "jumping off a treadmill," he says. "I pretty much collapsed, and I really didn't have any idea what to do next."

Dennis was exhausted at the time of retirement, but he was also used to the adrenaline high of a nonstop job and a staff—not to mention a dining room full of people—dependent on him. "I was used to taking care of people. It gave me purpose and a mission every day. Now I have no idea what my day should involve."

When I suggested that he try thinking of ways he could take care of himself, he admitted this was foreign territory for him. "I have a nice house, a nice car—but there are things I've never had, like a nonbusiness vacation or a massage." Working through his Memoir, Dennis noted that in his midforties, as he took over the restaurant he would call his own for the rest of his career, he remembered a time of almost-panic. "I felt like I had to 'make it,' and soon," he says. "I look back at my younger self and see that I was willing to give up anything for my career. No wonder that letting it go now feels like I'm losing a huge part of myself." Dennis, like many, feels a sense of compassion for himself when he looks back on his Memoir.

"If it's hard to think of self-care now, try thinking of it as caring for your former self," I suggested to him. "What did that forty-six-year-old man need that he didn't get?"

Dennis thought about this and ultimately realized his younger self didn't have a real mentor. "I felt alone," he says. "I felt like I had to forge my own path through the wilderness. That I couldn't count on anyone else. Now that I say that, I realize it's sad. I wish I could go back and mentor my former self."

The good news is that in a certain way, he can. Slowly, Dennis worked to reach back to his younger self. "At first, I thought I should

Self-compassion is simply giving the same kindness to ourselves that we would give to others.

—CHRISTOPHER GERMER

188

go to the beach for a month. But now I realize that's not what I really want to do. I want to talk to other people. I want to meet other restaurateurs, other people who have retired and succeeded at finding a next step that worked for them." Self-care is a very specific art, and we must be very honest with ourselves about what we *actually* need. If what we need is advice, a pint of ice cream won't do. If what we need is rest, an overbooked agenda will only distress us. If we have spent many years in service to others, the sleuthing it will take to arrive at what we need may take some time. Please be patient. It *is* worth it.

Fred had been retired for some time when his wife fell ill. Acting as her caretaker, he ultimately spent all of his days by her side. "I'd have done it no other way," he says. "But it was very painful, on many levels." The stress of her decline has taken its toll on him. "I'm physically exhausted, but mentally and spiritually exhausted, too. I've almost not had time to be sad." For Fred, signing up for a massage felt like a radical act. "I can't believe my plan is to do this—but I'm going to try," he told me. During his massage, he found himself feeling deeply the loss of his wife. He realized he had missed being touched. He remembered moments of happiness and moments of struggle. He felt compassion for himself and realized that it had been years since he had considered his own needs. As his massage neared an end, he signed up for another. For Fred, this felt like productive therapy. He would allow himself one massage a week, he decided.

For many retirees, self-care is a difficult art. But its rewards far outstrip the time and money it involves. When the next step is elusive, we do well to look at our younger selves in our Memoirs for clues to what we would once have wanted. When we are exhausted from service, we can make our best guess toward helping our bone-weary selves. Reaching a hand toward ourselves is often so unfamiliar that it may be shocking to see the result we are able to achieve—and how little we will actually respond to. Asking ourselves what we really need, we may be surprised that we have an answer—and surprised at how simple that answer is.

Love yourself first, and everything else falls into line. You really have to love yourself to get anything done in this world.

—LUCILLE BALL

TASK
Caretaking Ourselves

Have you ever been a battery for someone else? List three times you put more energy into a relationship than you got out of it. If a memory is loaded or painful, allow yourself to write for five minutes about this relationship.

Now, number from 1 to 10. List ten things you could do to spoil yourself—things you would easily do for others, but rarely (or never) do for yourself. Choose one thing off that list. Do that thing.

What lies behind us and what lies before us are tiny matters compared to what lies within us.

—RALPH WALDO EMERSON

Forward Motion: The Next Right Thing

Many find themselves feeling confused as they face their retirement. During their work life, they knew what came next. Their boss, or their company, or their client, would dictate their agendas. Retired, with no one dictating their agenda, they may have moments of feeling at loose ends, unsure of what to do next. Suddenly at home midday and mid-week, they may abruptly realize they've been standing in front of the refrigerator or staring at a newspaper without reading it for the last few minutes, trying to figure out what to do.

It is common to have these moments of confusion. When this happens, I tell people, "Just do the next right thing." Instead of focusing on the big picture, focus on the small. For most of us it is not too difficult to figure out a small step forward. The next right thing might be very simple: make your bed, do the dishes, take out the trash. Each small step dictates the next small step. For example, making your bed leads to hanging up your clothes, or, if you wish, hanging up your clothes leads to making your bed.

While these actions may seem too small or simple, a body in motion remains in motion, and even the smallest action—taking out the trash or taking a shower—inevitably leads to another action. If we think of God as GOD—good, orderly direction—it is easy to see how doing the next right thing is an act of spiritual housekeeping. The next right thing might be physical, like walking around the block to clear the mind, or putting the logs into a neat stack outside, or playing catch with the dog. It might be emotional—calling a friend or relative, writing about a loaded memory in our Memoir, screaming into a pillow. It might be spiritual—listening to music or reading from a work that inspires us. The trick is just to move from stagnation to action in any way we can think of.

I often find that cleaning or tidying something has great payoff in terms of forward motion. If we believe in the phrase "cleanliness is next to godliness," then we are on the right track as we neaten and clean our environment. Many students remark that as they clean, they receive ideas of the "next right thing" in many arenas. I myself often find that doing dishes helps me plot my plays.

Another "next right thing" that is almost always timely is to take ourselves on an Artist Date. Easily avoided but always rewarding, Artist Dates are a great choice of forward-moving action. When I feel stuck or unsure of what to do next, a quick drive downtown to the Georgia O'Keeffe museum brings me into a state of spiritual alignment and clarity. I come home from my excursion energized to do something else.

A student of mine, Joseph, was frustrated by the process of doing Morning Pages because he was "overcome with panic" whenever he wrote. "I have no good reason," he said, "I just feel very anxious. I think it has to do with feeling like I don't know which direction to move. I almost don't want to write about it because it's too painful to think about."

I asked him if he could think of one thing to do—no matter how small.

"Well, I could go to the grocery store," he said.

"Perfect," I caroled, delighted.

Courage doesn't always roar. Sometimes courage is the quiet voice at the end of the day, saying, "I will try again tomorrow."

—MARY ANNE RADMACHER

"Why are you so excited about me going to the grocery store?" he asked me suspiciously.

"Because it's a good idea and it will lead to another one," I told him. "Call me back later and tell me you've done it."

When he called, his voice was noticeably lighter. He'd gone to the grocery store and stocked up on things he needed and things he "just found delightful." Once he left the grocery store, it occurred to him that he was near the bank—and he stopped by to take care of his unfinished business there. Returning home, he suddenly seemed to have the energy to tackle the mail that he had been procrastinating about opening. In it, he found a note from a long lost friend.

He noticed that he now felt a sense of accomplishment, but his house felt lonely to him and he didn't quite know where to begin, tackling his loneliness. It seemed much too large. Stocking the refrigerator was one thing. But . . .

"Just do the next right thing," he reminded himself, and it became clear to him that he could send a note to the friend of his who had dropped him a line. It didn't have to be much—just, "Hi, I'm newly retired and grappling with what to do next. It occurred to me to write to you; you were so good to write to me."

Note written, it was time for a trip to the post office. There he bought a sheet of stamps, and used the first one on his note to his friend. Returning home, Joseph stopped at a new gas station, where the gas was thirty cents less per gallon than he had been paying. Wiping his windows while the gas pumped, he realized a car wash was long overdue. Finished fueling, he drove a mile to the carwash. He piloted his car onto the tracks and settled back to enjoy the scrubby flood of soapy water. It took less than ten minutes to wash his car and another ten minutes to vacuum the interior. He drove home with a sense of well-being. Doing the next right thing had proved happy and productive.

As he relayed this story to me, I had to laugh. "It sounds like you've had a wildly productive day, Joseph," I ventured.

Do what you can, where you are, with what you have.

—SQUIRE BILL WIDENER

"Yes. I have to admit it was an insightful one, too. Once I just broke out of my immobile state, it was pretty easy to do 'just one thing'—and then just one more. To be honest, knowing I had to call you and tell you that I had gotten groceries got me out the door."

The "sandwich call" trick—calling a friend, committing to an action, and then calling them back when the action is complete—is one that shouldn't be underestimated. While it may feel ridiculous to enlist a friend's help in getting ourselves moving, I would suggest that it is more painful to stay stuck than it is to make the call. And who hasn't been there? If we choose our friend wisely, we can rest assured that they will relate—and maybe even call us when they need to be held accountable to their day's agenda.

Progress lies not in enhancing what is, but in advancing toward what will be.

—KHALIL GIBRAN

Whether helping ourselves find our next right action or helping a friend, it is useful to ask the question "What small thing have you been putting off?" For Paco, it was getting a library card. "But that can't be what you mean, can it?" he asked me. "Isn't it *too* small?"

Not at all. No such thing.

"Go get it," I urged him.

"Oh, all right," Paco grumbled.

The very next time I spoke with him, he bragged, "I got my card, and our library really is quite good."

"What next, then, Paco?" I asked.

"There's this photography exhibit at a coffeehouse . . ."

"So go," I urged him.

When next we talked, he boasted, "I met the photographer himself. Tomorrow, I'm going to his studio to see more of his work. I just might buy a piece." Paco was discovering the art of gentle exploration. He was finding that he could fill his days easily once he overcame his inertia.

Doing the "next right thing" can feel almost magical when the cycle of motion is initiated. Don't overthink what the next right thing is. It will be something small, something easy, something that appeals to the imagination.

TASK
Do the Next Right Thing

Clue: the next right thing is tiny, nonthreatening, and right in front of you. Do that thing.

WEEKLY CHECK-IN

1. How many days did you do your Morning Pages? How was the experience of doing them?
2. Did you do an Artist Date? What was it? Did you discover anything in your Memoir that you'd like to explore in an Artist Date?
3. Did you take your Walks? What did you notice along the way?
4. What "ahas" did you discover this week?
5. Did you experience any synchronicity this week? What was it? Did it give you a sense of humility, a sense of being somehow guided by a higher power?
6. What did you find in your Memoir that you would like to explore more fully? How would you like to explore it? As always, if you have a loaded memory that you feel requires further attention but aren't yet sure what additional action to take, don't worry about it. Just keep moving forward.

Reigniting a Sense
of Vitality

This week focuses on developing a healthy sense of self-protection, thus giving us the strength and clarity we need in challenging situations. Looking back in your Memoir, remember how you spent your energy—on yourself and on others. Today, you choose again where to spend your valuable inner resources, and as you choose correctly for yourself and your values, you are rewarded with energy and strength. Writing, you are led forward. Taking Artist Dates, you are inspired. Walking, you are connected to a limitless spiritual resource and, committing to its care, you receive the strength you need. Revisiting your Memoir, you connect to, and learn from, your former self. Often, buried dreams are the calling cards of a true identity. When we honor our true identity, vitality is the reward.

The Inner Well

It is not length of life,
but depth of life.

—RALPH WALDO
EMERSON

Whenever we do something creative, we fish from our inner well. What do I mean by that? I mean that all of us have a supply of images that we employ when we create. It is worth thinking of ourselves as an ecosystem. When we write, paint, sew, or act, we draw on images from our inner well. If we learn to restock our store of images, we will find ourselves able to work more easily. Conversely, when we draw from the well without replenishing it, our work becomes labored, and we wonder what's "suddenly" gone wrong.

What's wrong is that we are fishing from the well without restoring our stock of images. The very best way to restock the well is to take an Artist Date. As we consciously refill the well, we regain a sense of ease. A weekly Artist Date is usually sufficient. However, when we are working flat-out, an extra Artist Date may be called for.

The Artist Date feels frivolous: an expedition to do something that is sheer fun. But many students report that it was on an Artist Date that they first felt a sense of conscious contact with a higher power, and it is true that Artist Dates give us a sense of a benevolent universe. An Artist Date may be extravagant or modest; something as simple as a visit to a floral shop may gently restock the well.

Working through the Memoir always brings up topics for possible exploration in an Artist Date. Taking specific "remembering" Artist Dates can be a very powerful tool for us, both in connecting to our past and fueling our present. Some people revisit the roads they once lived on, or walk their former route from their elementary school to their childhood home. Some re-create recipes, watch a favorite childhood movie, reread a favorite childhood book. There are many small details—the specific shapes of a mobile, the cat's red mouse toy, the scent of a grandmother's perfume, the song we listened to obsessively in middle school—that can trigger these powerful memories. More than memories, these images and senses connect us to ourselves. These are all still a part of us, and reconnecting to them, we are stronger for making contact with them.

Keep in mind that an Artist Date can be anything; it just needs to speak to a sense of fun. Any Artist Date will fill the well because an Artist Date always connects us to fresh images. The images do not have to be directly related to the piece of work at hand. Any images will do.

Genevieve is an English teacher-turned-novelist in her midfifties, hard at work on her second book.

"Julia," she complained to me, "I was writing up a storm, and then it all dried up."

"Don't worry, Genevieve," I assured her. "All that has happened is that you have overfished your well. Take a few Artist Dates and you'll soon be writing again. And remember that the dates do not have to have anything to do with the story you are trying to tell."

Genevieve set out on her Artist Dates as planned. "I always feel resistance when I leave the house," she shared. "All of a sudden it's too windy, or I should do the dishes, or any other number of inane excuses. My resistance isn't logical. An Artist Date only takes an hour, and I get such a sense of inspiration from doing it—my good mood lasts for days afterward. I just find it hard to get motivated."

For her first Artist Date, Genevieve visited an artisanal doughnut shop a town over. "I had heard of the place and their strange and fascinating doughnuts. My interest was piqued—blood orange persimmon doughnuts? *Dulce de leche*? But I never happened to be near the shop, and I certainly wasn't going to go out of my way just for a doughnut."

But when she did go out of her way "just" for a doughnut, she felt a sense of magic and naughtiness. "It seemed so frivolous! But the doughnuts were delicious—and yes, I did have two," she confided with mischief. "I felt like a kid getting a special treat."

It is a very powerful creative act to allow ourselves to feel like a kid getting a special treat. And when we choose treats that we did enjoy as kids, the payoff is even greater. Revisiting a childhood treat can trigger a flood of memories and ideas.

The debt we owe to the play of imagination is incalculable.

—CARL JUNG

For her next Artist Date, Genevieve did something very much outside her comfort zone: she went dress shopping.

"I was never one of those girls who shopped as a hobby," she told me. "So shopping for the sake of shopping was a bit unfamiliar. But trying on dresses—that was another level of unfamiliar! I don't think I have tried on dresses since I was in third grade!"

Genevieve did find—and purchase—a simple dress on that Artist Date. And a month later, she had an unexpected occasion to wear it.

Just living is not enough . . . one must have sunshine, freedom, and a little flower.

—HANS CHRISTIAN ANDERSEN

"I got a call from my literary agent that a new publisher was being formed and she thought it could be a match for my novel," she said. "I was so happy to have something to wear to the meeting. I felt comfortable in my new dress, but I also had a secret: that dress represented me taking care of my inner artist. I felt confident, sitting there in it. The meeting went very well, and I think it was in a big part due to the fact that I was feeling creatively free with the extra Artist Dates. I felt clear about my goals and able to talk about my work in the meeting. It really does put me in touch with what matters to me when I take these dates."

Genevieve let me know that her writing on her new project was now flowing along smoothly. "I can't believe it's so simple," Genevieve told me next, excited to be back on the page. But I am not surprised. I have consistently seen Artist Dates bring people into powerful contact with themselves, and, consequently, their world.

In planning an Artist Date, we should aim for enchantment. In other words, we are out to explore a mystery—something that captures our imagination. An Artist Date need not be—and perhaps should not be—high art. Taking a trip to a children's bookstore and rereading our favorite childhood book can unleash large amounts of emotion and energy. Cooking a favorite childhood recipe or revisiting a favorite movie from another time in our lives connects our past to our present. Artist Dates are enlightening—and I treat that word quite literally. We are "lighter" at the end of the date than we were at the beginning.

One of my favorite Artist Dates remains the one that resulted in my desktop paperweight, when I visited the open studio of a glassblower. I watched with fascination, and a little fear, as the artist worked with a molten blob of glass, shaping it into a paperweight. It was, by all accounts, outside my normal realm of experience.

"Would you like to try it?" she asked me. I heard myself say yes, and I held out my hands to receive the rod with the molten glass at the end.

"Dip it in a color," the artist directed, pointing to a palette. I chose scarlet and twirled the rod in that color.

"Now choose a second color," the artist directed. This time I chose fuchsia and spun the rod, picking up hot pink. Step by step, I followed the artist's lead.

"There," she explained. "Place it down. Now, spin it off." I did as I was told and found I had made a creditable paperweight. Next, I watched in fascination as the artist fashioned a koi fish, silver dappled with gold. She made it look easy, fanning out the tail to give the illusion of motion. The koi fish took great delicacy and expertise. It was a pricey item, and I could see why.

I love colored glass, I found myself thinking. I love seeing shapes coming into recognizable form. I love the magic and artistry of making something from nothing. This, to me, is the essence of a fruitful adventure.

As simple as these insights may sound, it is very empowering to celebrate what you love and celebrate that you are the person who loves it.

Cadee, a playwright, found herself drawing heavily on her inner well when she was on deadline. Aware that she needed extra "inflow" at a time when she was under deadline with heavy "outflow," she took herself to a bird store.

"I chose the bird store because I remembered, when working through my Memoir, that my grandmother had a great love of birds," Cadee says. "I wanted to connect with her. I wasn't sure exactly how to do it, but I thought heading to a bird store for a few minutes was a step in the right direction."

"I have blue jays and little birds in my backyard," Cadee explained to the clerk.

"Well, then," said the clerk, "you'll need two kinds of feed. Blue jays love peanuts and the little birds love seeds." Cadee hadn't gone into the store expecting to expand her own bird-feeding endeavors, but she purchased both kinds of feed and took them home to fill the small bird feeders hanging behind her house. True to the clerk's word, as soon as she put out the peanuts, she was swarmed by blue jays—sometimes as many as five at a time. Her little birds were slower on the uptake. They came singly and in pairs, pecking at their feed. Cadee's feeders hung just outside her living room windows. Perched on her living room couch, she could see all the action. She had a small birding book, and she looked up the birds as they arrived: juncos, chickadees, finches— they were all delightful. And, of course, there were the bold and beautiful blue jays. Watching the birds, she felt close to her grandmother. Thinking of her grandmother, more memories came to light. She remembered that, as a child, she would sit on the screened porch of her grandmother's house, where Audubon prints lined the walls. Her grandmother had a coloring book filled with birds on that porch, left out for the grandchildren to use when they visited.

On breaks from writing her play, Cadee looked up Audubon on the Internet. She found a source for posters and ordered a dozen of them. When they arrived she went straight to the framer, selecting beautiful frames for them all. As it happened, Cadee lived in a small town that featured a National Audubon Society refuge. The first warm spring day, she took herself to the bird sanctuary. To her delight, many birds flocked there, evidently sensing that they were loved and safe. At the sanctuary's bookstore, she purchased a coloring book—one very similar to the one on her grandmother's porch. Once home, she took great pleasure in coloring in each of the species that flocked to her feeders.

"I realize I love birds," Cadee says. "I live in the mountains, far away from the herons and egrets I saw growing up, but now I have two posters, one of a snowy egret and another of a blue heron. Surrounding myself with birds connects me to my grandmother and to my former young self. Bird-watching brings me great joy and gives me great inspiration as a writer."

It is hard to underestimate the power of revisiting early fond memories. Remembering them is one thing, but going out looking for the memory—or a physical representation of it—is another. As we reach out to our past self, that self reaches back, full of ideas for tomorrow.

TASK
Fill the Well

This week, take yourself on an additional Artist Date; one, as usual, that simply delights you, and one "remembering" Artist Date, where you consciously chase a memory from your past. If you feel indulgent taking two dates—good! Stocking the pond fuels your current project and readies you for the next one.

TASK
Memoir, Week Ten

AGES: _____

1. Describe your major relationships in this period.
2. Where did you live? Did you live in more than one place?
3. Where did you spend the bulk of your energy during this period?
4. Describe one sound that brings you back to this period.
5. Describe one taste from this period.
6. On whom did you spend your energy during this time? Did you put your own needs aside in the service of someone else?
7. What was a source of joy during this period? Is it still a source of joy today, or could it be?
8. Did you deal with health issues, yours or someone else's, during this time?

9. What was a source of pain during this time? Now, in hindsight, what did you learn from it?

10. What other memories feel significant to you from this time?

It takes courage to grow up and become who you really are.

—E. E. CUMMINGS

Healthy Selfishness

In retirement, many of us must learn to practice what might be called "healthy selfishness." No longer tied to a job, we have freedom, but some of that freedom must be used on our own behalf. For many of us, this is surprisingly difficult. We find ourselves only too ready to make sacrifices in the name of family, or home maintenance, or promises to help at church, or long-deferred duties or obligations. The point is, we sometimes sacrifice our own wishes in the name of external demands.

When Geraldine retired from her job as a kindergarten teacher, one of the things she looked forward to most was spending more time with her grandchildren. She offered to help out her daughter-in-law with occasional childcare only to find herself enlisted as a full-time free nanny. While she loved the children and loved feeling needed, she did not love feeling taken for granted. "I must sound bitter, but I feel like I am supposed to be a cultural stereotype of the sainted grandmother, with endless stores of patience and stamina. I love my grandchildren, but I am tired!"

Scratching the surface of Geraldine's complaint, I found there was truth to her discomfort. Her daughter-in-law wanted to resume her place in the work world and leapt at Geraldine's offer of childcare. One thing led to another, and soon Geraldine was working eight to five, five days a week. Her grandchildren, a boy and a girl aged four and two, were active, healthy, and rambunctious. Riding herd on them took all of Geraldine's energy. She found herself resenting her role as caretaker. "You're so good with them," her daughter-in-law often remarked, and Geraldine *was* good with them, but she was more and more distressed as she began to feel herself run ragged. While her grandchildren were charming, she did not realize the extent of her need for adult activities and conversations.

"I messed up," she said. "I offered—and gave—way too much. Now I'm in a place where I feel guilty trying to back out, but I resent the assumption that I'm always available. I'm afraid it could hurt my relationship with my son and daughter-in-law, and with my grandchildren."

When I met Geraldine, it was easy for me to make the diagnosis: too helpful. I suggested she try writing Morning Pages, and when she did, she was astounded by the anger she had kept bottled up. I assured her that it was okay to vent her anger in the Morning Pages—that's what they're there for, why they are for her eyes only.

"What you need," I told Geraldine, "is a little healthy selfishness. Tell your daughter-in-law you can help with the kids some days, but not all days." Geraldine was relieved at my diagnosis, but she found herself balking at my prescription. Wasn't it selfish, she wondered. After all, she had "nothing" to do.

"That's just it," I told her. "You need to find hobbies and interests of your own." Geraldine was reluctant to set new boundaries. She was up for sainthood, it seemed, although sainthood and martyrdom were standing perilously close together. Geraldine's Morning Pages kept suggesting she needed a life of her own. Finally, one day at the end of a long week of babysitting, she found herself having a difficult conversation with her daughter-in-law.

"You know that I love you," she said. "You know that I love the children. But it's really too much for me, watching them day in and day out."

Her daughter-in-law laughed uneasily. "I thought it was too good to be true," she confessed.

"I can watch them three days a week," Geraldine volunteered, "but you'll need to find someone else to cover the other two days."

"I can do that," her daughter-in-law anted up.

Geraldine found herself relieved. "I don't think it would hurt them

The person who says it cannot be done should not interrupt the person who is doing it.

—CHINESE PROVERB

203

to try day care," she ventured. "Socializing with other children might be good for them."

"Perhaps you're right," allowed her daughter-in-law.

And so, Geraldine found herself possessed of two full days each week. "What should I do with them?" she wondered. Then she found herself answering, "I can go to museums, galleries, and plays. I can take a class. I can do many things. If I don't know what to do, I'll just do *something*—and then something else." Before long, Geraldine saw herself practicing a healthy selfishness for the first time. "I had to become clear on my own position and stand up for myself," she says now, "and that was the hard part. I didn't want to admit that being a full-time childcare provider was more than I wanted right now. But once I accepted that as a respectable request to make, I was able to move toward a more balanced life—without being angry or, maybe worse, passive aggressive and resentful because I was trying to hide how I felt. I notice I'm more patient with everyone now—including myself."

Finding healthy selfishness can take a delicate balance of honesty about our emotions and compassion for ourselves, but happiness is the inevitable result.

As we undertake our creative recovery, we need to draw a sacred circle around ourselves. Many of our friends will not understand the boundaries that we draw. We need to protect our new activities. For example, our Artist Dates must be done solo, not undertaken with curious friends.

Clarice found she had many friends who were skeptical of her excitement about her creative recovery. Nonetheless, she forged ahead with the basic tools—Morning Pages, Artist Dates, and Walks. Working through her Memoir, she was surprised by vivid memories of her mother taking up quilting in her own retirement. Moved and inspired, she searched for an upcoming quilting show that she could attend. But when she shared her plans with one particularly pushy friend, the friend immediately invited herself along.

When I stand before God at the end of my life, I would hope that I would not have a single bit of talent left and could say, I used everything you gave me.

—ERMA BOMBECK

"I'd like to go alone," Clarice ventured cautiously, feeling both self-ish and sure. "I want to be with just the memories of my mother, if that makes any sense."

"Oh, come on, Clarice," her friend importuned her. "Why are you so selfish all of a sudden?"

Clarice, though hurt, stuck to her guns, suggesting that the friend join her for a meal afterward instead. Her friend reluctantly agreed.

When Clarice attended the quilt show on her own, she was flooded with memory. Her mother's thimble collection filled her mind, as clear as it had once been decades before as she watched her mother first learn to quilt. She saw bits of fabric with giraffes in one quilt that trig-gered thoughts of her own childhood quilt, one her grandmother had made for her. Walking through the quilts in her own silence, she felt as if both her mother and grandmother were there with her. She knew what she had to do.

As she left the show, she approached the elderly woman at the front.

"Could you suggest some steps for a beginning quilter?" she asked shyly. Quilting had never occurred to her, but at the end of this partic-ularly powerful Artist Date, the urge was undeniable.

"Of course I can," the kindly woman answered, handing her a card and some brochures. "Here are some resources you might find interest-ing, a good local fabric shop, and my personal phone number. And remember, dear, the first one can be small if you want it to be."

Clarice walked back to her car feeling as if she had both visited her past and seen a glimpse of a future that would bring her joy and mean-ing. "How important it was that I did this alone," she thought to herself. Had anyone else been there—especially her pushy friend—the experi-ence would not have been so intimate.

As Clarice continued to take Artist Dates, it became evident which of her friends respected her wishes to take certain adventures alone. They became, for Clarice, believing mirrors—people who appreciated her power and potential. They became the people with whom she would choose to spend her time and share her insights. And choosing to share time and insights should be done with care; in doing this, we are choosing to share ourselves.

At its base, art is an act of autobiography that brings to light family secrets that are a part of our personal history. For this reason, making art may feel a lot like telling a family secret. "How could you?" may greet the work. It takes daring to forge a piece of art, and that daring may not be welcomed. It's as if the artist has thrown open the door to the cellar, the attic, or the closet, and is breaking a family taboo.

Eliza was a fine-arts painter who specialized in plain-air landscapes. Working with her Morning Pages, she felt an itch for portraiture. She began to paint her family and herself. Her family met Eliza's new work with horror. "I'm not really so fat!" one sister exclaimed. "Did you have to paint Dad with a martini?" demanded another. "And Mom looks angry."

Eliza's work was airing the family skeletons.

"Our brother looks stoned," exclaimed another sister.

"Our brother *is* stoned," Eliza replied. To her credit, Eliza's gallery owner was able to accept the new work. "I always thought there was more than met the eye in your lovely landscapes," she declared, arranging the details of a show of Eliza's portraits. Capping the show was a painting of Eliza herself, painting. In the piece she looked fierce but happy.

Allowing ourselves to admit what we desire—and to make the art that we desire to make—takes an act of courage. As we travel through our creative recovery, we will find large and small ways that we need to be more selfish. Exploring these desires in our Morning Pages, we come into contact with ourselves and are guided in how to act on our wishes. Acting on our wishes appropriately, we have the self-esteem that comes from authenticity. Grounded in solid self-worth, we meet others more fully.

TASK
Healthy Selfishness

Complete the following:

1. If it weren't too selfish, I'd . . .
2. If it weren't too selfish, I'd . . .
3. If it weren't too selfish, I'd . . .
4. If it weren't too selfish, I'd . . .
5. If it weren't too selfish, I'd . . .

In Sickness

During our work lives, many of us enjoyed a sense of our own competency and strength. Moving from project to project, we felt vigorous and filled with self-esteem. When we let go of our work life, many of us find ourselves floundering. Our sense of our own strength has diminished. We no longer feel hale and able-bodied. We miss the feelings of accomplishment our work life provided. Baffled by our feelings of weakness, we worry that we will never again regain our sense of strength. But this feeling is an illusion. What we need to do is actually quite simple: we need to set new goals for ourselves. In accomplishing them, we will find a renewed sense of vigor. It is really as simple as taking pen in hand and listing categories in which we can set these goals. Our categories can be simple: spirituality, friendships, creativity, physicality.

When I do this exercise, I set a small, doable goal in each category. For spirituality, I may choose a small daily reading of spiritual literature. For my friendships, I may plan a shared meal. For creativity, I pledge myself to Morning Pages and then three pages of writing on my current project. I set goals that I can accomplish and, when they are

207

accomplished, I feel the strength and desire to do more. Meeting our goals gives us a sense of satisfaction. As we accomplish them, we feel ourselves growing ever stronger.

I became vegan two years ago when a few of my friends started a vegan diet and I saw the way they began to thrive physically and mentally. Today, forty-five pounds lighter, more energetic and clearer-minded, I am grateful I took this step. On the surface, my clothes have been replaced several times over for smaller ones and my stamina is much improved. My cholesterol is lower and I sleep better. But I also sense that the benefits of my new program run even deeper than those I can measure or see. To be proactive about our health is a manageable goal, and one that benefits us greatly as we enter our new phase of life.

Vincent retired and spent the winter mall-walking in Indianapolis. "It's very convenient," he says, "because the mall has markers and I can see how far I walk. I can also avoid the snow. Indianapolis isn't a place with too many places to walk, especially in the bad weather. I've found there's a whole culture of mall walkers. We get to know each other and it's fun to show up and see the same people every day." Vincent has found not just a healthy habit but one that connects him to like-minded people and encouragement. "I even walk with my daughter sometimes, which is fun because we bond, and safe because the stores are closed in the early morning," he jokes. "She can't pull me off course to shop." Vincent, twenty pounds lighter at the end of the winter, is now walking ten miles a day and his doctor is thrilled with the improvements in his blood work. Once prediabetic, Vincent is now "a picture of health."

My friend Kevin has a different attitude from Vincent's. Kevin struggles with his health, and, resigned, often says, "Aging is getting used to ill health—in yourself and others." While the chronic pain of arthritis, the need for a pacemaker, or a knee that calls for a replacement are among the ailments aging can bring, even the most humble work to combat the effects of age is not only productive, but, I would say, essential. Mary Elizabeth, at eighty-four, suffers from all three ailments. "I am physically quite limited now," she says, "but I can still do

In the middle of winter I at last discovered that there was in me an invincible summer.

—ALBERT CAMUS

something positive every day." Mary Elizabeth is diligent about her physical therapy and passionate about poetry, which she turns to for spiritual solace. My friend Elberta, at eighty-six, runs a horse farm and a paving empire. Her health is not as strong as it once was, but she takes care of herself with balanced nutrition, humor, and gentle exercise, and allows her work to distract her.

Edmund, newly retired at sixty-five, finds himself suddenly suffering many aches and pains, and a general sense of malaise.

"I think I need to do something," Edmund says. "When I was working, my health seemed fine." It was with a sense of excitement that Edmund settled on taking a beginners' carpentry class. "I'm putting my toe back in the water," he said, having enjoyed building simple tables and bookshelves in his father's garage forty years earlier.

Once he began the class, Edmund noticed his energy returning and his aches and pains disappearing. Like many retirees, he found the act of commitment itself to be a cure for what ailed him. His conundrum was more spiritual than physical, although it manifested physically. As his spirit was revitalized by the work—and the inspirations of his classmates—he noticed that he seemed to naturally return to better health. "The carpentry was what I needed," he says. "It seems like a circuitous—or at least surprising—route to better health, but I'll take it. I'm feeling good and having a great time." Encouraged and invigorated, he threw himself wholeheartedly—and quite effortlessly—into the class.

At age seventy-eight, Kaida, a school psychologist, suffered from a bout of breast cancer. Her operation was successful and she decided to retire. "My health was a wake-up call. How did I want to spend my final years?" Kaida had many interests. She needed to choose among them. After years of listening to others, it was time to listen to herself.

Kaida loved horses and decided to treat herself to box seats at Denver's Arabian horse show. The horses were beautiful and restored Kaida's feeling of optimism. She bought some Arabian note cards and used them to communicate with her far-flung friends. "It's all the little

Don't cry because it's over; smile because it happened.

—DR. SEUSS

209

things," she says, "like reconnecting with people today as opposed to tomorrow. I am clearer about what I want, and having a health scare, I'm now living more intentionally. I've heard people talk about that before, but experiencing it, I see how important each tiny choice is and how much it really matters to me."

Sometimes, as we age, we are cast in the role of caretaker. Our significant others are aging, too, and sometimes their infirmity becomes our responsibility.

Angie takes care of her husband, who suffers from Parkinson's disease. Her husband has good days and bad days, but the overall trend is bad. Daily, Angie watches her partner failing. The dynamic man she married is dynamic no longer. Angie still loves him deeply, and she prefers to care of him herself, but the constant struggle with his health has taken a toll on Angie, as well. She finds herself feeling cranky, restless, and irritable. When I suggested she take an Artist Date, entrusting her husband's care to another for a few hours, her eyes filled with tears of frustration.

"I don't want to leave him," she confessed.

"It's only a matter of hours," I countered. "The break will do both of you good."

Angie was not convinced. She broached the idea to her ailing husband, and to her surprise, he brightened considerably.

"Take a break," he told her. "It will do you good."

And so, Angie, against her better judgment, hired a helper to come in once a week, allowing her to get out of the house.

Feeling guilty, she took her first Artist Date: a visit to an aquarium. As she examined the many tanks of fish, she began to relax. In the half-light of the aquarium, she found herself softly weeping. She let herself feel—a luxury she had not allowed herself in months. Emerging into the sunlight after an hour, she felt more herself than she had in a very long time.

Back at home, she discovered her husband also brighter. He and his caretaker had managed a game of cards, and he wanted to know all about her Artist Date. She told him of the aquarium, of the moray eels and sharks. "I'm so glad you went," her husband told her, and Angie resolved that she would go out once a week—a resolution her husband heartily seconded.

Taking care of ourselves always helps those around us. My improved health improves my dog's life, as she gets longer and more consistent walks. I have more energy for my friends, my daughter, my granddaughter. I have more clarity as a teacher and a writer. When we give to ourselves, others benefit by our improved state—and they may even be inspired to improve their own lives, as well.

TASK
To Your Health

List five simple things you could do for your health—physical, emotional, or spiritual. For example:

1. Walk to the library instead of drive.
2. Take time to visit the chapel I love the next time I'm downtown.
3. Call Laura—our long newsy talks always cheer me up.
4. Reinstate the morning smoothie habit I have let slide.
5. Etc. . . .

Can you realistically add one or more of the things on your list to your daily routine?

The Partnership Balance

One wag puts it this way: "Having a retired husband is like having a piano in the kitchen." This solicits a laugh, but can feel like no exaggeration. When a partner retires, he or she is suddenly "around" 24/7.

This requires a huge adjustment from the spouse. A homemaker whose husband retires may go from having time for herself to suddenly feeling under scrutiny and perceived criticism. "I got along fine without my husband's 'help,'" says one wife. "I feel like I have a toddler underfoot," says another. "My husband expects me to entertain him," says a third, "at least I think he does."

It's an equal adjustment when the working wife retires. "My wife was used to earning. Her retirement meant less money and less autonomy. I had grown up in another time, and my mother had never worked. I think I unconsciously expected my wife to become like my mother—and I deeply offended her with that assumption. And it's no wonder she was offended. I see the error in my thinking—but I think her retirement caused an emotional upheaval for us both."

If you think of the family as a mobile, retirement causes all the pieces to jiggle wildly. Every piece is affected by the movement of one.

"I retired," says Jim, "but my wife kept on working. I found myself restless and discontent. In a word, I was lonely. I missed my colleagues at work, and I unconsciously expected my wife to be a playmate. In the meantime, she still had her job, with its many obligations. I guess, if I was honest, I was jealous in some ways."

"We really went through the mill," recalls Jim's wife. "I felt torn between my job—which I enjoyed—and my husband. It seemed to me he spent his days devising more and more jobs for me. I would come home from a day at the office only to find a list of things Jim wanted done: a grocery list, a stack of filing, a series of repairs that were needed on the house. He was used to being a boss, but I didn't like the feeling that I was his employee instead of his wife."

"My poor wife," says Jim now. "I gave her task after task. I was used to having a staff and having my orders carried out. Retired, I unconsciously made my wife my staff. When she balked at my expectations, which I now realize were unreasonable, I found myself thinking of divorce."

"I'm the one who daydreamed of divorce," says Jim's wife. "We'd

There can be no deep disappointment where there is not deep love.

—MARTIN LUTHER KING JR.

212

had a solid marriage for more than thirty years, but retirement really rocked the boat."

Jim shared what finally proved to be a solution for their newly rocky marriage. "My wife suggested we see a counselor. I was offended—if she would just shape up, everything would be fine. But my wife was stubborn and finally I gave in to her demands. The counselor helped both of us to see that we were underestimating the shift in power that came with retirement. To her credit, my wife saw that I needed her understanding. To my credit, I saw that she was not my employee, and that rather than load her down with projects, I needed to find some projects of my own. When I put the focus on myself, our marital ship righted its course. I had really been 'king baby,' I realized."

To love oneself is the beginning of a lifelong romance.

—OSCAR WILDE

The balance in the partnership will inevitably shift at the retirement of either—or both—parties. Accepting that the change is inherent will help partners find a new equilibrium.

When Beatrice, a Jungian analyst, reached seventy, her life partner pressured her to retire. "I'm not ready to retire," Beatrice protested. "I'm finally old enough and wise enough to do some good." And so, against her partner's protests, she continued to carry a full patient load, and even to take on new cases.

"You'll burn yourself out," protested her partner, who was happily retired and eager for Beatrice to join him. Beatrice pointed to Jung's teachings on the value of elders.

"I enjoy being useful," she told her partner. "I've got too much energy to retire."

"I'd like us to travel," retorted her partner. "I'd like to go to Egypt and to Machu Picchu."

"I'd like to go, too," Beatrice replied. "And I think I can arrange my schedule."

But arranging her schedule to carve out some travel time wasn't really what her partner wanted. His desire was to be the focus of her attention. Realizing this, Beatrice made the difficult decision to sever their bond. She continued to work another ten years, and would do some of her finest work in the decade between ages seventy and eighty. At eighty she gracefully, and happily, retired.

As the dynamic at home is affected by the retirement of one or both partners, it is helpful to remember that Morning Pages are for our eyes only. As we work through change, it is often best that at least some of that work is done alone. We do not need to verbally process everything with our spouse. We can write "I wish Jim wouldn't sleep so late" in our Morning Pages, perhaps then writing in the next sentence, "What does it matter, actually, if he does? He's gotten up early for forty years. It's not really a big deal."

May this marriage be full of laughter, our every day a day in paradise.

—RUMI

Morning Pages help us process our feelings. If we were to stop and talk about every sentence in our pages before we had thought it through ourselves, drama would likely ensue. This is why it is so important that Morning Pages are private. I have been grateful that I have never lived with anyone who would read my pages. But I have had students hide, burn, lock up, or shred their pages. This is just fine. Often both partners do Morning Pages—one tries them, and the other joins in, citing "self-defense." But these partnerships also tend to weather change and benefit from more openness and honesty.

When we focus simply on cleaning up "our side of the street," we are happier and more empowered, and we naturally make ourselves more present—and pleasant—to those around us.

TASK
Balance

Take a quick personal inventory: Has your retirement shifted the balance in your household? Is there anything that has made you short-tempered? If so, look closely: What is your part in it? As we take responsibility for ourselves, our partners and intimate others often do the same.

Pain as Energy

The world is not flat, although the ancients believed it to be so. It took Magellan's voyage to prove that the world was round. Many people hold a belief as false and damning as the belief that the world is flat. They believe they are not creative. And it is only by setting sail in the direction of their dreams that they are able to prove that the world is round.

One day in retrospect the years of struggle will strike you as the most beautiful.

—SIGMUND FREUD

It is painful to believe that one is not creative, and the reason is that it is never true. I have never in my career met a noncreative person. The hard thing about pain is that it's painful. But the good news about pain is that it is energy, and with a little conscious effort, we can redirect it toward our own good.

Jesse, at age fifty-five, retired believing he "did not have a creative bone in his body." After spending years in a corporate management job, he was convinced he was "as boring as the life I have led." But upon closer inspection, Jesse—and his life—were anything but boring. He had moved and traveled, gone skiing and hiking, kept a close-knit friend group, read piles and piles of literature, and raised a family. Still, he saw himself as uninteresting—although he was a charismatic, charming man, and often the life of the party. It was when he worked through his Memoir that he noticed an early dream of acting that he had abandoned long ago. "I figured, I could read, at least, and so I dove straight into Shakespeare," he recounts. "It was a great dream come to fruition, just to interact with these plays on the page. I believed I couldn't act; yet I had the craving. Eventually, I decided to give it a try. And I took a monologue class at the local college. It was incredibly fun, and I'd like to do more. Now I'm torn by two diverse emotions. On the one hand, I am proud to have attempted acting. On the other hand, I feel regret for the years wasted believing I couldn't act." Jesse must now use the pain of regret as energy for forward motion. But being aware of this is a giant first step, and one that will likely ensure his success.

We may arrive at our seniority bearing psychic as well as physical pain. Over the years we may have been wounded and find that, for the most part, we have buried those wounds. Morning Pages and Memoir writing may bring our pain to the surface. Writing about our pain, we transform our wounds into energy. We can then use that energy to heal and to move beyond our pain toward our long-waiting dreams.

Jonah was a distinguished academic specializing in medieval literature. He wrote several scholarly books but dreamed of writing fiction. When he turned sixty, he said to himself, "I'm sick of saying I can't do this. It's now or never," and he wrote his first novel. The book was published by a small press, but no royalties ensued. For a while, Jonah allowed the situation to slide, grateful to be published at all. Then a veteran writer read the book and said to Jonah, "This deserves broader publication. It's a wonderful book." Embarrassed, Jonah confessed that he was receiving no royalties. The veteran writer was outraged. He sent Jonah's book to his own literary agent, who seconded the writer's vote of confidence.

"Hire a lawyer," the agent advised. "If you can break your contract with the small press, I will take your book on and sell it."

Jonah screwed his courage to the sticking point. He hired a lawyer as directed. The lawyer was able to break his contract, citing the lack of royalties as a breach of contract. Jonah signed on with the literary agent, in effect placing a bet on his own talent.

"I had to get frustrated enough to make a change," he says. "But it's true. My frustration was productive in that way. I'm proud of myself for moving ahead instead of staying stuck. Brooding didn't do me any good, even if I theoretically had the time for it."

Many of us find we have time to spare as we enter retirement. And too many of us spend this time wallowing in self-inflicted despair. Creative people are dramatic, and we can use negative drama to scare ourselves out of our creativity. It is important to be on guard and watch out for this. We may find ourselves picking fights with loved ones, dream-

Nothing is predestined: The obstacles of your past can become the gateways that lead to new beginnings.

—RALPH BLUM

ing up worst-case scenarios of a dark and foreboding future, or nursing frustration and resentment. Retirement is not easy, and we feel caught off guard by its challenges. "Retirement was supposed to be fun," we fume. Instead, we find it hard. This makes us angry, and we are often uncomfortable with this anger. This is because we do not recognize that anger is also actually fuel. If we have a dream, anger helps us accomplish it. Anger is a dare, and it's up to us to rise to the occasion.

Cari had worked as a paralegal for forty years. She retired physically, but was mentally still tied to the office. She found herself brooding about the one partner who she never seemed able to please. He had always intimidated her with his sharp criticisms of her work.

"I could please everybody else," Cari thought, "but not him. I should have pointed that out to him. I should have made him see that I was competent and confident. Instead, I was tongue-tied." Cari rehearsed in her mind over and over what she could have done and should have said. "I really resent him," she admitted to herself. "I don't even work for him anymore and his criticisms still sting." Retired, she was spending as much—or more—mental energy on the job than she did when she was working, and it was a tragic waste of her creativity.

At my suggestion, Cari wrote a letter—not to be sent—to the offending partner. I suggested she put everything in the letter, no matter how petty; that she say everything she wished she had said. Cari began writing the letter, hoping and believing that on the far side of the letter was freedom.

"You never liked me," she wrote. "You never praised me, no matter how hard I worked. You hurt my feelings." She noticed that her resentments had a childlike ring. "I think you're selfish," she wrote. "I think you're stingy. No matter how well I did, you never said anything. I did a good job. I never dropped a ball. I was trustworthy. Again and again, I was successful at what I set out to accomplish—and I helped you to be successful."

When Cari finished the letter, I asked her to read it to me.

I will prove by my life that my critics are liars.

—PLATO

"But it seems so babyish," she protested.

"Yes," I said. "Resentments are often childish. That's all right."

Cari read me the letter. As she read, her voice grew stronger. She claimed aloud that she had been a good worker. As she did so, her resentment began to fade. It was her own acknowledgment of her pain, as much as anyone else's, that set her free.

Having put her resentments down on paper, Cari felt a huge weight lift from her shoulders. No longer weighed down by the anger she stoked by playing and replaying the situation in her head, she felt exhilarated. "I'm ready to take on my next challenge," she told me. "The letter was hard, but holding the resentment inside was harder. Whatever I choose to do next surely won't be as difficult as that." The last I heard, Cari was taking an improv class—a bold and courageous thing to do, but not the hardest thing she'd ever done, not by a long shot.

Sometimes elders find themselves addicted to sympathy. Rather than solicit positive attention for their accomplishments, they solicit negative attention instead. At first, this seems harmless enough—after all, any attention is good attention, right? Wrong. An addiction to sympathy is an addiction to weakness.

Jude retired from a busy career in advertising and found himself hungry for the attention he used to receive as a matter of course. Rather than take affirmative actions on his own behalf, he sulked, believing that attention should simply come to him. His wife and his children continued to have busy lives. Jude's life felt empty. Six months into retirement, he found himself fighting depression. He took up smoking for the first time in thirty years. He knew he was being self-destructive, but he didn't stop. Once a week, he got together with friends for poker night and his card-playing buddies noticed his lethargy. One poker night, a friend stayed late after the game was done. Jude confided that his life felt empty and that his smoking was an empty diversion.

"My wife nags me to quit smoking," he confessed, adding, "but at least her nagging is a form of attention."

Jude's friend did not mince words. "I think you're addicted to negative attention," he said bluntly. "You want our sympathy, not our friendship." Jude protested, but in his heart, he knew his friend was right. He had a long-standing interest in Web design, and, with his friend's goading, he explored master's programs, finding an online degree program he could pursue from home. He became excited as he read the credits of the faculty. "I'm a little bit old," he told his wife, "but I think I'm going to go for it." He applied, was accepted, and now found his empty evenings filled with a new challenge. No longer interested in eliciting sympathy, he found himself attracting the admiration of family and friends.

"I'm finding purpose again," Jude muses, "and it's exciting. I'm learning about a younger person's business, but my advertising background is proving to be a great base for it all. I also quit smoking—I've got to keep up with my young colleagues!"

The truth is that turning our pain into energy for good can be one of the great assets of age. With a little willingness, we can draw on stores of experience—and heal our wounds—as we work to create the life we want.

TASK
Pain as Energy

Pain does use our energy, but we can consciously channel it toward productive and positive action if we are willing to look at our options with fresh eyes. Writing very quickly, so as not to censor yourself, complete the following:

1. The truth is, I'm frustrated by . . .
2. The truth is, I'm frustrated by . . .
3. The truth is, I'm frustrated by . . .
4. The truth is, I'm frustrated by . . .
5. The truth is, I'm frustrated by . . .

Now, take the energy you have just uncovered and use it toward a creative act.

WEEKLY CHECK-IN

1. How many days did you do your Morning Pages? How was the experience of doing them?
2. Did you do an Artist Date? What was it? Did you discover anything in your Memoir that you'd like to explore in an Artist Date?
3. Did you take your Walks? What did you notice along the way?
4. What "ahas" did you discover this week?
5. Did you experience any synchronicity this week? What was it? Did it give you a sense of humility, a sense of being somehow guided by a higher power?
6. What did you find in your Memoir that you would like to explore more fully? How would you like to explore it? As always, if you have a loaded memory that you feel requires further attention but aren't yet sure what additional action to take, don't worry about it. Just keep moving forward.

Reigniting a Sense of Adventure

This week you will dream a little: what would be fun, if you chose to stretch your limits just a bit? Look back into your Memoir and consider those risks you took—and those you did not. What excites and intrigues you? Even in the second act of life, there is unlimited potential for growth. It is not too late to take creative risks for the first time, to form new relationships and new kinds of relationships, to see new places and set—and meet—new goals. These years are years of freedom, and this is a time for adventure.

Risk for the Sake of Risk

You miss 100 percent of the shots you don't take.

—WAYNE GRETZKY

In the movie *Raging Bull*, boxer Jake LaMotta's manager-brother urges him to enter a match that he might not win. "It's worth the risk," his brother explains. "If you win, you win. And if you lose, you win."

Embarking on creative endeavors, we always "win," in that we are better for having tried than not tried, whether or not the results meet our expectations. Stretching ourselves, we discover new strengths and interests. We expand ourselves into a fuller potential. We write a song, and no matter what happens after that, we've written a song. Our next song will come more easily. We now have something in common with all other songwriters. We inevitably increase our sense of self-worth, just by having done it. As in *Raging Bull*, it's not about winning or losing. It's about gaining experience and coming out the other side the person who dared to get in the ring.

Just as for Jake LaMotta, the most important moment is when we step into the ring. This is the moment that our fears, our doubts, our doubting friends, or any number of things can impede us. We must be willing to begin anyway. Creative risks come in all different styles and sizes. Perhaps it is taking pen to page. Perhaps it is leaving the house to take an especially unfamiliar Artist Date. Perhaps it is sharing a newly remembered story with a relative. Perhaps it is picking up the phone to call a friend's sister, a gallery owner, who might be able to provide some advice. Creative risks, big or small, expand our world, and we grow by taking them.

Art is an act of faith that we practice practicing. No matter what form our creativity takes, it boils down to making something from nothing. It is always a risk to make something from nothing. We put ourselves out there. We say, "I see this. I think this. I could imagine this . . ." Taking a risk always requires courage. The blank page or easel, the empty stage or podium, all call for an act of faith, for the willingness to risk. Speaking for myself, as a writer, I find the blank page a daily challenge. I pray for guidance, then I listen and write down what I hear. I try to let the great creator create through me, and I am often surprised by the wisdom of what I write—as if the idea came from somewhere just beyond me.

My daughter tells me that she, too, considers writing a step into the unknown. In a year when acting jobs were scarce, she accepted the challenge of writing into the void and produced sixty-nine poems. My friend Robert Stivers, the photographer, began his career as a dancer. When an injury to his spine permanently sidelined him, he made a fresh start in a brand-new direction: he took up photography as a means of capturing the fluid forms he could no longer embody. It was a great risk for him to begin anew, in another art form, but he has spent the second half of his career in this new form, and it is a large part of what now defines him. He is a deeper, stronger photographer for having been a dancer.

All our dreams can come true—if we have the courage to pursue them.

—WALT DISNEY

Age may bring with it newfound courage. Risks we were afraid to take now become risks we must take. Looking back in your Memoir, you may see risks that you avoided, repeated yearnings toward a certain art form or goal that you turned away from more than once. Sometimes, the dream we have closed our eyes to the most repeatedly is the one that looms the largest. Dreams do not die. We may not act on them, but the ember of their desire burns on. Some may cite a fear of failure as a reason for not pursuing a dream. When we are young, many of us are concerned with what others think, what effect taking a risk might have on our personal or professional life. Later in life, these concerns may not loom as large, but fears of being too old or underqualified may distract us. In the end, the reasons we ignore our dream do not matter. The dream still waits.

Doreen has for years dreamed of becoming an actress. Yet she always balked at auditioning. It was simply too frightening, and so year after year went by with the dream still burning within her. Turning sixty-five, Doreen began working with her Memoir and saw how, in each decade, she had consistently turned away from her call to act.

223

"I knew I'd had this thought, but it was only in looking back that I saw just how often I'd had it," she says. "I'm devastated to see it—but also, in a strange way, excited. I know now what I have to do. It's not about being a movie star or accepting an Oscar like I acted out as a child. It's about realizing, admitting, *I want to act.* That's it. There's something within me that is called to do this, and I see now that it's a call to action."

Imagination is more important than knowledge.

—ALBERT EINSTEIN

When her local community theater announced plans to put on *Arsenic and Old Lace*, Doreen knew she was cornered. She was aware of what she wanted, and here was her opportunity. "I'm the right age, and I love this story. I can take a hint." Screwing her courage to the sticking point, she scheduled an audition.

"Making the phone call was hard," she says, "but then the woman on the phone was so friendly, and she didn't seem to think it was a big deal that I was auditioning. She took my name and gave me a time. Somehow, just talking to another person, it all started to seem like a bunch of small steps instead of one giant leap off the cliff."

On the day of Doreen's audition, she woke up early, counting the hours until her ten-minute slot. "I promised myself I just had to go," she says. "It didn't matter if I got cast. It just mattered that I got out the door and showed up. That's it. I'd be proud of myself—even celebrate—for trying." This is risk for the sake of risk. By setting her goal on the part she was able to accomplish—showing up—as opposed to the part she was not in charge of—getting cast—she was taking the only risk she needed to take.

"I walked into the theater and read my lines. I was nervous. I took notes from the director. I read a scene with another actor and then I left. It almost happened before I could process it. But I had done it. I had done it!"

Imagine Doreen's delight when she got the call to say that she was cast in the play.

"I just about jumped out of my skin," she says. "To think that the thing that almost stopped me was going to that audition," she says. "I hadn't auditioned since I did a community theater show as a child. So—almost sixty years. But I had to ask myself, what was I going to do, wait another sixty? And you know what? Auditioning's not so bad. I just needed to take it all a moment at a time." Doreen then continued to take small risk after small risk: showing up early even though she was nervous on the first day, asking questions of the director when she didn't understand a scene, asking her husband to read lines with her at home as she memorized. "Step by step, it got easier," she says. "Once I'd successfully done something that felt scary, I could do something else. It was all okay. In fact, it was pretty thrilling to have a sense of raw excitement and emotion every day. I guess that's what taking risks feels like."

Many of us have lives that are, in some areas at least, risk-free. We may have even cultivated these risk-free lives because we think we want stress-free lives. But while stress from negative situations can be damaging, stress from confronting challenges or taking a healthy risk can be energizing and motivating. When our lives feel lackluster, it can help to ask ourselves if there is a creative risk we could take but are not taking. A little healthy risk goes a long way toward giving us a rewarding sense of aliveness.

It is important to remember that risks can take many forms. The possibilities are unlimited, yet we ourselves contain the answer to the risk we'd like to take. The answer is ours alone to define. Making art always involves risk, and the reward in artistic actions is experience and a body of work. Artists, as Agnes de Mille famously said, "take leap after leap in the dark." When I first wanted to write songs, it felt like a great risk to sit down and begin. But, meeting my own challenge, daring to risk showing up at the piano and writing—whether it was "good" writing or not—I did show up for myself. I took "leap after leap in the dark" and eventually built a very large body of work. Many of my songs went on to be performed. I am now in the process of recording an album. Had I not dared to write that first song, what a different place I would be in today.

When I was little, my pony Chico could out-jump many horses. It was always a risk, taking him in a jumpers' class. But it was a risk I learned to take and enjoy. Often, Chico emerged victorious. And if he didn't, we still had the self-respect of having tried. I still take pride in the courage I was willing to display, arriving at the class week after week. Jumping a horse mirrors any other risk; once you aim for the jump, there's no turning back. Making the decision and then acting on it brings a great sense of momentum and satisfaction. I still refer to risks I take in my life today as "jumps." A day might contain many "jumps"—a live interview where I have to be "on," a difficult phone call, a large travel agenda. But I have learned to take these "jumps," and learned, too, that I nearly always land on my feet.

TASK
Risk

Complete the following:

1. A risk I could take is . . .
2. A risk I could take is . . .
3. A risk I could take is . . .
4. A risk I could take is . . .
5. A risk I could take is . . .

TASK
Memoir, Week Eleven

AGES: _____

1. Describe your major relationships in this period.
2. Where did you live? Did you live in more than one place?
3. What were the risks you took during this period?

4. Were there risks you wanted to take but did not take, during this time?

5. Describe one sound from this period.

6. Did you travel during this time? Where? Why? With whom?

7. What goals did you have during this period? Did you accomplish them?

8. Do your goals from this period have anything in common with your goals today?

9. What was a source of adventure for you during this time? How does it compare to today?

10. What other memories feel significant to you from this time?

New Relationships

It is a paradox that as we undertake the seemingly monotonous routine of Morning Pages, we undertake a life of adventure. As we mine our psyches for insights, we meet an inner—and then outer—world of deep interest. As we explore what it is we really feel, we find adventure in making authentic new connections.

Perry would have told you his life was dull, but when he began writing his Morning Pages, he found quite the opposite. Writing about his daily life, he experienced a deepening interest in the people, places, and things that crossed his path. Soon, an interest in modern art became a passion. On his Artist Dates he was drawn to galleries and museums. Looking at the work of others, he felt an uncanny sense of relationship with many of the artists. It seemed to him that their art was somehow expressing deep feelings of his own. One gallery exhibited a show that was particularly interesting to him and, to Perry's delight, he was able to meet the artist.

He and the artist forged a friendship. The artist's work was based on abstractions of trees. Perry appreciated the artist's deep craft. The artist appreciated being appreciated. Both Perry and the artist were in their sixties. The artist had only begun painting full-time once he retired. It was only when Perry retired that he became a full-time appreciator of art. Now, they enjoy a lively and inspiring friendship.

Faith is taking the first step, even when you don't see the whole staircase.

—MARTIN LUTHER
KING JR.

"I'm glad I took that Artist Date," Perry says. "You never know when doing something alone will introduce you to a new friend." I have seen many times that new relationships are "chanced" upon once people undertake the tools. As we know ourselves better, and take ourselves on the adventures that call to us, we often meet kindred spirits along the way.

Being seen by another person is wonderful indeed. And feeling unseen is a painful and common plight of a retiree who is suddenly surrounded by fewer people on a daily basis. Stripped of their "working" identity, many people find themselves feeling invisible. Where before they had daily contact with many colleagues, now they find themselves spending much more time alone. It is up to each of us to forge a new identity in retirement. Our identity begins not with how others see us, but with how we see ourselves. Morning Pages reveal our daily emotional terrain as we reflect on the past and plan for the future. Artist Dates put us in touch with an ageless, lighthearted part of ourselves. Allowing ourselves to blossom and explore in these ways, we find ourselves more secure in who we are—and more able to connect authentically with others.

As we age, we may find that we further lose our identity from a sexual point of view. Ours is a youth-oriented culture, and as our youth moves behind us, we find ourselves seen differently—or not at all. This is true for men as well as women.

"I don't get looked at," Randolph says. "I feel like I'm over the hill and when I look appreciatively at a younger woman, I feel like a predator." An attractive man in his midsixties, Randolph finds each new wrinkle a cause for despair. What he once called laugh lines, he now calls lines. A widower, he tries to resign himself to a future without women. Recently he got a new driver's license with a new photo. "That's what I look like?" he exclaimed with dismay. "I still feel young, I just don't look it." At the airport on a trip to Europe, Randolph was asked if he had yet turned seventy. If so, he could keep his shoes on while going through security. "Don't rush me!" he told the attendant. He willingly relinquished his shoes, eager to claim the five years he is shy.

When pushed to explore his pain further, he admits, "I guess I feel replaceable." This is the core of much of the struggle retirees have with age—and it ignores a central fact. No one is replaceable. In the words of the great spiritual teacher Ernest Holmes, "It is right and necessary that we should be individuals. . . . The Divine Spirit never made any two things alike—no two rosebushes, two snowflakes, two grains of sand, nor two persons. We are all just a little unique, for each wears a different face but behind each is the One Presence—God. . . . Nothing is ever twice alike. "

My friend Andrea, divorced twice, is now dating a man ten years her junior but is constantly aware of the difference in their ages. "You look great," he tells her, but she thinks, "If only we'd met ten years earlier. . . ." Andrea admires and envies younger women. While she feels that age has brought her wisdom, she worries that wisdom does not translate to sex appeal. But again, Andrea's sense that she could be replaced by someone else is at the core of her fear and has very little to do with the reality of the situation. She "holds back from getting 'too involved' because she is afraid he will leave her for someone younger." But as long as we are focused on what we are not, we prevent ourselves from celebrating and sharing who we are—and from forming true connections with people who would appreciate our best selves. Focusing on who we are, in the here and now, we embrace ourselves, allowing others to embrace us, as well.

People who consider themselves young at heart in the second act of life often find mates who match. Graced with the wisdom that comes with age, they appreciate and cherish their new romance.

"I never expected this to happen. I'm so happy!" exclaims Elizabeth.

If you have knowledge, let others light their candles with it.

—MARGARET FULLER

229

Newly married, for the second time, Elizabeth cannot believe what she calls "her luck." Her husband is a retired engineer and he is "just full of projects." After her first marriage ended catastrophically, Elizabeth worked to support herself and her horse farm by her work as a portrait artist. She succeeded in her goal, but money was always very tight, and sometimes she wondered where her next mortgage payment would come from. "It was always nip and tuck. I couldn't really enjoy my art. There was too much riding on it." When Elizabeth met Kjell, he was recently widowed after a seven-year battle with his late wife's breast cancer. "Here was this wonderful man, but I didn't just want to be a rebound relationship." For his part, Kjell knew immediately that Elizabeth was a miraculous second chance for happiness. Their courtship took in the creativity of both partners. Kjell was impressed by Elizabeth's portrait work, and Elizabeth was impressed by Kjell's "projects." Retired, Kjell had time and energy to devote to a relationship. He turned his considerable creativity toward wooing Elizabeth. For her part, Elizabeth had to practice being in a relationship and juggling her career.

Kjell was fun, and Elizabeth had not had fun in a very long time. She found herself having to work hard at play. She tried not to panic as she felt herself falling ever more deeply in love. When Kjell proposed, he took on both Elizabeth and her farm. He built new fences and gates, then added the extravagant touch of an indoor riding arena. He threw an extravagant wedding, too, as if to announce to all of his friends: "This is the woman I love, and nothing is too good for her." For the first time in years, Elizabeth found herself painting for sheer joy. As she matched her new husband's joie de vivre, she declared, "We're always very busy. We both love working. Kjell's retirement gives us both a full-time job."

It is possible to forge new relationships with the people who would bring us friendship, adventure, and love. Working through our Memoir helps us to do this. As we revisit, understand, and thus heal our past, we weave our former selves with our present selves. Doing this, we become stronger. Stronger, we have more to offer the world—and the people we will share it with.

TASK
Visibility

The first step toward allowing yourself to be seen by new others is to look clearly at yourself. Looking back in your Memoir, choose a time in your life when you felt invisible or believed that what you were doing was not worth acknowledging, and allow yourself to write about it. Dig deep into detail here: Did you spend long days on a farm doing work that only you saw the results of? Was it cold and windy? Did your red plaid scarf have a tear that you knotted up? Describe all you can re-member of this memory. You may wish to write in the third person: *He awoke at 3:30 a.m. and boiled water in the rusty pot on the stove as he pulled on his familiar layers of clothing. . . .* When you are done writing, you may feel that you have been able to bear witness to yourself, or you may wish to share it with another. You may surprise yourself—and your reader—with the depth of emotion in a memory you might have brushed off as forgettable.

Travel: Reaching New Horizons

Retirement can mean freedom. No longer tied to a job and a routine, we are free to travel. During our work lives, many of us traveled only on business. We may have attended conferences in exotic locales only to find our work kept us so busy we couldn't enjoy the beauty all around us.

When Fred retired and began to consider what might be fun as a next endeavor, he found himself thinking "travel" over and over. "But

I've already traveled," he mentally protested, only to realize, upon reflection, that he had gone to many wonderful places without truly exploring—or really enjoying—any of them. Working through his Memoir, he recalled a trip to Hawaii in his fifties that left him wishing he could spend more time there. The culture and landscape had enchanted him, and he'd looked longingly out the window during his full days of meetings, feeling he was missing out. "I'd like to go back to Hawaii," he thought to himself, but then promptly scotched the idea as "too expensive."

Once we accept our limits, we go beyond them.

—ALBERT EINSTEIN

"Fred," I urged him, "explore your options."

"I'm like the kid at the candy store window," he fumed stubbornly, "not allowed to go in. But I'm so frustrated, because I'm the one stopping myself."

The next day in his Morning Pages he remembered that he numbered among his acquaintances a travel agent named Parker.

"Just call her," I urged.

Fred protested, squirming at the idea of taking the action he so wanted to take. "But what if it's beyond my means? I can't very well put her to work and then back out at the last moment due to costs."

"Fred," I said, "you don't know the costs, and Parker's job is exploring the costs for you." It was clear that, no matter how powerful his blocks, Fred truly desired to take this trip.

"I can't spend a nickel more than my monthly social security," Fred allowed.

"That's fine," I assured him. "You know the limit you are comfortable with. That should make it easy for her."

Reluctantly, he called Parker and asked her about an economy trip to Hawaii.

"You're in luck," Parker assured him. "I've got just the ticket for you." She named a price $400 below Fred's budget.

"Book me," he said with delight. And so, he found his dreamed-of travel becoming a reality. He just had to get in touch with the desire and then do a little research. All it took was a willingness to explore his options—and a little encouragement—and now he was about to embark on a great adventure.

"The hardest part was picking up the phone to call Parker in the first place," he admits sheepishly.

Of course it was. There's a reason for the saying that when we need help but don't want to ask for it, we need to "pick up the phone that weighs a thousand pounds." It does not mean we have some grave emotional disorder. It just means that it's sometimes hard to pick up the phone.

It's good to pick it up anyway.

George, like Fred, found travel on his list of desires, but he did not call a travel agent. Instead, he contacted AAA, and with their help, planned a road trip to national parks.

"I lived in the Southwest for twenty years, but never took a trip to the Grand Canyon, the Painted Desert, Monument Valley. I loved to drive, and I found my travel delightful. Going at my own pace, stopping when I wanted to stop, I took the trip of a lifetime. I resolved that I would travel yearly, heading next to the Pacific Northwest. I had never camped, but I found myself intrigued by the campsites along my route. I decided I could afford to buy a tent, and a good one. It would pay for itself with my savings on hotels."

A few years into his retirement, George began dating a widow. He expected her to think his camping excursions were crazy, but instead she was enticed, responding wholeheartedly, "Oh, George, how romantic!" And so, on his next expedition, he had company.

Travel in all forms, near and far, breeds adventure. Changing surroundings, even if it is just a brief day trip to a nearby town, fills our well of images and reminds us of the vast world around us. Some take to the road in a mobile home like my friends Arnold and Dusty, who traveled from their house in Santa Fe to the northernmost regions of Alaska. Next, they traveled south to the Mexican border. Their mobile

One's destination is never a place but rather a new way of looking at things.

—HENRY MILLER

home gave them a feeling of security and flexibility. There are many ways to travel, many ways to expand our horizons and explore the mystery of new places.

Crista ended a stifling thirty-year marriage and entered her retirement with the determination to travel to half a dozen countries she had longed to see. Her husband had traveled frequently for work and preferred to stay put in his time off rather than travel for pleasure. Now, on her own, she was ready to follow her yearnings. And as she did, she found great rewards.

"As for travel, I used to be intimidated by the planning process—especially because I was doing it alone. There was the tedious searching and the multitude of decisions and possibilities. Then there was the packing and the getting there—it always seemed like so much work. But of course, once I was on my way, it was all worth it."

Crista eventually discovered that while the planning was daunting to her, the rewards of travel far outweighed the hassle. "I'm finding my way," she says now, "and I'm finding myself."

For Allison, an interest in travel was revealed to her slowly. Working with her Memoir, Allison diligently sought clues to buried artistic interests that she might have suppressed during the many years when she was focused on her work or marriage. She was convinced that she was "supposed" to have a dream of writing or painting. But traveling kept floating to the forefront—location after location. The countries she longed to see had been calling to her for years. And one day, in her Morning Pages, she wrote the sentence: "Traveling is my artistic calling." This was a breakthrough, and it was accompanied by the realization that she could use her longtime love of photography to document her trips.

"Now that I view travel as my artistic calling, I see all this effort as the equivalent of converting the rough draft of 'let's go to . . .' into an experience worth the time and money it takes to do it," Allison says. "If I think of my trip as a symphony, the advance work is the rewrites, it's

One doesn't discover new lands without consenting to lose sight of the shore for a very long time.

—ANDRÉ GIDE

the rehearsals, and it suddenly becomes wonderful to make it part of the creation. I'm not trying to create the perfect trip, but a trip full of experiences to gain new perspectives and add more richness to life."

Today, Allison has visited almost half the places she dreamed of, and the next one is currently entering the "rehearsal" stage. She also has a wall in her home office dedicated to the many photographs she took during her travels. "That wall brings me joy every day," she beams.

Chester retired from a long and successful career as a business manager. In his work life, he gained a sense of satisfaction from helping others to attain their goals. Retired, without the goals of others to focus on, he found that he needed to focus on himself and his own goals. He had a longstanding dream of European travel. Counting his funds, he found he was solvent enough to make his dream a reality. Planning his trip gave him a sense of anticipation and adventure. When he booked his tickets, his excitement was palpable.

"I realized that during my work life, my sense of adventure had come from serving others. Now, I booked an adventure for myself alone. The feeling was wonderful."

Amanda, a minister for more than twenty years, found that she could fulfill her sense of adventure by attending conferences focused on her interests, where she heard diverse speakers sharing their theories of the Christian life. She took these theories into account in planning her own sermons. She found that encountering new ideas expanded both her work life and her personal life, keeping her ideas as fresh and as exciting as in the early days of her ministry.

For some of us, travel involves great amounts of time and planning. For others of us, a weekend in a nearby town is plenty to satisfy our travel bug, giving us ample raw material for creative production. Everyone's idea of the perfect trip is unique. But the rewards of a change of scene will always impact our creativity, bringing with it both fresh images and fresh insights.

TASK
Exploring Travel

Complete the following:

1. A big trip that sounds fun is . . .
2. A small trip that sounds fun is . . .
3. I've always wished I could see . . .
4. A place I wish I could spend more time is . . .
5. Close to home, I'd love to explore . . .
6. It would be fun to travel with . . .
7. I'd rather not travel with . . .
8. One thing that worries me about travel is . . .
9. One thing that excites me about travel is . . .
10. Maybe I should plan a trip to . . .

Setting New Goals

When we come into our retirement, we become our own boss. Accustomed as we may be to reaching goals set by, or at least involving, others, we are often unaccustomed to setting goals pertaining only to ourselves. As we undertake the practice of Morning Pages, we may find ourselves naturally setting self-determined goals.

I have a vinyl grocery bag printed with inspirational quotes. One of them urges setting goals on paper four times a year. Setting goals sets your "inner computer," the quote explains. I use Morning Pages to set my goals. My goals emerge on the page as desires. "I'd like to write a play, but about what?" my pages may ask. And then, a day or so later, "I'd like to write a play about suicide." This dark wish soon becomes an agenda. "I'll start tomorrow" becomes "I'll start today." As the goal becomes concrete, I find myself taking small steps in its direction.

"I'd like to feel more spiritual" becomes the goal "I'd like to read more Ernest Holmes prayers." This in turn becomes the goal "I'll read three prayers a night." Beginning as desires, my goals become plans. "I wish I were more fit" becomes "I think I'll try jogging." This goal is fine-tuned to "I'd better start gently—jog ten paces, walk ten paces, jog ten paces, walk ten paces." There is no area in my life that doesn't benefit from gentle goal setting.

You are never too old to set another goal or to dream a new dream.

—ARISTOTLE

I can set goals in any arena I choose. Creativity, spirituality, fitness, and more. As I set goals, I transform the vague and undoable into the doable. "I'd like a new headshot" becomes "Talk to Robert about executing one." "Lose weight" becomes "Maybe I should talk to Dick about eating vegan. He's lost fifty pounds that way." Goals can start as musings, wishes, thoughts, and as they come into form, action plans emerge.

Setting goals and making progress toward them is energizing. Beginning in our Morning Pages, we explore our desires in a free-form way. Day after day, ideas come into focus. From the page, concrete plans emerge. We are getting to know ourselves—a word at a time—and, a word at a time, we become empowered.

I like to write longhand. Each sprawling scroll leads to a new thought. Recently a friend sent me an article that posits handwriting as "more creative" than writing by machine. And so I happily continue to scrawl my first drafts, pleased to be scientifically proven to be opening more neural pathways. But then what? I've gotten my thoughts on the page, and it's time to use the computer. At the part of the process where I am entering the editing and publishing stage, I must enter the electronic age as well. Recently, I wrote in my Morning Pages, "It would be helpful to feel more proficient on the computer." That became "I should look for someone to help me. I could ask around. . . ."

I now have a helper, Kelly, who is tutoring me in the art of computers. For me, making small progress toward my simple goal of learning to be more proficient with my devices is liberating and enlivening.

We can also set large goals in retirement, and it is not uncommon that at this point in the Memoir, larger goals are whispering to us.

Sometimes we are well aware of them. Other times, they sneak up on us. We may feel jealous of others doing something we wish we could do, and it may take an outside eye to help us see what we are looking longingly at.

Andrew had enjoyed a long and illustrious career as a movie critic. Retired, he found himself jealous of those who were, as he put it, "still in the game."

"Screenwriters are lucky," Andrew told me. "They don't need to retire."

When I suggested to Andrew that he try his hand at writing a movie himself, he was horrified.

The breeze at dawn has secrets to tell you. Don't go back to sleep.

—RUMI

"I'm a critic, not a writer," he protested.

"Just give it a try," I wheedled. Against his better judgment, Andrew agreed to try. His ego was what stood between him and writing. As a critic, he had been accustomed to critiquing writing. Now he was putting himself on the line.

"Just find something you care about and write about that," I urged him.

"I could write about my experiences in movies," he finally volunteered. "The truth is, I've always loved movies. No matter how harsh my tongue may have been when I wrote about them. All my most formative experiences happened at the movies." Once he began writing, ideas flowed to him. He found he enjoyed the process and that he felt closer than ever to the many screenwriters he had met during his career.

"My jealousy was a clue to the goal I was avoiding," Andrew told me. "For now, I'm loving writing. But once I finish a draft, I think I know which writer I'd love to ask for notes from. He's someone I've written about many times. It's ironic, but I see the humor in it now. I'll welcome his honest feedback, if he's willing. I finally feel like part of the group—no longer the outsider." Andrew has a plan. One of the great fruits of goals is that they often lead to other goals.

Writing Morning Pages keeps our goals in our sight. It is nearly impossible to write, day after day, and not have inklings of what we'd like to do next. And these inklings, ignored, will only grow stronger. Working through our Memoir often puts us in touch with our authentic dreams. Naming our goal, we may then work backward, a technique my piano teacher calls "chunking it down." We see the ultimate dream on the horizon, but between us and that horizon are many small steps. Remembering that each step is, in fact, accomplishable, we are able to move forward. There is no such thing as jumping from here to the horizon—or "suddenly" being able to play a Bach invention when we have not studied the piano before. But we can learn. A step—or a note—at a time, we make progress forward. Moving ahead is always an option. Moving ahead, we are inspired to move ahead yet more. With the willingness to name our dream and then acknowledge—and take—the first step toward it, we move into the life we have previously only dreamed of.

The significance of a man is not in what he attains, but in what he longs to attain.

—KHALIL GIBRAN

TASK
Set a Small Goal

We are always only one goal away from a feeling of accomplishment. Some of our goals are large, and some are small. Accomplishing a small goal primes the pump and inspires us to set another. Choose one small goal that you can accomplish today. Name and accomplish it. Note your feeling of satisfaction. Does another, larger goal now wink at you? Do you wink back, ready to take it on?

WEEKLY CHECK-IN

1. How many days did you do your Morning Pages? How was the experience of doing them?
2. Did you do an Artist Date? What was it? Did you discover anything in your Memoir that you'd like to explore in an Artist Date?

3. Did you take your Walks? What did you notice along the way?

4. What "ahas" did you discover this week?

5. Did you experience any synchronicity this week? What was it? Did it give you a sense of humility, a sense of being somehow guided by a higher power?

6. What did you find in your Memoir that you would like to explore more fully? How would you like to explore it? As always, if you have a loaded memory that you feel requires further attention but aren't yet sure what additional action to take, don't worry about it. Just keep moving forward.

Reigniting a Sense of Faith

This week you will focus on celebrating the now. In the moment, you are safe. In the moment, you are guided. You will finish your Memoir this week, and become "current" with your current self. Having re-covered the terrain of your life, you are able to be present and aware of today. You will gain perspective and appreciation for the path you have followed. Do you sense that you have been led, looking back at your life now? Do you have a sense of what you would like to do next? Inklings of what would bring you happiness? Do you find that you appreciate yourself and your own unique journey more than you thought you did? Do you feel a renewed sense of purpose? Do you suspect that you have been more aware of your purpose all along than you might have assumed? The past and present "you" meet in the now, bringing you strength and wholeness.

Art as Alchemy

At age sixty-five, we may be officially considered a "senior," but our inner artist is always a child. We take on the role of elder and hope to be a source of wisdom and discernment for our family and friends. We often fill that bill very well, but we fill it even better when we remain connected to our inner child. On our Artist Dates, we allow our inner artist a chance to play. We are soon rewarded by a strong, new flow of creativity. We discover an inner resource that serves us—and others—very well. No longer tapped out, we find new stores of energy and faith.

For many of us, the term "senior" is abhorrent. "It just sounds so old," I would frequently complain as my birthday approached. At sixty-five, we may yet feel ourselves to be decades younger. In writing this book, I had to overcome my own denial. Like it or not, at sixty-five, I was officially a senior, and so were many other baby boomers who had worked with my book *The Artist's Way*.

"But, Julia," many of them told me. "I'm not ready to be an elder, and I'm certainly not ready to be a sage." But to some, we are elders, and to some, we are sage. Our life experience has rendered us wise—or at least on the verge of wisdom. Accepting that, we empower ourselves, and can offer the wisdom of our experience to help others. The paradox is that when we share our "senior savvy" with those around us, we connect to a younger and more vibrant part of ourselves.

In the moment of creation, we are ageless. We feel both young at heart and old and wise. "Artists work until the end," my photographer friend Robert said to me yesterday. Yes, they do. This is why retirement from one career—even if it is our major career—is not, by any means, "the end." Because the act of creating something, anything, renders us timeless, because the act of creation is led by that inner, youthful part of ourselves, we continually reinvent our lives through our art. The capacity to create is as innate as our very life force. I would even say that our creativity and our life force might be one and the same.

Study and in general the pursuit of truth and beauty is a sphere of activity in which we are permitted to remain children all our lives.

—ALBERT EINSTEIN

Carla retired from a career as an optometrist with no real thoughts about what to do next—but plenty of energy that she needed to channel into something. "It was a series of Artist Dates that gave me the idea," she says, "to open a small bakery." Carla had learned to bake as a child. A series of Artist Dates in search of some of her favorite childhood confections led her to go home and try baking them herself. "I remembered what joy these desserts brought me and was disappointed to find that there wasn't a bakery nearby that carried what I was looking for. So I started to think that this was something I could contribute to the town that would also give me great pleasure."

It is your light that lights the world.

—RUMI

Carla now runs a small gourmet bakery. Her offerings are delicious as well as beautiful to behold. When she is baking, Carla feels timeless. She has a child's delight and an elder's discernment. "I love to bake," says Carla. "Nothing makes me happier. Before opening my bakery, I had a period where I was beset by boredom and depression. I needed to find something that I loved, but I didn't know how to find it. I'm so happy I took those Artist Dates that eventually led me to the memories and passions that would bring me fresh life now. For me, baking is that fresh life."

Carla takes pride in her creations, ranging from delectable gingersnaps to key lime pie to dark chocolate pistachio cake to pumpkin cheesecake.

"I never tire when I'm baking," says Carla. "I feel so young. I hope to keep baking for years to come."

Making art of any kind is an alchemical process. Making art, we turn the dross of our life into gold. Making art, we re-create ourselves. When we work through our Memoir, we transform the events of our life into golden adventures. As we write, the ordinary becomes extraordinary; the commonplace becomes special. We transmute our memories into priceless episodes. We make our past present. Moving our hand across the page, we create a handmade life. As we share our perceptions and findings with those we are close to, we give them a window to our world. Often they are amazed—even astonished—by our tales and memories. Often they share their own. As we come to know and appreciate ourselves, we have more to share, and, with more to share, we find our connections with others are deeper and more abundant.

When I revisited my own Memoir, I was interested by some of my early memories that had risen to the surface. When I wrote out my story of trying to eat magical mushrooms, inspired by Alice in Wonderland, it became a cautionary tale for my grandchild, Serafina. Looking back at this adventure, glad my mother had known what to do, I still appreciated my own daring. I could follow the logic of that child who was looking for magic. I could see that, while I do not eat mushrooms from the backyard today, I do still look for magic.

To invent, you need a good imagination and a pile of junk.

—THOMAS A. EDISON

Another tale I recovered from my own childhood was the story of our boxer Trixie, giving birth to puppies. They were so tiny they could not be held. Trixie had chosen the antique shower stall in our basement as the perfect place to give birth. "Puppy," I learned to say. When Serafina became interested in dogs, I told her, "Puppy," and soon she made the sound herself.

The stories from my childhood could become a part of hers, living on, timeless.

"How come you never told me these stories?" Domenica, my daughter, wanted to know.

"I hadn't turned them into gold yet," I explained.

Recalling in detail a life event, we transform it through the magic of our imagination. We honor our experiences. We carry them forward with us as energy and strength. Our inner youngster still thrives as we honor its past—and its present desires. Writing about the adventures my childhood best friend Lynnie Lane and I pursued in the "Rough Riders" club, I transformed them into the tasks of Hercules. My memories became golden.

The youthful part of ourselves is alive and well, eager and curious. This is the part of us that creates and cherishes our golden memories. Cherishing our stories, and acting on our dreams, we re-create ourselves today. As we come to accept our age, we must also accept what that youthful part of us would like to do next. Perhaps it is adopting a health regimen or indulging a baking habit—or both. Perhaps it is buying a new tray of watercolors or forging a new friendship. Whatever it is, we will be intrigued by it, called to it, enlivened by it. Whatever it is, we must pursue it.

Creativity should feel easy, not difficult. Our inner youngster will lead us if we listen.

TASK
The Fountain of Youth

We have all experienced the sensation of our age slipping away. Try to recall ten activities that have made you feel youthful and then pick one and do it.

1. I feel youthful when . . .
2. I feel youthful when . . .
3. I feel youthful when . . .
4. I feel youthful when . . .
5. I feel youthful when . . .
6. I feel youthful when . . .
7. I feel youthful when . . .
8. I feel youthful when . . .
9. I feel youthful when . . .
10. I feel youthful when . . .

TASK
Memoir, Week Twelve

AGES: _____

1. Describe your major relationships in this period.
2. Where did you live? Do you still live there?

245

3. What were the major changes during this period?

4. Describe a time where you felt guided during this period.

5. Looking back across your Memoir, do you see the hand of guidance in your life?

6. Do you have a sense of purpose or calling now, looking fully at your life?

7. What is one thing you saw in your Memoir that you can now appreciate about yourself?

8. What patterns do you now see, related to your creativity, as you look back on your life?

9. What other memories feel significant to you from this time?

10. What would you like to do next?

A Life of No Regrets

In writing our life stories, we come in contact with our inner wisdom. Many times we lay to rest the regrets of the past. Writing "if only I had . . ." often reveals the wisdom in the path we did take. Dr. Carl Jung believed that every life contained the tracery of destiny. Writing our story, our destiny becomes clear to us. We see the many choices we made and we appreciate their meaning.

When I wrote *The Artist's Way,* my then–movie agent read the manuscript and told me, "Julia, go back to writing movies. Who is going to be interested in a book on creativity?" Nearly four million readers later, I can see the wisdom in having written a book rather than a movie. Since that turning point, I have written forty more books.

The Artist's Way was what I came to call a "creativity support kit." Its tools helped artists learn to trust themselves. I gained fame as a helper—a very nice kind of fame, indeed. And as for the movies, *The Artist's Way* has supported many a film actor and director. Recently, I taught in New York and was startled midway through my seminar to recognize a well-known movie actress. She had used *The Artist's Way* as a support kit for her booming career.

Working through our Memoir helps us to make peace with ourselves. Sometimes we see the wisdom in the course we have taken. Other times we encounter a buried dream that we now have the courage to pursue. Often, something we assumed was a regret reveals itself as destiny when we revisit it in our Memoir.

Experience is not what happens to a man; it is what a man does with what happens to him.

—ALDOUS HUXLEY

Many of us enter our retirement disappointed in ourselves. During our work life, we may have fulfilled the goals and dreams of others while often ignoring our own. Free at last to pursue our own agendas, we find that we need to focus squarely on our own dreams so that we may have a life of no regrets.

In recovering from our creative blocks, it is necessary to go gently and slowly. We are aiming to heal ancient wounds, not create new ones. Cammie, an advertising creative director, was a fine musician who often wrote music for the commercials she oversaw. "I'm a composer," she joked, "but I only compose thirty-second spots." Then, Cammie fell in love and got married. Her husband was a studio musician. Often he played on the spots Cammie had written. But before much time had passed, Cammie stopped writing. Her husband was the "real" musician in the family, she decided. She stopped composing and contented herself with sitting on the sidelines. Although she couldn't admit it, she missed writing her own music. When she worked through her Memoir, watching her composing slowly slip away over the years, her grief over her abandoned creative outlet came to the fore.

"I regret all the time I lost," she confided. "I feel like I spent my life wrong."

"Treat your music like your Morning Pages," I told her. "Let yourself write, but keep your writing private. Your inner artist got spooked by your husband's art, so for now, just write and keep it to yourself. You need to rebuild the trust with your inner artist." In the mornings, she would write her Morning Pages and then go to the piano, listening for a scrap of melody. As the days passed and the melodies built upon each other, she was overcome by relief. "I am expressing myself in the way I need to now," she told me. "It's almost more about the act of expression itself than anything else. Sure, maybe I'll share my music with someone when the time is right, but for now, the act of writing is healing my sense of regret. I was afraid to write music because of the pain of all the time I 'lost'—but what I didn't realize is how that pain would heal through composing. Maybe I'll come to see that the 'lost' time—the pain itself—will make me a deeper musician."

Everybody is a genius. But if you judge a fish by its ability to climb a tree, it will spend its whole life believing it is stupid.

—ALBERT EINSTEIN

Vahn began his Memoir nervous to revisit a time in his late teens that he had long regretted. As a young man of eighteen, he had gotten his girlfriend pregnant, and after much soul-searching, they decided to have an abortion. Now, fifty years later, he was still haunted by the decision. He wanted to write a book that would help other young men.

"I want to write, but I'm afraid to write," he told me. I urged him to start with Morning Pages. He did so, and after a month found himself starting his dreamed-of book. "It is as if I take one step toward my dream and the universe takes two more," he explained. "The act of writing is, in itself, healing." As Vahn reconciled with his own past through his Memoir, he was able to share it, finally connecting with other people on a topic that he had long harbored as a secret.

"Once a month, I speak at a recovery center. I tell my story of substance abuse and I include the abortion. Afterward, men come forward to thank me. 'That's my story, too,' I am told. I started drinking and using with a vengeance after the abortion. It left me with a large wound. I tried to self-medicate but, of course, the drinking only made the wound worse. I could not seem to forgive myself. I was Catholic, and I went to a priest for confession. He all but told me I was damned for what I had done. I reacted by leaving the Church. It was twenty years before I started reading about spirituality. I met a minister who helped me to change my idea of God from punishing to loving. This is the message I want to carry to young men. I realized, speaking to other men, that abortion is something more often discussed by women. I didn't have any men to talk to about my experience, and I am learning that these men often don't have that, either. My pain can be a source of wisdom or healing for others. Helping others helps me let go of my pain and regret."

We all carry wounds from our youth. Art brings healing. Art airs out the basements and the attic, flings open the closets and balms the sometimes ancient wounds we carry. Art is a spiritual vacuum cleaner, poking into corners. In this sense, all art is autobiographical, and all art contains the power to heal.

Sometimes, our wounds are severe. Adrienne came to me because she desperately wanted to write but was afraid. I urged her to try Morning Pages, but she was reluctant.

"Let's make a deal," I told her. "You'll start writing, and if all hell breaks loose, you'll get a therapist."

And so, Adrienne started writing. About six weeks in, she came to class excited. She handed me a plain manila envelope and announced, "It's my first short story." I took the envelope home and the next night settled in to read. The story was wonderful but disturbing. It concerned incest. I called Adrienne and suggested we meet for coffee. When we met, I asked her whether it was autobiographical.

"Yes," said Adrienne. "This is the ghost I was afraid to confront."

"Well, remember our bargain?" I said. "Find yourself a good therapist."

A few weeks later, Adrienne handed me a second manila envelope. "Another short story," she said. "And, PS, I found myself a therapist."

I opened the manila envelope that night. Once again, the story concerned incest. But the fictionalized heroine confronted her abuser. Adrienne and I met again for coffee.

"I loved your story," I told her. "Your heroine was so brave."

"Yes, I liked her, too," Adrienne answered. "In real life, my abuser is dead. In fiction, I was able to gain some resolution. My therapist said my writing was therapeutic. I think it was."

As long as you're breathing, it's never too late to do some good.

—MAYA ANGELOU

Not all wounds are as severe as Adrienne's. But whatever the damage, making art can help heal it. Regret is painful, but we always contain the power to take positive action—and lessen our pain.

TASK
Change for Good

At this point in the course, you may sense that you would like to make a change in an area that feels intimidating to you. Take pen to page and write about a time when a change appeared to be negative but in hindsight was positive. Remembering this time, allow yourself to imagine that a current change you may be resisting may also be for the best. What silver lining could exist in changing your current situation?

The Magic of Today

Life is lived one day at a time. But many of us find ourselves straying out of the day at hand into the past or into the future. The past is finished; the future is not yet here. Only the day that we are in can be lived. Each day well lived is a thing of beauty, giving us a more satisfying past and more promising future.

As I pray each day for knowledge of God's will for me, I am led to the next right action. Whether our daily habit is asking for God's will, or simply writing in our Morning Pages to see what they will reveal, there is always some small something we can do to make our present productive. As we focus on the now, we are rewarded by a sense of well-being. Our daily life becomes fulfilling.

Dr. Carl Jung believed that the latter part of our life was a time for reflection. Thinking back over the years that had passed, we would be able to understand their meaning. When we honor our life story through exploring our Memoir, in art or words or teachings to others, we leave behind a legacy. We tell our descendants who and what we were. We see how our past has brought us to where we are today. Writing our Morning Pages, by contrast, we focus not on the past but on the present. The pages help us to "stay in the now." They help us to find meaning and grace in our days as they unfold.

Our work lives depended on us paying attention to the present, to the agendas and schedules of the moment. Freed from the harness of such a life, we may find ourselves frightened and adrift. We need to anchor ourselves one more time in the present day. Each morning, our pages help us become wise, possessed of the knowledge we need for the exact current moment.

For many of us, the pages prove addictive. We become "hooked" on processing our own lives, just as they are, right here, right now.

Rae started writing Morning Pages reluctantly. She was certain the pages would lead her to divorce. She had a nagging sense that her marriage was failing, and she constantly imagined a dark and dismal future. Writing the pages, she found herself pulled quickly into the present, where she discovered, to her surprise, a sense of responsibility for her troubled marriage.

"I wish my husband would be more open with me," she wrote, and then, a scant paragraph later, "I think I need to be more open with my husband." With the urging of the pages, she began to communicate more fully. To her surprise, her husband responded in kind. Within weeks, she found herself starting to feel happier and more fulfilled in her marriage. Instead of spending time and energy worrying about the future, she focused on improving—and enjoying—the present.

"In the end, I didn't need to make a huge and dramatic—and destructive—change. I needed to sort out some complex feelings that weren't, in the end, as complex as I feared." I urged her, as I often do with students who see a positive change from the Morning Pages, to keep writing. The pages keep us on course. Rae did keep writing, processing the variations of each day's emotional terrain. "The pages are like a good marriage counselor," she one day wrote. "They kept me from making a terrible mistake. Divorce was not the answer—

We must be willing to let go of the life we have planned, so as to accept the life that is waiting for us.

—JOSEPH CAMPBELL

communication was." How simple this advice sounds, but when clarity comes from within us, it is truly profound. When we come to our own solutions, we have internalized their wisdom and can act on it as an authentic part of ourselves. Taking advice from the outside is only a fraction as powerful, even if it is the same advice.

Some of us think the most interesting years of our lives are behind us. Focusing on the present day, we see that our lives are still fascinating, our insights profound.

Recently I received a letter from a woman in her sixties named Nicki, who began the pages when she was in jail. Her crime? Possession of marijuana. Her sentence? Seven years. "Pages gave me a way to survive the boredom of prison," she says. Ten years later, released from jail, pages still give her a way to process her life.

"I learned," she says, "to live in the now, not to think of how many days ahead remained of my sentence. I found the 'now' was filled with insights. Even in prison, my imagination took wings."

Many of us think of time like one long bolt of cloth: "today until I die." Such thinking—looking at time as "all we have"—doesn't serve us. It allows us to procrastinate and keeps us from using our time productively. How much better it would be if we were to try to live one day at a time. Waking in the morning and heading into Morning Pages, we provoke, clarify, comfort, cajole, prioritize, and synchronize the day at hand. "What can I do today?" we ask ourselves. The answer comes in a manageable bite.

For forty-five years, my friend Jane has been on a spiritual path. When I call her with problems, she inevitably says, "That all sounds hard, but just for today, you are all right." No matter what arena my worry inhabits, Jane brings it to scale by her practice of being in the now. Recently hospitalized for a health scare, Jane practiced staying in the now on her own problems. The doctor said she had three days to live. She received this news with equanimity. When panicked friends would call her, she always said, "I'm *fine*," refusing to engage in any drama. Now, months past the doctor's three-day verdict, her teaching

[D]o not grow old no matter how long we live.... [N]ever cease to stand like curious children before the great Mystery into which we are born.

—ALBERT EINSTEIN

of staying in the now set an example for me and all her other many concerned friends. It is the small things in life that are the blessings of the now.

"Easy does it" is a saying we have all heard, and I always interpreted this to mean "Oh, calm down." But when I considered that "easy does it" could actually mean "easy accomplishes it"—"it" being the daily project at hand—I started to see how a gentle approach, one day at a time, would move me forward much more quickly than imagining a future I had yet to create. The magic of staying in the day is that there is only so much that can happen in a day—and when we accept, and then accomplish what the day offers, we will find that, before we know it, we have moved further than we might have ever imagined.

There are only two days in the year that nothing can be done. One is called yesterday and the other is called tomorrow.

—THE DALAI LAMA

TASK
Just for Today

Staying in the present day is often easier said than done, but when we can successfully focus on the moment at hand, there is always magic to be found there. Often we jump backward into the past or forward into the future because we feel that it is "too late"—or "too early"—to begin. We assume the next step is too large for us or has passed us by. When we focus our attention on the time we actually have available to us—today—we see the possibility of what we can accomplish, "just for" today.

Complete the following:

1. Just for today, I can . . .
2. Just for today, I can . . .
3. Just for today, I can . . .
4. Just for today, I can . . .
5. Just for today, I can . . .

Never Alone

In the morning, I write my Morning Pages. In the evening, I ask for guidance from those who have passed on. I pose questions and listen for answers, for example, "Could I hear from Mom?" And then I "hear," *Julie B., I am with you always. You are on track. Do not be discouraged. Your aunties and I work to give you wit and wisdom. We are with you always, as near as your breath.*

All goes onward and outward; nothing collapses.

—WALT WHITMAN

I find my mother's messages reassuring. Next, I turn to my father. "Could I hear from Dad?" I ask. And I "hear," *Julie B., I guard and guide you. Ask me for guidance and it will come to you. You are safe and protected.*

Unfailingly, the messages I receive from "beyond" are positive and helpful. I have often wondered if the messages are "real," or figments of my imagination. They certainly *sound* real, and I find, reading them over, peace and calm. When I ask to hear from more generalized higher forces, I hear messages that begin with "We," as in, *We guard and guide you. You are well and carefully led. We lead you gently. We lead you a step at a time.*

Like the messages from my parents, the messages from the more mysterious higher forces are both calm and kind. If I am making up their content, it nonetheless serves to comfort me. Instead of simply "missing" those who have gone before me, I find myself enjoying an ongoing sense of connection.

We can all try writing to those who have passed on. Unexpectedly, we may find those who have passed on seem to answer us back. In time, we develop a real dialogue, seeking answers to problems and hearing solutions.

June began seeking contact with her deceased friends because without them she felt lonely. She missed their wisdom and companionship. Imagine her surprise when she heard back from them that they missed her, too.

"It was a relief for me to hear from my friends. I found they had passed in body, but not in spirit. Our relationship was subtle but ongoing. I found them eager to help me."

Carl, too, found an ongoing connection to those who had passed on. "I was shocked," he says. "I didn't expect contact, but found contact, indeed. I had many questions and received many answers. It became routine for me to seek help from my deceased friends. I thought I was a little crazy until I talked to a Jesuit priest who told me he sought the help of his friends who had passed on. He opened his desk drawer and took out a pack of cards. On each card was a name and an obituary. 'If I have a medical problem, I ask for help from a doctor friend,' he told me. 'If it's a legal question, I ask my friend the lawyer. I find my friends are my personal saints, and they are only too eager to help me.'"

Tell them stories.

—PHILLIP PULLMAN

Gradually, we learn that there seems to be no arena of our life that cannot be improved by spiritual help. In the privacy of our pages, we experience a spiritual awakening. We gradually find ourselves asking for help and expressing our gratitude for help given. Our significant others may notice a difference in us and our attitudes. We do not need to share that the difference is spiritual. Our awakening is personal, but awaken we do.

Seeking to contact those who have passed on, I find myself comforted. There is an afterlife, I believe, and as we move toward—and through—our golden years, the veil between our world and the next grows more sheer. Asking for guidance, we find ourselves led. As we mentor those younger than ourselves, we are, in turn, mentored. As we seek to forge an ongoing relationship with those who have passed on, we are, indeed, never alone. Finishing our Memoir, we are possessed of a new and firmer faith. We are part of all that has gone before, and all that leads ahead. We are connected to other realms, and we pass on our belief in this connection as our final—and finest—legacy.

TASK
Ask and Listen

This week, experiment with asking direct questions to those who have passed on and "listening" for a response. Do you sense a higher wisdom? Do the answers have a simple ring of truth, the familiar voice of those you reach out to? Are you starting to suspect that you are not alone?

Progression—that is the key to happiness.

—RUTH MONTGOMERY

WEEKLY CHECK-IN

1. How many days did you do your Morning Pages? How was the experience of doing them?

2. Did you do an Artist Date? What was it? Did you discover anything in your Memoir that you'd like to explore in an Artist Date?

3. Did you take your Walks? What did you notice along the way?

4. What "ahas" did you discover this week?

5. Did you experience any synchronicity this week? What was it? Did it give you a sense of humility, a sense of being somehow guided by a higher power?

6. What did you find in your Memoir that you would like to explore more fully? How would you like to explore it? As always, if you have a loaded memory that you feel requires further attention but aren't yet sure what additional action to take, don't worry about it. Just keep moving forward.

Reborn

Here, at the end of the book, it is my hope that in finishing the work, you have found yourself to be larger and more colorful than you had imagined. I hope you have reconnected to your own story and come to appreciate all that your unique journey has to offer those you may touch. I hope that you have found an inner strength and source of energy that will propel you forward into your "second act" of life. I urge you, as you move forward, to continue doing Morning Pages, Artist Dates, and Walks. These tools ensure future creativity. Using these tools, you will continually find the answer to the question "What shall I do now?" to be simple, profound, and doable.

"Try this," our pages invite, and we do try "this." As we age into sages, we have great wisdom to share. A belief in our own creativity is a gift we pass on. Our children and grandchildren, friends and colleagues all benefit from our conviction. As they see us forging new and more vibrant lives, they are often inspired to pick up the tools themselves. We can lead by example. Our actions encourage those around us to see that they, too, can dare to dream.

We are all creative, every single one of us.

TASK
Wish List

A final, parting tool, which is one of my very favorites: the simple but potent "wish list." Number from 1 to 20 and fill in the blanks.

I wish . . .

I wish . . .

I wish . . .

Wishes range from the petty to the profound—and often fall well within our range of possibility.

What do you wish?

Acknowledgments

Tyler Beattie
Dorothy & James Cameron
Sara Carder
Joel Fotinos
Gerard Hackett
Linda Kahn
Joanna Ng
Martha & Rob Lively
Susan Raihofer

Index

Also from TarcherPerigee

An international bestseller, *The Artist's Way* has inspired
millions to overcome the limiting beliefs and fears
that can inhibit the creative process.

978-1-58542-146-6

$16.99

Focusing on parents and their children, newborn through age twelve,
The Artist's Way for Parents builds on the foundation of *The Artist's Way*
and shares it with the next generation.

978-0-39916-881-9

$16.95